היסטוריה

ArtScroll History Series®

Rabbi Nosson Scherman / Rabbi Meir Zlotowitz
General Editors

Once Upon a

by Chaim Shapiro

Published by

Mesorah Publications, ltd

Shtetl

A fond look back at a treasured slice of the Jewish past

FIRST EDITION
First Impression . . . June 1996
Second Impression . . . August 1998

Published and Distributed by
MESORAH PUBLICATIONS, Ltd.
4401 Second Avenue
Brooklyn, New York 11232

Distributed in Europe by
J. LEHMANN HEBREW BOOKSELLERS
20 Cambridge Terrace
Gateshead, Tyne and Wear
England NE8 1RP

Distributed in Israel by
SIFRIATI / A. GITLER — BOOKS
10 Hashomer Street
Bnei Brak 51361

Distributed in Australia & New Zealand by
GOLDS BOOK & GIFT CO.
36 William Street
Balaclava 3183, Vic., Australia

Distributed in South Africa by
KOLLEL BOOKSHOP
Shop 8A Norwood Hypermarket
Norwood 2196, Johannesburg, South Africa

THE ARTSCROLL HISTORY SERIES ®
ONCE UPON A SHTETL

© Copyright 1996, by MESORAH PUBLICATIONS, Ltd.
4401 Second Avenue / Brooklyn, N.Y. 11232 / (718) 921-9000

ISBN
0-89906-642-9 (hard cover)
0-89906-643-7 (paperback)

Typography by Compuscribe at ArtScroll Studios, Ltd.

Printed in the United States of America by Noble Book Press Corp.
Bound by Sefercraft, Quality Bookbinders, Ltd. Brooklyn, N.Y.

Foreword

"*Blessed is he who remembers what is forgotten*"
(Agnon)

This book does not intend to describe life in the *shtetl* in its entirety; that would be an encyclopedic undertaking. One line alone suffices: "In a thousand years, no Jew was ever charged with murder." (This, of course, excludes blood libels devised by the government, often hand in glove with the Church, as a stimulus for fresh pogroms against the Jews.)

The *shtetls* of Eastern Europe had many different sizes and populations. The Talmud tells us, "A large town is one that has ten men of leisure who attend synagogue. A settlement that has less is a village" (*Megillah* 3:8). A major city in Poland or Lithuania would be considered a small town in America. My own home town of Lomza had some 25,000 to 30,000 residents, 12,000 of whom were Jews. This constituted a major city in Poland but would have been considered minor in America. When you read about one town, you know them all. As the Talmud states, *Sadna d'ara chad hu*: The earth is one solid block. In other words, human nature is much the same the world over.

People speak about the *shtetl*, some with nostalgia, others with a desire to plumb their own roots, but — with the older generations gradually "moving out" — there is hardly anyone left who is capable of describing that life. Over the course of many sleepless nights I squeezed my brain like a sponge, trying to remember, to dig up episodes, to give the younger generation a key-hole view of what life in the *shtetl* was like. As one philosopher put it, "Your memories of the past, bound up inside you, live in the present and follow you into the future."

Every night a new item, long forgotten, would pop up, substituting living memory for passive sleep. I would like to share some of those memories with you, dear reader. Use your imagination to inflate this small token into an enlarged picture of a world that is gone forever.

Acnowledgments

I wish to express my gratitude to several individuals whose efforts made this book a reality: to Libby Lazewnik (née Shapiro) who so masterfully edited this work, to my daughter Chava Roth whose illustrations grace the cover and endpapers of the book, to Rabbi Moshe Kolodny who offered valuable comments, to Mrs. Tova Finkelman who reviewed the manuscript, to Avrohom Biderman who shepherded this memoir to completion, and to all those at ArtScroll/Mesorah who contributed their many talents to this volume.

May the angel who redeemed me from all evil bless my wife Haddasah and our children Alter Pinchas and Shirah Tzipporah, Chava Rivka and Dovid Elimelech, Esther Feige and Aharon Baruch, Eliezer Nosson and Mindel Bracha, and Avrohom Shimon and Ahuva Libba, and all our grandchildren. May my name be declared upon them — and the names of my forefathers — and may they proliferate abundantly within the land. Amen!

Chaim Shapiro
Baltimore

Table of Contents

Chapter 1: Shtetl Geography

*W*here were the *shtetls* of Europe?

To place these small Eastern European villages, or *shtetls*, in their proper geographical and historical context, take a pencil and draw a line on the map, beginning with Finland in the north and continuing down to Yugoslavia and Bulgaria in the south. All the territory to the east of this line made up the Russian Empire. Up until the end of the first World War, Finland, Latvia, Estonia, Lithuania, Poland, White Russia, Ukraine, northern Romania, Czechoslovakia, Bulgaria and Yugoslavia were integral parts of the brutal Czarist Empire. It was only in 1918 that the Russian Empire, as well as the German and Austro-Hungarian Empires, fell apart. When United States President Wilson proclaimed the right of individual nations to "self-determination," all these small countries stood up and declared their independence.

Under the czars, Russia was divided into 89 provinces, called *gubernies*. Each *Guberny* was headed by a *gurbernator* (governor), appointed by the czar. A full 80 of these provinces were

"The streets were unpaved and sidewalks virtually nonexistent"

off-limits to the Jews! This led to the development of the *Cherta Osedlosti,* the few sections in which the Jews were permitted to reside. Here, in cramped, neglected little towns, the Jewish population of Russia struggled to live. Some of these villages belonged to big landowners known as *pritzim.* Neither the governor of the province nor the *poretz* of the town was interested in improving the lives of the people; their major concern was in squeezing taxes from them. *Shtetl* life was primitive. The streets were unpaved and pavements virtually nonexistent, though some villages boasted wooden sidewalks. During the rainy season, the streets wallowed in deep mud. There was no running water, no sewer system, no garbage collection. Peasants would enter a town two or three times a year to collect the accumulated rubbish and clean the outhouses for use as fertilizer, for which they paid with farm products.

Autocracy

In no place in the world were the differences between democracy and dictatorship as glaring as in czarist Russia. A democratic government — "by the people" — is obligated to the people; it "owes" them a living. In czarist Russia, the reverse held true: The people were there to serve the czar. They owed him their livelihood and, indeed, their very existence. The czar, in a word, owned the country and everyone in it! This was more than just a dictatorship. It was a *samo-derzavye* — an autocracy.

A typical Russian story illustrates this point. Yeketarina (Catherine) the Great, czaritza of all the Russians, was traveling in her coach, pulled by six horses, when she came to a little brook without a bridge. The chief of her guards suggested that they arm the soldiers with shovels and order them to fill the brook with earth so that the horses and coach might pass.

"No," the czaritza commanded imperiously. "Place the soldiers on the ground, one next to the other, and the coach will pass over *them*." Coolly, she explained her decision: "An army grows. Every year I get new soldiers via the draft. But the holy Russian earth — it does not grow!"

As the Russian Empire expanded — and especially after it incorporated Poland, the Baltic states, and other lands westward — its Jewish population doubled. This was not at all to the liking of the czar and the Church. They were annoyed to find that some of the laws of the old empire did not apply in the new territories. In Russia proper, for instance, Jews were prohibited from owning land — not necessarily the case elsewhere in the expanded empire. Also, the big Russian cities were off-limits to the Jews, except to prominent Jewish businessmen or those who had served in the Russian Army for 25 years. This sometimes had curious ramifications, as the following story illustrates.

When Rabbi Yitzchak Blazer became *Rav* of St. Petersburg, Russia's capital, he was not permitted to reside in that city, since he was neither a veteran nor a businessman. The Jews were forced to circumvent the law by registering him falsely as a family member of a certain Jew by the name of Czarski, who was in fact a 25-year army veteran. (It was common for Russians to claim a distant relationship with members of the royal family, in the hopes of receiving better treatment at the hands of local officials.) One day, the *Rav* was seated on a park bench as the czar and his aides strolled past. Noticing the *Rav's* long gray beard, and knowing that Jews as a rule were forbidden to live in the capital, the czar approached the *Rav* to ask his name and whether he was indeed a resident of the city.

The *Rav*, fearful of being arrested, replied that he was a member of the Czarski family.

Smiling, the czar repeated, "Czarski, eh?" Turning to his adjutant, he said, "Congratulate me. I've discovered a new member of the family!"

Oppression and Charity

The royal Romanov family was "appointed" by Heaven, not only as the rulers of all Russia, but also as spiritual head of the Russian Orthodox Church — of which the czar was "Pope." The Russians called him *batyushka* (father). On seeing him, they would sink to their knees and cross themselves. The Russians were a very religious people, and a major part of their religion revolved around their hatred of the Jews. As a fish stinks from the head, so did this hatred dribble down from the czar, through the Church and the provincial governors, to the district governors, mayors, police chiefs and village constables, all the way down to the very lowest official in the farthermost village. Each in his own way made life miserable for the Jews, enforcing evil laws and inventing new ones, all with the aim of further oppressing them.

Oppression embittered the lives of the Jews. A Russian governor asked a rabbi: "Why are the Jews so competitive with each other?" The rabbi replied, "In the animal world, you will never see one species swallowing its own kind. The exception is fish. They swallow one another. Why? Because fish are the only species that is locked up in one habitat. So has the government locked the Jews in a limited space, which is beneficial neither to the Jews nor to the government."

Yet even under the most oppressive conditions, living in dire poverty among antagonistic neighbors, the Jews' culture and education blossomed and far outshone that of their gentile counterparts. The lifeblood of the community was charity. Let a

Jew's horse die, and in a single day a collection would be taken up to raise the necessary funds for another one. Let a house or a store burn down, and its neighbors or competitors were the first to help put the owner back on his feet. (Fire insurance — or, for that matter, any other kind of insurance — was unknown.) Charity preserved the life of the *shtetl* Jew, and imbued it with a rare dignity very much at odds with his dismal physical surroundings.

An Open Hand

Although poverty was rampant and most Jews lived from hand to mouth, there did exist a middle class of wealthy Jews. These were the big businessmen, prosperous landowners, and government contractors. These Jews were the ones who dealt directly with representatives of the government.

When a new official arrived, the first question the Jewish community asked was: "Does he keep an open hand?" In other words, would he take a bribe? Bribery was the way of life, the *minchah l'Eisav* (gift to Eisav)[1] that helped lessen the community's unreasonable, unbearable burden. The *shtadlan*, or mediator, was always one of the leaders of the community, a well-to-do businessman who spoke perfect Russian and, in Polish-Russian territory, was fluent in Polish as well.

My grandfather, Reb Chaim Velvl Szeniak, was one of these mediators. He was in constant contact with the various officials by virtue of his personality, as well as his status as a large landowner. He would visit the new official, welcoming him in the name of the Jewish community. These visits always took place in the official's home, never his office. The reason for this was simple: The office contained too many curious eyes and ears, and — most important — was missing a wife. In his private residence not only was discretion possible, but the official's wife was also present to see that her husband did not reject a welcome gift.

---

1. Yaakov, upon learning that his brother Eisav was approaching with an army, prepared a lavish gift with which to placate him (*Bereishis, Vayishlach* 32).

After some polite conversation, the *shtadlan* would rise to go, leaving a bundle of rubles under the tablecloth. The next day the community would hold its breath to see whether the gift had been accepted — whether *"vayikach Eisav"* (*Bereishis* 33). They would look to the official's wife for evidence. If she took off on a shopping spree (in Jewish shops of course; there were no others), the *shtetl* felt relieved. "He has an open hand — *mazel tov*! Blessed be Zeresh, *eishes mafchidi* (the wife of my oppressor)."[1] Woe to the community where Eisav did not take.

Sacrifice

Periodically, in one town or another, Jewish blood would be spilled in pogroms that flared up for no reason — except the simmering anti-Semitism that was never far from the surface in both the Polish government and its Church. These blood libels were often, in fact, organized by the police themselves, hand-in-glove with the clergy.

Rashi relates a heartrending tale of one such blood libel that took place long ago, in the city of Lud (*Taanis* 18b). When a king's daughter was found dead one day, the Jews of the city were accused of killing her and sentenced to a collective death — until a pair of Jewish brothers stood up and "confessed" to having committed the crime. The king had the two put to death in place of the entire community. In this way, these two holy individuals redeemed great numbers of their falsely accused brethren.

A similar episode occurred much closer to our own time, in the city of Minsk. To avenge the killing of a young Christian girl found dead in the town, a bloodthirsty mob screamed for Jewish blood! The Minsk police, putting a decent face on the affair, piously explained to the anxious Jews that they would not be able to restrain the mob from seeking retaliation — unless the killer was found.

---

1. A reference to Haman.

A Jewish volunteer by the name of Ashkenazi went to the police and "confessed" — just as long ago those brothers had — that he was the killer. Everyone in town, including the police, knew very well that Ashkenazi was innocent. They knew he was offering himself as a sacrifice to spare his fellow Jews another devastating pogrom.

The sacrifice was accepted. Ashkenazi was hanged to satisfy the bloodthirsty Christian mob. For years afterward, the entire Jewish community of Minsk would light a *yahrzeit* candle and recite *kaddish* for his soul on the day of his death.

The maiden name of Rabbi Ruderman's mother was Ashkenazi. The *Rosh Yeshivah* of Ner Israel of Baltimore was a descendant of that holy sacrifice.

The Jews and Agriculture

The ancient Polish kings, pressured by the Church, prohibited Jews from owning land. This state of affairs lasted some 800 years. Then Poland invited the Jews to come and help build the economy of the underdeveloped land. Jews began entering the country in large numbers in the 16th and 17th centuries — and immediately came face to face with the fanaticism and hostility of the clergy, who ignited the masses against them. For their own protection, the Jews were forced to settle around the palaces of the kings and high government officials.

The edict against Jewish ownership of land continued unabated, though some Jews found a loophole. They would lend a farmer money, placing a mortgage on his farm or using it as collateral. If the farmer did not pay back the loan, the Jew could foreclose on the farm. However, the Church quickly closed that loophole, too.

On page two of *Sprava Catolicka*, the organ of the Lomza Archdiocese (no. 27), under the headline, "When Will We Buy Out Polish Lands From Jewish Hands?" was the following:

Arenders at work

"We talk a lot about raising the agricultural and spiritual level, about the nationalization of businesses, artisan shops, and industry. But we completely forget about removing Polish land from Jewish hands! This is not a minor problem. There are still three million acres of land in Jewish hands."

The issue was dated September 4, 1938. Clouds of war were already hovering in the Polish skies. One year later, the Germans attacked Poland, and the country fell apart in days. But the bishops weren't worried about that. What really concerned them was the fact that Jews still owned land in Poland.

Arenders

The story was the same in Russia and the Ukraine. Forbidden to own land, the Jew was forced to rent it from the wealthy *pritzim*. Leasing a farm was known by the Russian legal term *in arenda*, and the leaser was called the *arender*. Hundreds of Jews farmed on leased lands. They raised crops, with the usual worry about rain. They raised cattle, with the usual worry about dry noses. They

A cattle merchant

raised sons who became farmers after them. They almost forgot that the land did not actually belong to them. Then, after some 25 years or more, the *poretz* died and his son would order the Jew off his land. Now the Jew was forced to remember that the land was not his.

Where did a Jewish farmer go in his old age — to the city? He longed for a piece of land covered with grass, not cobblestones and wooden sidewalks. After so many years of hard work, what was left?

"A horse has four legs," they would say in great pain. "Still, he falls sometimes, and then he gets up. I have only two legs. When I fall, do you expect me to get up?"

Sadovniks

An orchard was called *sad* in Polish and Russian. Because the owners didn't want to be bothered with them, they rented the orchards to Jews, who became known as *sadovniks*. These Jews were soon fruit experts, with an expertise handed down through the generations. Each spring, they counted the number of trees in their orchards and appraised their size. They counted the blossoms on one tree. By tasting the blossoms, they could tell whether the apples would be sour or sweet. Weighing all these factors, they were able to estimate the number of bushels to be harvested from each tree.

After paying the owner, the *sadovniks* still faced many risks: too much sun, too much rain, wind, thieves, birds and insects (chemical spraying was as yet unknown). With the absence of refrigeration, storage was also a problem. But if they had a good summer, they had earned their living for the entire year.

The Poretz

In the Eastern Europe of yesteryear, there were houses —and there were houses. There were people of wealth, and there were wealthy people. There were *pritzim* — and there were *pritzim*. A world of difference existed between them.

The Yiddish word *poretz* signified a man of large estates, a huge landowner. In Russian he was called *graf* (Count) and in Polish, *hrabia*. The *pritzim* lived in palaces. They owned countless acres of land, plus hundreds of serfs who filled a role similar to that of the American slaves. The estates were run by managers while the noblemen and their families lived in luxury in Paris, Berlin, Moscow or St. Petersburg. This nobility lived sybaritic lives, dedicated to physical gratification and devoid — as were their enormous, lovely homes — of any spiritual content. Pretending to be cultured, they filled their libraries with books they would never read; they vastly preferred hunting and horseback riding. In Russia, they were known as the Romanovs, the Plekhanovs, the Chernickins, etc. In Poland and Lithuania, the names were Potocki,[1] Czarnecki, and Radzivil. The homes of the *pritzim* were notorious nests of infidelity and immorality. Most of

---

1. One of the Potockis was Polish Ambassador to the United States for 20 years; he could afford to pay for his own keep. The Radzivils lived in London, and their son married President Kennedy's sister-in-law.

these noblemen were mean to their servants, cruel to their serfs, and brutal to the Jews living on their huge estates.

Then there were the Jewish *pritzim*. They owned small estates, but never possessed serfs. (There were no Jewish serfs.) The homes of these Jews were large, as were their families, but these *pritzim* did not dedicate their lives to the pursuit of lust and power. On the contrary, their homes were bastions of religion, and their libraries always in use. Living in the country, where there were no schools, they always made sure to hire teachers for their children, paying them well in cash, plus room and board. The parents also formed study groups for themselves.

Kitchens were strictly kosher. The heart of the Jewish *poretz*, like his hands, was always open to the needy. Any traveler passing through was welcome to a free meal and a bed for the night.

My *zeide*, Reb Chaim Velvl Szeniak, was known as the Kollaker *Poretz*. Kollaki was located in northeastern Poland, between the cities of Lomza and Zambrow ("Zembrove" in Yiddish). The entire village, along with the surrounding land and forest, belonged to Reb Chaim Velvl. He was no match for the Potockis or the Radzivils, whose estates were a thousand times larger than his. Still, he was a *poretz*, entitled to the honor and dignity the title carried.

Standing tall, with a wide, reddish-gray beard and tall *yarmulke*, he looked like a *rosh yeshivah*. He was a *talmid chacham*, yet he was also a farmer. He bought acres of land and forests and employed many peasants. Chaim Velvl's mind was like a calculator. When he visited a forest, he would observe its size, the thickness of the trees, and the diameter of the trunks. Then he would think for a moment and produce figures for the number of cubic feet of lumber and firewood that could be derived per acre. The non-Jewish landowners called him Voolvki, and would consult him before buying or selling land and forest. His estimates were almost always correct.

My mother would tell us how, as a child, she awoke one night and heard someone crying. Frightened, she crawled into her mother's bed. Her mother comforted her: "It's Father. He is praying, saying *Tehillim,* and crying. Weeks have passed with no rain. The crops are dying; he is crying for rain."

Life on the Estate

There was a windmill in the village that was used to power the flour mill, but being wind driven it was unreliable; days might pass with little or no wind. To solve this problem, the *poretz* Velvl crossed the border to the city of Koenigsburg in East Prussia, and purchased a gasoline motor for the mill. This machine also supplied electricity to the entire village for three hours each evening, except for Friday nights. Later it was upgraded to deliver six hours of power, but never on Shabbos or *Yom Tov!*

No other village in the vicinity — or, for that matter, any of the area's small towns — enjoyed the benefits of electricity. As none of the local peasants was versed in the running of the power mill, Chaim Velvl imported a mechanically inclined Jew by the name of Shmuel Solomon. Reb Shmuel was a *talmid chacham* as well, and also served as *chavrusah* (learning partner) to the *poretz.* The two established a daily routine to study *Gemara* and *Rambam.*

Bobbe Shoshe, the "queen" of the estate, was a tall woman with a look of authority and a lovely face under a big *sheitl* (wig). She, too, enjoyed the arrival of the Solomon family. Her daily yoke of watching out for her children as they played with the non-Jewish village youngsters was lifted. Now they had the Solomon children to play with.

In the *shtetl,* Jew and gentile lived so close together, and yet were so far apart in their lifestyles. Nowhere is this illustrated more clearly than in studying the daily routines of a Chaim Velvl and comparing it to those of the typical nobleman of his time. Every morning, Chaim Velvl the *poretz* would ride into town, either by coach or on horseback, to *daven* with a *minyan.* On Saturdays and holidays, poor men from the neighboring villages walked to Kollaki to make up a *minyan*. After *davening*, Bobbe Shoshe would serve a *cholent* with plenty of meat to all the guests.

Life was good. The only worry Chaim Velvl had was for his children. Determined to prevent revolutionary ideas from tainting their young minds, he handpicked the teachers he hired to educate them. He wanted his children to receive the best Hebrew, Polish and Russian education — minus the revolutionary notions so prevalent at the time. Winds of revolution had begun to blow all over the Czarist Empire. The Poles were revolting against the Russians, the Russians against the tyranny of the czar, the workers against the capitalists, and the peasants against the *pritzim*. Kollaki, however, seemed immune to the trend. There were no Russians in the village for the Poles to rebel against, and the *hrabia* (*poretz*) Voolvki treated them very, very well. So content were the villagers that there was no need even for a policeman to patrol its streets.

Happiest of all were the children. They rode horses and ran with the dogs, racing as far as the eye could see. Without a care in the world, they grew and enjoyed life in the sun and fresh air, played out against a panorama of forest, field and garden. They knew they were different from the non-Jewish children, though the differences were still a little vague.

Two restrictions, however, served to underline the differences. When playing, the Jewish children would never, ever enter the church or the cemetery, while the Polish children freely entered both.

The Cemetery

The *shtetl's* non-Jewish cemetery was a place where dead people were buried and that live people visited once a year. The Jewish cemetery was a different story entirely. It was part of the daily life of the *shtetl*, the umbilical cord binding the living to the dead. Ironically, the Hebrew term for cemetery is *bais hachayim*:

The entrance to the "new" cemetery in Lomza

the "house of life" or "house of the living," for all living beings eventually wind up there. In Yiddish, it is called *der heiliger ort,* the holy place.

Just as the life of the *shtetl* was ruled by laws and customs, so too, in death, was the cemetery. First, a fence was erected around its perimeter. A resting place for the dead is a holy place, and holiness must be clearly delineated and set off with borders. A dedication ceremony and the recitation of special prayers sanctified the Jewish cemetery.

One corner of the field was set aside for the burial of *sheimos,* holy books. Whereas other nations discard their sacred tomes — indeed, it is not uncommon to find prayer books and Bibles in the trash can — the Jewish attitude is very different. Our holy books contain sacred names;[1] thus the books themselves are considered sacred and must not be burned or trashed. Rather, they are buried with respect, just as with a human being. Once every year or two a collection of *sheimos* would be taken up in the *shtetl* and a burial conducted, complete with special prayers.

---

1. The term *sheimos* derives from the Hebrew word for "names."

Another section of the cemetery was designated especially for mothers who died during childbirth. This was considered the holiest and most respected section of the cemetery. The reason for this is explained by our Sages as follows. There is an etiquette in burying the dead; for instance, we do not bury a wicked man next to a righteous one, and even among the righteous we distinguish between a lesser *tzaddik* and a greater one, for each *tzaddik* has his own level of *kedushah* (holiness). The highest level of holiness one can attain is in the giving of one's life for the good of the Jewish people. And can there be a more heroic deed, or a greater service to the Jewish people, than delivering a baby? After all, this is the act that ensures the perpetuation of the Jewish nation!

According to Torah law, only men have an obligation to bring children into the world. Women may choose to remain single their entire lives. Despite this — and to their lasting honor — the women of the *shtetl* did marry, in the full knowledge that many of them would die in childbirth. In marrying, a bride took her life into her hands. If she subsequently lost her own life in bringing a new life into the world, she was duly buried in the holiest part of the cemetery, the one set aside for *tzaddikim*. Their place in Heaven, too, is the one reserved for those who risk their lives for the sake of the Jewish people.

In the *shtetl* of Zembrove, "that fence" — the border of the Jewish cemetery — stood at one end of the village. Enveloped in legends and fearsome stories, no child or pregnant woman was ever encouraged to enter there. At midnight — so rumor had it — the dead gathered to pray. If you passed nearby and heard your name called, it meant you were being called up to the Torah reading! In that case, you had to enter backwards and never, ever open your eyes, lest you recognize some of the dead and be prevented from leaving. If you refused to enter when called, you would die within a month's time.

As the story goes, a daredevil of a Jewish boy once laughed at the superstition and declared that he would enter at midnight.

"I'm not scared," he boasted. The other boys gave him a stick to place in the ground near a grave, as proof that he had really been there. They waited fearfully at a distance, cowering in the dark.

It was winter, and the daring lad wore a long coat. He had a good laugh calling out the names of people who had recently died in the village. Then he tried to thrust his stick into the ground near some old graves, but it would not enter the frozen earth. Finally, he forced the stick into some loose earth near a freshly dug grave. He turned to leave — but found himself held fast. The dead were pulling him back!

The brave boy became hysterical. He began to scream for help. In the silence of the night, his voice could be heard a long way off. His friends heard the screams, but were too terrified to help. Then the screaming stopped. The boys waited, but he did not come out.

In a panic, they ran to their parents, overcome by guilt for encouraging him in his reckless act. "We killed him!" they wailed. The adults hastily ran to the cemetery, where they found the young hero, who had passed out beside the new grave — the hem of his coat held fast in the ground by the tip of his stick!

People laughed. The boy could simply have taken off his coat and run. But in those terrifying moments, he was convinced that the dead were indeed pulling him into the grave because he had disturbed them in their prayers. How could a Jewish child not be afraid of cemeteries after hearing a story like that?

Still, watching the Polish children make their way freely into both the Jewish and the Christian cemeteries and picking the beautiful flowers that grew there, the Jewish children of Zembrove gradually lost their fear. They still believed implicitly in the truth of the tales, but decided that the danger was present only at midnight. During the day, the dead slept peacefully — everyone knew that they couldn't stand the light of the sun. During the day, the cemetery was perfectly safe.

Then the children met Chaveh the Klaperke, and quickly changed their minds.

Chaveh the Klaperke

The doctors in the *shtetl* knew very little. There was no real medicine, not even aspirin. Most babies were delivered at home by a midwife, and the mortality rate among both infants and delivering mothers was extremely high. As a result of this situation, a special poetic prayer was written and recited during *Selichos*, the penitential prayers said prior to Rosh Hashanah. Pleading for a cure to children's illnesses, the prayer was enough to bring tears to anyone's eyes: "Oh, L-rd, please cure the illnesses of the fruitful vine . . . Perfect from the womb, do not shrivel [his] roots." Today, most congregations omit this poignant prayer. However, to this very day, guests at a wedding sing out their wishes that the new couple bring into the world *zara chaya v'kayama* — living and surviving offspring.

Given the deficiency of medical skill in the village, it is not surprising that the villagers were especially fervent in their prayers for good health, sometimes calling on the merit of those who had passed from this world. That was old Chaveh's job: to act as intercessor between the living and the dead. She was an expert at talking to the dead. Chaveh had all the family trees in the village at her fingertips, as well as the names of all the living relatives of every person buried in the Jewish cemetery. If you had trouble locating a generations-old grave, Chaveh found it for you. Like a woman in her own garden, she bossed around the living as well as the dead!

If the regular midwife was called away from the town, Chaveh was her substitute. If the baby died, it was she who personally delivered it to the grave. People would say: "She brings them to this world, and she sends them right back." The villagers were afraid of Chaveh. She was considered the "partner" of the *Malach Hamaves*, the Angel of Death. Who dared stand up to such a partnership?

When orphans became engaged, they would not marry until they had visited their mother's or father's grave and invited

The Klaperke

them to the wedding. The young bride would soak the headstone in tears as she begged her mother to be present at her *chuppah*. When Chaveh noticed a young girl crying over a stone while a youth waited in the distance, she immediately sized up the situation. She would wait until the girl was done, and then approach. First Chaveh blessed the bride with a *"Mazel tov!"* Then, holding the girl's right hand, she performed her duty. She knocked on the stone three times with her cane — her customary way of announcing her presence. (From this practice came her name, *Klaperke*. In Yiddish, to *klap* means to knock.)

"Perl Dvoshe!" she would begin, "It's me, Chaveh. I've come to give you *mazel tov*! Surely you will not insult your daughter, and you'll come to her *simchah* (celebration)! She looks so beautiful, and the *chassan* (groom), so handsome. Give them your blessing. After all, it's your own flesh and blood. Stand up for her before the *Kisei HaKavod*, the Holy Throne of the A-mighty. Let them be blessed with *parnasah* (sustenance) and living children!

"Don't sleep, Perl. Do something, or I'll not leave you in peace. I'll knock on your grave every day! May you have lots of *nachas* (pleasure) from the young couple. Amen!"

Then she led the bride toward her betrothed and blessed them both with tears in her eyes, her ever-sorrowing face wreathed in smiles. People said that ever since she buried her own daughter at the age of two, she had made it her business to support every bride who came to the cemetery and to attend her wedding — invited or not.

Although pregnant women were advised not to visit the cemetery, many broke the rule. A year after the wedding, the erstwhile bride could often be found crying at the same stone, pleading with her mother to intercede for her and pray that her delivery be without complications: "I'm scared, Mama!" Another year, and the same woman at the same grave might be wailing, "Mama, we named the child after you, and now she is sick. The doctor doesn't know what to do. Do something, Mama! The Master of the Universe is my only hope, and you are my avenue to Him!"

At this point, old Chaveh would again step in. Gently pushing the young woman aside, she would *klap* three times with her cane, announcing her arrival. She embraced the young mother while talking to the dead one: "Perl Dvoshe, wake up! It's me, Chaveh. I came to tell you that your Miriam is here. Her baby, named after you, the beautiful little bird, is ill — something in her sweet little throat. So don't waste any time. Get up! Stand before the *Pamalya Shel Malah* and plead for your child! Don't take 'no' for an answer!

"Your daughter Miriam needs *parnasah*, too. Her husband is not very well. She herself is just as beautiful as the day you departed, but so skinny; apparently there isn't much food on the table. So hurry and do something for your *nachas*! She'll give candles to the *Bais HaMidrash* (House of Study) so people can learn Torah by their light. It will be a help for your soul!"

In especially difficult cases, instead of candles she would advise the supplicant to donate linen: "Measure in meters the length of the cemetery fence. Give the exact amount in linen to the old-age home, and some to the hospital. That will fence off your child from the cemetery!"

And so, when the village children stepped inside the cemetery to pick the flowers, they came face to face with Chaveh the Klaperke, dressed in her old bulky clothes with her cane thumping ahead of her. Normally, she would have raised her cane and chased them out — and the children would have run for their lives on meeting such a frightening old figure in the cemetery. But Lazer, leader of the "gang," wanted to impress the others with his bravery. He stood up to the old woman, declaring, "We are picking flowers for the new family, the Solomons!"

Chaveh, about to raise her cane, instead pushed it deeper into the ground. "Who are you? And who are the Solomons?"

The children erupted in giggles. This was the first time anyone had asked them who they were. Surely, the whole world knew that!

"The *poretz* is our father, and Shoshe is our mother. Now you know?" Lazer and the others replied.

For the first time, Chaveh had met up with children who were not afraid of her. The respect she bore the *poretz* and his wife extended to their children. In a motherly voice she asked them to sit down in a circle around a tree stump, the only place she could find to sit. She lifted the pince-nez from around her neck and perched them on her nose. Then the lecture began. "You see, *kinderlach* (children), a cemetery is a holy place. The human body is holy and so is the grave. A person is forbidden to make use of them. That's why one cannot sit on a grave. Luckily, I have found this tree stump to sit on to relieve my aching feet. One cannot raise crops in a cemetery, for that would mean making use of a body or a grave. Your mother Shoshe would never approve of these flowers if she found out where they came from.

"Besides," she added sagely, "it's bad luck!"

Transportation in the Shtetl

Motor cars were unknown in the *shtetl*, as was asphalt.[1] Some village streets were paved with cobblestones, which rattled every bone in a passenger's body. The standard mode of transportation was by horse and buggy, and in the winter months, by sled.

The ubiquitous ba'al agalah

---

1. The peasants (known as Muziks) had never even *heard* of motor cars. Once, during the Bolshevik revolution (in which the peasants sided with the "Whites," or the czar's men, against the Red Army), a Bolshevik lieutenant by the name of Clementy Voroshilov was driving a steel-plated armored vehicle. He lost his way near a village, and the motor chose that moment to die on him. The local Muziks had never before seen a moving object that was not pulled by horses or oxen. Terrified, they armed themselves with rifles, scythes, and pitchforks and waited for the "devil" to emerge.

The "devil," Red Lieutenant Voroshilov, waited inside, certain that he would be killed by the peasants if he dared come out. Finally, the Muziks decided to hook up a pair of oxen to the vehicle and pull it into the village, where the blacksmith would find a way to open the "devil box." They set this plan into action. However, once the car was moving the lieutenant was able to put the stick in gear. The motor roared! Panic stricken, the peasants ran for their lives. The oxen broke loose, and Voroshilov drove off. (He later became Marshal of the Red Army, Defense Kommissar of the USSR, and Stalin's right-hand man.)

Main street in a Shtetl

Every big landowner owned a troika, which was a coach or sled pulled by three horses. The Russian poets idolized the troika. Here is a free translation from a few of them:

> *Hey troika on the soft snow,*
> *The night is young, frost over all*
> *Shine, you silvery moon*
> *All is white, all is mute!*
>
> (Turgenev)

> *Over the gray winter path*
> *The troika pulls the sled.*
> *The sleigh bells are ringing*
> *Like a funeral dirge.*
>
> (Pushkin)

> *Swiftly speeding horses' hooves*
> *Pounding feet on icy roads*
> *And the decorated troika*
> *Over the snow steps apace!*
>
> (Nekrasov)

With horses and wagons the primary means of transportation in the *shtetl*, the *balagole* (a Yiddish contraction of the Hebrew *ba'al agalah*), or wagon driver, was a vital figure. When the railroads finally made their appearance in Russia, that most primitive of lands, the men contracted to lay down the rails were mostly Jewish. Knowing that the trains would ruin the livelihood of the local *balagoles*, the contractors made sure that, except in major cities, every station was built a few kilometers from the town — thus securing the need for professional horse-and-wagon services.

In one particular *shtetl*, the very first train ever to be seen arrived during the night and was scheduled to depart on Shabbos. Normally, every Shabbos after partaking of the *cholent*, the entire Jewish populace of the *shtetl* took a nap. (After all, the letters that make up the word "Shabbos" — *shin, beis, taf* — stand for s*heinah b'Shabbos ta'anug*: Sleeping on Shabbos is a pleasure!) On Shabbos, all transportation came to a halt. Even non-Jews, knowing there was nothing to be bought on that day, did not travel to town. The street was usually so empty that one could lie down and go to sleep right in the middle of it! But that Shabbos was different. On that momentous afternoon, the entire village walked down to the station to watch the spectacle of the first train's departure.

Reb Mendl, "wise man" of the *shtetl*, was voluble in his skepticism. "They claim these 'houses on wheels' will move. Ridiculous! How can anything move unless it pulled by horses or pushed by oxen? They claim that water is boiled inside, just like we make tea, and turns into steam, and the steam turns the wheels. *Meshuggeh* (crazy)!"

The villagers waited for a miracle. Reb Mendl repeated his assertion: "It won't move." Suddenly, a whistle shrieked: *Whee! Whee! Whee!* The "houses on wheels" began to move. Not only were they moving, but they were picking up speed every minute! The folk were astonished. They were *preechmelet* (a combination Yiddish-Russian word not to be found in any dictionary), which meant petrified, mesmerized, stupefied and hypnotized, all at once.

Reb Mendl was one of the first to recover. He said, "Well, they puffed and sweated and steamed and whistled, and they got the thing moving. But I'll bet my life they'll *never* be able to stop it!"

Trains and Mussar

The trains arrived in Russia from Koenigsberg in East Prussia. Koenigsburg was the home of Reb Yisrael Salanter, founder of the *mussar* movement. Allegedly, on contemplating the train, he was inspired to write a song, entitled, *"Der Eisenban"* ("The Railroad"), which the Novarodoker used to sing. I used to wonder whether Reb Yisrael really did write the song; but after listening to the lyrics, it is not difficult to believe that it might well have been Reb Yisrael who composed it, for it is a classic lesson in *mussar*.

By way of explanation: When the railroad first came to Russia, people thought they could treat it just as they were used to treating the local *ba'al agalah*. When asked, "When are you leaving for Minsk?" the wagon driver might reply, "At 8 in the morning." However, what with waiting for this passenger and that package, he was lucky if he left at 10. Assuming that the same free-and-easy attitude toward time applied to the rail system as well, people at first often missed their trains. They soon learned that if the train was scheduled to depart at 8 a.m. sharp, that was when it left. If you got there at 8:01, that was just too bad. The lesson is implicit: As the Talmud states, "One can gain eternity in one minute" (*Avodah Zarah* 6b). One can also, tragically, lose eternity in the same minute.

One could bargain with a *ba'al agalah*. "Reb Fievl, how much will you charge me for a trip to Vilna?"

"Ten rubles," Fievl might reply.

"Make it seven."

"No, I can't. I'll take you for nine."

Finally, driver and passenger would settle on a fare of eight-and-a half rubles. With the train, on the other hand, if you were short just one cent, you couldn't buy a ticket. How analogous this is to life! On Rosh Hashanah, we are required to have a certain number of *mitzvos* in order to acquire our "ticket" for the coming year. Short just one *mitzvah,* we run the danger of losing our seat on the train, G-d forbid.

And if, on Rosh Hashanah, you get a "ticket" to ride third class, you cannot switch to the first-class car. As the Talmud states: "A person's income is decreed from one Rosh Hashanah to the next" (*Beitzah* 17). Inscribed for a specific income, you will not, for all your efforts, make a single extra dollar.

Finally, an individual can only ride to the destination that is stamped on his ticket. Should he attempt to take the train to a different place, the conductor has the power to force him off despite all his tears and protests. And who is the conductor in life? The *Malach Hamaves* — the Angel of Death! As it says in the Yom Kippur liturgy: "May this Yom Kippur to next Yom Kippur pass over us only to the good!" (*Kol Nidrei*)

These are some of the ideas expressed in *"Der Eisenban."* The average person looks upon the train as a mere vehicle to transport him from one place to another. A *mussar* giant like Reb Yisrael looked upon it as an allegory for life.

Der Eisenban

A railroad, new, has just been built.
It carries passengers, poor and rich.
Hurry, run to see the invention
But don't forget — it's a reflection of you!

People are sitting in the cars.
The locomotive represents time.
It drags along millions of people.
It runs like a bullet from a gun!

Each single rail is a minute,
Each station a year,
Each wagon an hour.
The entire train is a generation!

Ticket in pocket,
That's the travel plan — a man's mazel.
How far to go, and what class?
As assigned by the Director in Heaven!

The conductors check the tickets,
Place each one accordingly:
Some first class, full of luxury,
Some third class, where it's crowded and wet.

The conductors are agents
From Heaven above.
Some get health and money besides,
Some to live in overcrowded flats, in poverty.

Health and wealth and everything else
Children like apples on the tree
Some loneliness, sickness and poverty
Or to be a wanderer, far from home!

Don't argue with the conductor.
The world is run according to a plan.
Each one receives what's on his ticket
Decided by the Almighty, Director of the train.

At the station, bells are ringing.
Conductors jump up and down,
Passengers are running with luggage.
Some getting off, some getting on.

Our stations are the years.
On Rosh Hashanah we are marked:
Who shall continue traveling,
Who shall get off the train.

Our cashiers are the Heavenly Court.
The tickets are sold according to the mitzvos and law.
Some travel longer, some less,
Some miss the train altogether.

When ordered to get off, don't argue
Even if you are still young.
Your ticket is null, it's no use crying,
It's the order of Hashem, Director of the train!

The machinist constantly watches the road,
Observes how much coal, steam or heat.
By taking off his eyes for a moment
The train might derail, endangering lives.

The machinist is the mind, the brain,
The leader of a person's life.
But the mind alone can derail a person —
Hence the Torah was given to him, to help.

A Torah given from Above:
When in doubt, study her and ask for answers.
In her you'll find faith, philosophy and more.
You'll then continue your journey in peace!

If you want to live according to your own dull logic
Laughing at the Torah, neglecting the entire plan —
Watch out! You are falling, derailed from the tracks
A punishment from the Director of the train.

To avoid a collision of two trains
Is the function of the telegraph man.
Our pedagogues, our teachers, are our telegraph men!
Be careful of contrasting ideas in our children's minds.

The old generation lives with faith;
The young are calling for a stop.
So you teachers, avoid collisions
Of two opposing ideas on the same line!

With one wrong word, you can twist a child's mind.
He may lose emunah, hope, and become a tyrant.
Broken, devastated, he'll jump off the proper line
Against the wishes of the Director of the train.

The imbeciles, the idiots, the stuffed brains
Ask, "How can a train run without horses?
How can air and steam have the strength
To pull wagons full of people along the earth?"

Those fools observe the world with eyes of flesh.
They don't believe; they don't want to understand
That the Heavenly steam lives in every creation.
That's the energy that moves, pulls, makes them walk!

Stones, trees, animals, fire, water, and wind.
The soul hidden in the human they can't see: They are blind.
They can't understand or grasp
The plan — the wisdom of the Director of the Railroad!

Chapter 2: Rabbanus — the Rabbinate

or all the poverty it suffered under the czar, Russian Jewry managed to turn the land of their oppression into a fertile spiritual ground. Here the holy Ba'al Shem Tov planted the seeds of *Chassidus* and Reb Yisrael Salanter brought forth the *mussar* movement. *Yeshivos* and great *roshei yeshivah* saw their heyday in the Russian Pale. Illustrious scholars abounded, along with their written works. In these muddy little towns and villages, Yiddish and Hebrew literature flourished. Above all, Russian Jewry gave us *rabbanim* — great rabbis.

Election of a Rav

In a country where the democratic ideal was unknown throughout its thousand-year history, the Jews alone practiced democracy. *Shabbos Bereishis*, the first Shabbos of the year, was

The last officers of the Lomza Kehillah. R' Moshe Shatzkes is seated in the center.

election day, when new officers for all the village institutions were chosen, including the *kehillah* (community) officials who oversaw all aspects of *shtetl* life and who bore the responsibility of representing the community to the government.

The single exception was the village *Rav*. In the matter of choosing their spiritual leader, the masses had no say. That task was delegated to the Torah scholars and the many *balebatim* (a Yiddish contraction of the Hebrew *ba'alei batim*), householders, who had *semichah* (rabbinical ordination). This was in keeping, apparently, with the procedure recommended by the Maharsha, who, in the 17th century, served as *Rav* in my second "home town" of Tiktin:

> ". . . the cause of these problems is that the lay leaders choose a rabbi according to their whim or fancy, with money playing no small role. Properly, the scholars and rabbis should select the leader from their midst, as was done in previous generations" (*Maharsha, Sotah* 40).

The town's learned men would travel throughout the country to seek out and "talk in Torah" with various candidates. A prospective *rav* would be invited to visit the town and deliver a *drashah*, or Torah lecture. Ironically, smaller towns had a better chance of attracting a rabbi of stature than the larger cities. Whereas the big-city *rav* was constantly occupied with communal affairs and problems, the true giants of Torah were drawn to the smaller *shtetls*, which offered more time for learning Torah and putting their scholarship into writing. If a *rav* did agree to accept an offer from a bigger city, it was either because he felt he could accomplish great things there or because his *rebbetzin*, tired of struggling to make ends meet, took the practical point of view: A bigger city meant a bigger income.

Reb Yoshe Ber Soloveichik, it is said, refused the position of *Rav* in Brisk. Two separate delegations of townspeople were not able to persuade him to change his mind. Finally, a third contingent arrived, with coach and horses. At its head was a wise man.

"*Rebbi*," he said, "there are 25,000 Jews in Brisk who are waiting for you!"

It took only a few minutes for the *Rav* to reply. "In that case, we mustn't keep the *tzibur* (public) waiting. Let's go!"

A smiling *rebbetzin* handed him his coat, and they entered the coach.

There were other considerations which could hold a great man back from the rabbinate. Some scholars took very seriously the edict, "Do not make the Torah a spade with which to dig" (*Avos* 4:7). Thus, it is said that the *gaon* and *tzaddik* Reb Yitzchak Blazer, foremost student of Rav Yisrael Salanter, approached his *Rebbi* with a plan. In need of a means of livelihood, he intended to become a house painter. All he needed, he said, were two buckets and two brushes — one for white and the other for black. What Rav Yisrael Salanter replied is not known; but he left for Petersburg the very next day and arranged for Reb Yitzchak to become its *Rav*, hence the name he is best remembered by: Reb Itzele Petersburger.

"Robber Barons"

In the smaller towns, which could not afford to pay the *Rav* a salary decent enough to live on, he and his family subsisted on G.Z.EI.L.H. (literally, "robbery"). These initials stood for certain taxable items, the profits from which would be turned over to the *rebbetzin* as a supplement to the *Rav's* regular salary. The *gimmel* stood for gasoline, the kerosene universally used in the absence of electricity. The *zayin* stood for *zaltz*: No one could live without salt. The *yud* was for *yayin*, wine; the *lamed* for *licht*, candles; and the *hey* stood for *heivn*, the yeast used for baking. Some villages would give the *rebbetzin* all five concessions, while others granted only one or two.

The *Rav*, like the *Rosh Yeshivah*, dressed in the same fashion as the town's other *balebatim*. To protect them from the elements — snow in winter, rain and the ubiquitous mud in summer — the men wore knee-high leather boots, with their pants tucked inside. The boots were most noticeable on Friday nights in *shul*. All week long the Jew worked hard to make ends meet; on Shabbos every man, from the *Rav* on down, was a king with freshly shined boots. As shoe polish still lay in the future, wagon grease was used to give the boots their special shine. The grease also gave the boots a very distinctive smell — but nobody minded. It was all *lekavod Shabbos*, in honor of the holy Sabbath!

It was customary for the parents of a bride to buy her *chassan* a suit — often the only new suit of clothes he received for the rest of his life. This tradition applied to the *Rav* as well: The only *kapote* (frock coat) he owned was the one he received at his own wedding. If a man was lucky, there might be a relative in America who sent a box of clothing. It was the tailor's job to remake the clothing to fit its new owner, who then proudly dressed up in his finery — *lekavod Shabbos*.

For a *rav*, life in the big city held different challenges. Very often there were litigations involving large sums of money, called *dinei Torah.* Not every *rav* was worldly enough to judge these cases, and sometimes certain expert *rabbanim* — men experienced at detecting subtle lies and business tricks — were called in to participate in other cities' *dinei Torah.* Rav Avraham Kalmanowitz of Tiktin (founder of the Mirrer Yeshivah in Brooklyn) and Rav Moshe Shatzkes of Lomza were two such rabbis.

Certain cities — my two home towns of Lomza and Tiktin among them — made a point of selecting a *rav* who was either a *posek* (halachic authority), a *mechaber sefarim* (author of scholarly works), or a *darshan* (public speaker) — and preferably all three. Another such city was Piotrkow. All the rabbis in that city were famous for their scholarly works. Reb Meir Shapiro was *Rav* there before he moved to Lublin, where he established his Yeshivas Chachmei Lublin. Once, on Purim, someone asked Reb Meir Shapiro: "*Rebbi,* what's going to happen after *techiyas hameisim* (resurrection of the dead), when all the great rabbis arise? Who will be *Rav* in Piotrkow then?"

Reb Meir, renowned for his wisdom, replied, "Each *rav* for his own generation."

"But, *Rebbi,*" he was asked again, "what will happen if the *Rav* wakes up and his *balebatim* don't?"

"A *rav* who cannot drag along his *balebatim,*" Reb Meir declared forcefully, "does not deserve to be a *rav!*"

Rav Shapiro served in six different cities. When asked why he could not stay in one place, he answered, smiling, "A *rav* is like a nail. As long as he has a head, he can be pulled out of one place and put into another." In fact, Reb Meir was about to move again — this time from Lublin to Lodz — when his soul passed from this world.

There are two types of speakers or writers. The first kind says much, but knows little. In a single speech or written work he will deliver to his public everything he knows. A thought that might be expressed in one line stretches out to ten, and by the time he's done you feel you've heard all he has to offer.

Then there are those who speak little but know much. These men are rich indeed in ideas, but they do not advertise their wealth. When you hear them speak or read their writings, you feel certain that there is much, much more in store. What they've delivered up until now is just a drop, lifted from the deep well of their wisdom and knowledge.

This second trait characterized the rabbis who graced the towns of Piotrkow, Lomza, Tiktin, and many others. The community willingly, and with great respect, followed the lead of such truly illustrious leaders.

"Yachol"

Unlike today's American rabbis, a *rav* in Europe delivered a speech only twice yearly. The first time was on *Shabbos Shuvah*, the Shabbos between Rosh Hashanah and Yom Kippur, when we read the *maftir* of "*Shuvah Yisrael*." The speech was usually a masterly combination of Torah, *mussar*, and *drash*, with a call to *teshuvah* (repentance) before Yom Kippur, the Day of Judgment. The second speech, which took place on *Shabbos HaGadol*, the Shabbos just before Pesach, was devoted to Torah, *halachah* (specifically, the laws of Pesach), and a call to remember the poor and supply them with all the holiday's needs.

If the *rav* was a big *talmid chacham,* a great Talmudist, he would place a notice on the *shul's* bulletin board weeks ahead of time, along with a *mareh mekomos,* announcing the topic he would discuss and the exact sources in Talmud, *Rambam,* etc. to which he would refer. This gave the townspeople and scholars a chance to study the sources and prepare themselves for the *rav's* lecture. They readied themselves to engage in Talmudic battle with the *Rav*, to state their opinions of the subject matter, sometimes in opposition to the *rav's* views, as Talmudic scholars are wont to do.

If, however, the *rav* was not such a great scholar, his speech was usually derived from the works of others. In this case, he preferred not to wage battle with the scholars of the town. He would put up a notice on the bulletin board on the day before his speech, so that no one had time to study the material or prepare himself thoroughly.

The *shtetl* folk described this system using a phrase from the Pesach *Haggadah*: "*Yachol meiRosh Chodesh, Talmud lomar, 'bayom hahu.'*[1] If the *rav* was a capable scholar (*yachol*), he put up the notice on Rosh Chodesh, two weeks ahead of time. If, however, he was not all that scholarly, if he was merely able to quote from the Talmud ("*Talmud lomar*"), then "*bayom hahu*" — he placed the notice on the very same day!

A History of Semichah

In every town and city there resided literally dozens of men who possessed rabbinical ordination, or *semichah*. However, the title of "Rav" was used only when a man was called up to the Torah — much as the title "*Kohen*" is used today. No one had the audacity to call himself a "Rabbi" unless he was actively engaged in the rabbinate or in *chinuch* (Jewish education). My own father, for example, was qualified to be a *rosh yeshivah*. He had *semichah* from the Aruch HaShulchan, the *Rav* of Navaradok. He also had *Yoreh Yoreh-Yaddin Yaddin* from his *Rosh Yeshivah*, Reb Eliyahu Boruch Kammai, the *Rav* of Mir. Nevertheless, since he was a businessman, he never referred to himself as "Rabbi."

How and when did the practice of *semichah* begin, and when did it end?

The original legal term "*semichah*" does not exist any more: It ended 1,500 years ago. What we call *semichah* today is really *semichas chachamim*, and the practice is a mere imitation of the ancient *semichah*, and does not have its legal validity.

---

1. Literally: "One might think (*yachol*) [that the obligation to discuss the Exodus from Egypt commences on] Rosh Chodesh, but the Torah says (*Talmud lomar*), 'bayom hahu' — on that day."

The very first *semichah* was given to Yehoshua by Moshe *Rabbeinu,* on Hashem's orders. "And he placed his hands upon him, and he charged him" (*Bamidbar* 27:23). This was the basic procedure followed for generations. Only a man who has *semichah* himself is authorized to give it to another qualified person. Also, *semichah* can be given only in Eretz Yisrael. Both the giver and the receiver must be within its borders at the time of the nomination: "*Ein semichah b'chutz la'aretz,* There is no *semichah* outside the land [of Israel]" (*Sanhedrin* 14a). The giver must tell the receiver, orally or in writing, that he is nominated for *semichah* and is entitled to be called "Rabbi." This process was known in *Eretz Yisrael* as *minui;* in Bavel it was called *semichah* (*Yerushalmi Sanhedrin* 1:2).

Thus, the line of *semichah* was handed down directly, through nomination, from Moshe *Rabbeinu* to Yehoshua to the *zekeinim* (elders of Israel). People would travel from Bavel and Surya to Tiberias, which lay within the borders of *Eretz Yisrael,* in order to receive *semichah* from those who possessed it. The golden chain was unbroken until the end of the fourth century of the Common Era. Travel to *Eretz Yisrael* became extremely dangerous. Qualified *talmidei chachamim* could not risk their lives in order to give or receive *semichah,* and eventually the few remaining holders of *semichah* within the land died out. The chain was broken.

Rambam, in his introduction to his monumental *Mishneh Torah-Yad HaChazakah,* which he began to write "in the year 1108 from the destruction of the *Bais HaMikdash,* which corresponds to the year 4937 from the Creation of the universe," gives the lineage of Torah teachers for 40 generations — beginning with Moshe *Rabbeinu* and ending with Rav Ashi and Ravina, editors of the Talmud. After Rav Ashi and Ravina, the Talmud was sealed.

The enemy occupiers of Israel appreciated the value and power of *semichah.* To crush the backbone of the people, they knew they must destroy the legal system and the Torah leadership. We find recorded:

"Once the vicious rulers ordered: Whoever gives *semichah* and whoever receives *semichah* shall be executed, and the city where the nomination took place shall be destroyed. What did R' Yehudah ben Bava do? He sat between two mountains, between two cities, Usho and Shifrom, and gave *semichah* to five men. When he spotted the enemy, he told them, 'My sons, run.'

'What about you?' they asked.

'I shall remain here like a stone.'

He was caught. His body was stabbed by three hundred bayonets and became like a sieve" (*Sanhedrin* 14a).

R' Yehudah ben Bava gave his life for the continuation of the golden chain.

The Rav as Teacher

From the very inception of the concept of *rabbanus* among the people of Israel, the *rav's* first duty was to teach Torah. Ruling on halachic questions and arbitrating *dinei Torah* were secondary. The very first *Rav*, Moshe *Rabbeinu*, was known not as a king, nor as a leader, deliverer, or even lawgiver. He filled all these roles, but his title became — and remains to this day —Moshe *Rabbeinu*, our teacher.[1] As he told his father-in-law, Yisro:

---

1. There is an old question: Why is Moshe *Rabbeinu* called by that name? Wouldn't a more proper name be *Rabbeinu* Moshe? The same question can be asked about the phrase we find throughout the Talmud: *tanu rabbanan* (literally, "they have learned, the rabbis"). Wouldn't it be more correct to say *rabbanan tanu* ("the rabbis have learned")? The ancient answer to this question reveals a hidden lesson: First they learned, and then they became *rabbanan*. Similarly, Moshe began as just plain Moshe; after a great deal of learning, he became *Rabbeinu*.

I have found another explanation. Reb Chaim, older brother of the Maharal, explains: If we called him *Rabbeinu* Moshe, it might imply that we accepted the Torah under the influence or persuasion of our great teacher. This is absolutely untrue. We accepted the Torah of our own free will. It was delivered to us by humble Moshe, directly from Hashem. Only afterward did he become "*Rabbeinu*," our teacher.

"The people come to me to inquire of Hashem." *Rashi* explains this to mean, "To ask for teachings from the mouth of the Mighty One." It was only afterwards that Moshe stated, "and I judge between man and his fellow" (*Shemos* 18:15).

The *rav* of the *shtetl* was neither fundraiser nor social worker. He bore the responsibility for such communal matters as *kashrus*, *chinuch*, charity and justice, but his primary task was teaching Torah. The *rav* would deliver *shiurim* (Torah classes) to the people on different levels, and *semichah* to those who qualified. Hence, every *rav* served a double function as a *rosh yeshivah*.

To make it easier for the *rav* to dedicate more time to Torah study and teaching, larger communities would hire a *dayan*, or judge. The role of the *dayan* (also known by the term *Moreh Tzedek*, Teacher of Justice) was to relieve the *rav* of the burden of ruling on questions of *halachah*.

As the Chassidic movement took hold, the title *Rebbe* was assigned to the Chassidic leader, while the spiritual head of the community was called, variously, *Rav, Rosh Bais Din, Av Bais Din*, or *Mara D'asra* ("Master of the Place"). The title *Moreh Tzedek* continued to be reserved for the *dayan*, who acted as assistant to the *rav*.

The role of the *rav* began to change with the opening of the first *yeshivah* in Volozhin and those that came later. Gradually, the duty of teaching Torah was removed from the shoulders of the *rabbanim*. The functions split: The dissemination of Torah became the *rosh yeshivah's* domain, while the *rav* was exclusively involved with the community. For a number of years, some *rabbanim* did continue to perform double duty as *rav* and *rosh yeshivah*. Today, this practice is virtually non-existent.[1]

---

1. Wherever the Jews have gone throughout their history, the Torah has gone with them. When Nebuchadnezzar expelled King Yehoyakim to Bavel, the so-called "*hacharash v'hamasger*" (*Kings II* 24:16) went with him. *Chazal* explain the roots of these words. *Hacharash* comes from the word *cheresh*, or silence: When the sages began lecturing in Torah, everyone fell silent. *Seger* means "closure":

Semichah in Europe

The giving of *semichah*, as we have said, belonged to the *Rav*. In Europe, it was not the *Rosh Yeshiva* who gave *semichah*. In fact, many *roshei yeshivah* did not themselves have *semichah*, and therefore could not give it to anyone else. They could easily have obtained *semichah*, but they did not need it. The situation is comparable, *lehavdil*, to a medical school professor who teaches future doctors but cannot legally write out a prescription.

The Chofetz Chaim was never a *rav*, and therefore never had *semichah*. When he was supposed to travel to Vienna for medical attention and to attend the *Knessiah Gedolah* of Agudas Yisrael, he was told by a foreign ministry official — a non-Jew, and a Pole at that — that the Chief Rabbi of the Jews, a Rabbi of all rabbis, needed to present documentation of his ordination. An odd problem arose: How to explain that he had never been ordained? They had to rush to R' Chaim Ozer Grodzensky in Vilna, who quickly wrote the Chofetz Chaim *semichah*.

A similar situation came about in Slutsk, where the *Rosh Yeshivah* was the *gaon* R' Isser Zalman Meltzer, author of the famous seven-volume *Even HaAzel*. The *Rav* of Slutsk was the famous *Ridvaz*, who wrote a commentary on the *Talmud Yerushalmi*. After traveling to America to raise funds for the publication of the *Yerushalmi*, Ridvaz took up a position as *Rav* of Tzefas. The *kehillah* of Slutsk then approached the *Rosh Yeshivah* to accept the *rabbanus* of the city. Suddenly, R' Isser

---

Once those 1,000 sages closed a subject in Torah, there was none to open it (*Sanhedrin* 38a).

Next came the generation of *Sofrim*, whose brightest light was Ezra *HaSofer*. These were followed by *Anshei Knesses HaGedolah* and then the *zugos* (pairs of sages), the *Tannaim, Amoraim* and *Savoraim*. After them came 450 years of *Geonim*, then the *Rishonim* and the *Acharonim*. With the passage of time, the level of the generations has diminished and so have the teachers of Torah. Yet to this day, the titles of *Rosh Yeshivah, Rav,* and *Rebbi* are borne with a mixture of pride and humility by those who are genuinely qualified.

R' Yechiel Mordechai Gordon

Zalman realized that he did not have *semichah*. R' Chaim Brisker was called upon to send him *semichah* by telegram!

In my home town of Lomza, R' Yechiel Mordechai Gordon served as *Rosh Yeshivah*. When the *Rav*, R' Archik Baksht,[1] departed Lomza to accept the rabbinate of Shavl in Lithuania, a committee of townspeople, including my father, came to the *Rosh Yeshivah* to offer him the position of *Rav* of Lomza. The *Rosh Yeshivah* rejected the offer, explaining that he already bore responsibility for a big *yeshivah* in town, plus another in Petach Tikvah. "Besides," he added, "I don't have *semichah*."

An interesting story is told of the *Rav* of Minsk. A young man once approached R' Dovid Tevl (*Rav* of Minsk and author of the famous work, *Nachalas Dovid*), requesting *semichah*. Naturally, they spoke together in Torah and Jewish *hashkafah* (ideology). In the course of their talk the young man expressed ideas that were not to the *Rav's* liking. Realizing his mistake, the fellow justified himself by explaining, "*Rebbi*, these are not my ideas. They come from *Rambam* in *Moreh Nevuchim* (Guide to the Perplexed)." The *Rav* of Minsk said, "Young man, let me tell you a story.

"A small-town businessman used to go every month to a wholesaler in the big city to restock his store. To bring the merchandise home, he would hire a *ba'al agalah* with a horse and wagon. Once, when his regular wagon driver was sick, he hired a young man who had never been in a big city.

"In the course of his shopping, the businessman pointed at

---

1. Incidentally, when R' Baksht gave *semichah* to his *talmidim*, he would add the words, *Afilu b'tiv gittin v'kiddushin* (including matters of marriage and divorce).

the various loaded shelves to indicate the merchandise he wanted. While pointing at a certain shelf, he accidentally broke a window. Apologizing profusely, he offered to pay for the damage. The wholesaler wouldn't hear of it.

" 'Calm yourself, Reb Yaakov,' he said genially. 'It was an accident. Thank Heaven you didn't cut yourself! Here, sit down and have a glass of schnapps to calm your nerves.'

"The young *ba'al agalah* watched and was very impressed. 'Funny people, these big-city slickers,' he thought. 'You break a window, and they give you schnapps!' He reasoned that the bigger the window, the bigger the schnapps. Without wasting any time, he went and smashed the biggest window in the place.

"Needless to say, the furious wholesaler set his salesmen upon the fellow. 'You crazy man! What do you mean by going about breaking windows?'

"The young driver was chagrined. 'I don't understand,' he cried. 'That man broke a window and he got schnapps. I break a window, and I get a beating.'

"The wholesaler replied, 'You fool! This is a man we've been doing business with for years. But you? What kind of business have we ever done with you?'

"Young man," concluded the old *Rav* of Minsk, "*Klal Yisrael* has done big business with *Rambam*. Even if other authorities disagree occasionally with some of his views, no one questions his greatness. After all, he gave us the *Mishneh Torah, Peirush HaMishnayos,* and much, much more! But you, young man — what kind of business has *Klal Yisrael* ever done with you? Request for *semichah* denied."

It was the influx of European Jews to America after World War II that changed the status quo with regard to *semichah* for *Roshei Yeshivah.* A young man once came to the offices of the *Agudas HaRabbonim* in New York, asking to be admitted to its membership. The President of the *Agudas HaRabbonim* in those days was Rabbi Eliezer Silver of Cincinnati. Rabbi Silver was known as a "live wire," a fiery flame for Torah, *chesed*, charity and love of his fellow Jew. He was also a great *talmid chacham*, who had studied in the *kollel* of the *gaon* R' Chaim Ozer Grodzensky of Vilna.

R' Silver's inner fire often expressed itself in sharp, witty rejoinders. In his conversation with the applicant for membership, he asked the young man if he had *semichah*, and from whom. The young man replied that he had *semichah* from a very prominent *rosh yeshivah* who'd come from Europe in the aftermath of the Holocaust. R' Silver laughed, "He gave you *semichah*? I never knew he had *semichah*!"

How, in fact, did the *roshei yeshivah* begin giving *semichah* upon their arrival in America? To trace the answer, we must understand the immigration laws of the United States at the time. Applicants for an American visa had to fill out a questionnaire and submit to an oral interview. Certain representations, including a position in the rabbinate, had to be documented. If a man was a rabbi, he could be asked to produce a certificate of ordination. The gentile immigration officers could not be expected to differentiate between a *rosh yeshivah* and a *Rav*. Thus, before applying for visas to America, the *Roshei Yeshivah* of Europe were forced to acquire *semichah*.

Kavod HaRav

From Bavel to Europe, from Europe to America, the title "Rav" has been synonymous with Torah and accorded a similar reverence. Before Moshe *Rabbeinu* died, he prayed that Hashem would appoint a man "over the congregation" (*Bamidbar* 27:16-17) so that "the congregation of Hashem be not like sheep that have no shepherd." *Malbim* explains: Sheep do have a leader to follow — the ram. The problem is that the ram is also a sheep, "one of the boys," with the same level of intelligence. What is needed is a being of higher intelligence and perception — namely, a shepherd.

The *Rav* has always been higher than his congregation, in Torah knowledge, in righteousness, in *middos* (good character) and in *mussar*. He is a shepherd. Nowhere were these traits seen in greater abundance than in the lowly *shtetl*.

The 33rd Infantry Division was stationed in Lomza. On Pesach, the community would arrange *sedarim* for the Jewish soldiers who had not been granted a furlough for the holiday. These were held in the huge Talmud Torah building belonging to the *kehillah*.

The entire upper story of this building was reserved for the living quarters of the *Rav* and his family, his library, and the *bais din shtub* (chamber where the *bais din* convened). The lower floor housed 10 classrooms for about 500 students. The basement contained the cooking and dining facilities for the *yeshivah*, which was situated nearby. It was in the basement that the Pesach *sedarim* for the soldiers took place.

The Talmud Torah in Lomza

The *Rav* would come down from his family *seder* to participate in the soldier's *seder* for a while and offer words of Torah.
An ex-serviceman named Medik, who was very active in organizing the affair, noticed the *Rav* about to ascend the stairs to his
apartment. Instantly, Medik appeared at his side.

"*Rebbi*, three large flights of steps are too hard for you to
climb."

Before the *Rav* realized it, Medik had hoisted him up and pro-
ceeded to carry him on his own shoulders all the way to his
apartment! Medik was not a learned man or scholar, yet his love
and respect for the *Rav* guided his actions absolutely.[1]

Then there was the opposite case. Something unheard of once
occurred in the village of Rutki, in the vicinity of Lomza. A butcher slapped the *Rav*!

Now, a butcher in a Polish village was not a butcher in
America. He was a poor man who had probably borrowed money from his entire family and all his friends, gone to the farmers
and bought three animals. If the animals were kosher, he would
sell the meat, make a profit, and pay off his debts. If not, he went
bankrupt. On this particular occasion, the *Rav* pronounced all
three animals *treif* (unkosher). The butcher, faced with financial
ruin, lost his composure and slapped the *Rav*.

When the shocking news reached Lomza, the *Rav*, R' Moshe
Shatzkes, declared that it was not enough for the community in
Rutki merely to punish the butcher. For the sake of *kavod harav*,
the honor due to the rabbinate, there must be a public *macha'ah*
(protest). The *Rav* rented three wagons, loaded them with *yeshivah* boys, and drove up to the village of Rutki. There, the boys

---

1. The *Gemara* records a similar incident in the Babylonian city of Nehardea. The
Rosh Yeshivah there was Ameimar. After delivering a *shiur*, he was carried off to
his home on someone's shoulders (*Beitzah* 25b).

Elsewhere, the Talmud records that the city of Semunya asked *Rebbi* to recommend a *rav* for them. *Rebbi* sent them his student, Levi ben Sissi. They placed
their new *Rav* on a golden throne and gave him so much honor that he later confessed to his mentor, *Rebbi*, "All this *kavod* has made me forget my learning."

went from house to house calling the townspeople to the *beis midrash* to hear the Lomzer Rav speak.

The following is an abridged version of Rav Shatzkes's speech to the people of Rutki:

"*Chazal* gave us a key to understanding the Torah. They stated that Hashem does not come with demands that are beyond human capabilities: *Ein HaKadosh Baruch Hu ba betrunya im briyosov* (*Avodah Zarah* 3). *Rashi* defines the word '*trunya*' as 'entrapment.' Thus, 'The Holy One, Blessed is He, does not seek to entrap His creatures.' In that case, it must surely lie within our capacity to fulfill every *mitzvah* and every requirement in the Torah. When the Torah states, '*v'ahavta l'rei'acha kamocha,* Love your fellow as yourself,' this, too, must be something we are capable of doing, for the Creator knows the character and the abilities of His creations.

"What about a brother? You won't find the Torah saying 'Love your brother as yourself,' because that can be *trunya* at times, when parents play favorites among their children. The story of Yaakov *Avinu*, Yosef *HaTzaddik,* and the episode of the *kesones passim* (the multicolored coat that Yaakov gave his beloved son, Yosef), is a perfect example. Such favoritism can remain engraved in a child's mind so that even many years later he finds it hard to love his brother fully. With regard to a brother, then, the Torah demands only, '*Lo tisna es achicha bilvavecha,* Do not hate your brother in your heart.' Granted, you may not be able to love him fully — but at least do not hate him.

"What about a *rav*? You'll never find it said in the Torah, 'Love your *rav* as yourself.' This would definitely be a case of *trunya*. A *rav* is someone who constantly criticizes: You don't learn enough, you don't give enough charity, your children are not sufficiently supervised. So how can you be told you must love him? The Torah goes one step further. It does not state, 'Do not hate the *rav* in your heart.' If, for example, you participate in a *din Torah* in which you are convinced that right is on your side, but the *rav* judges against you, you could conceivably hate that *rav*. Because of *trunya*, the Torah cannot obligate you not to hate him. Instead, what does the Torah tell us in reference to a *rav*? *Venassi be'amcha lo ta'or*, meaning, do not curse a *rav*. Granted, you may not be able to love him; granted that you might even hate him; but at the very least, do not curse him. And a patch, a slap — that the Torah will surely not grant you!"

I remember the *Yamim Tovim* in Lomza, when the *Rav*, R' Moshe Shatzkes, would give a *kiddush* for the townspeople. The *kiddush* took place in the huge *bais din shtub* — the *Rav's* living quarters plus the adjoining rooms. My father always took us

along so that we children could feel and absorb the atmosphere of respect and love for the *Rav* that permeated the crowd.

When the *Rav* delivered his talk, there was total silence. The huge rooms were packed with humanity, yet you could have heard the proverbial pin drop. R' Shatzkes had a tradition from the stepfather who raised him, R' Yitzchak Blazer (R' Shatzkes's father died when he was a small boy, and his mother then married R' Itzele Petersburger, the fore-most student of R' Yisrael

R' Moshe Shatzkes

Salanter), to sing a certain song every Shavuos and every Simchas Torah. It was called the *bite* (exchange) song, and had been composed by R' Levi Yitzchak of Berdichev.

Not many people are aware that the stock exchange was not invented on Wall Street. R' Levi Yitzchak invented it in Berdichev. But instead of stocks and bonds, sins were exchanged for atonement. Can you imagine the giant of *mussar* singing a song by the giant of *Chassidus*? To this day, when I sing the *bite*, tears come to my eyes as I remember the holiness and devotion that, as a child, I absorbed at the table of the Lomzer *Rav*. His thin, low voice still rings in my ears: "*Slicha-a-ah, mechila-a-ah, v'kapparah, Ta-a-atenyu!*" ("Pardon, forgiveness, and atonement, Father!") And the crowd would join in: "*Avoino-o-os, v'chatai-i-im, u'psha-a-a'im, Ta-a-atenyu!*" ("Iniquity, misdeeds, and sins, Father!") The emotion, the spiritual heights and the respect for the Rav were indescribable.

> *Ribbono Shel Olam,* I want to make a trade with You.
> Do you know what I'll give You in exchange?
> *Avonos, chatoim, u'pshoim, Tatenyu.*
> Do You know what You will give me in exchange?
> *Slichah, mechilah, v'kapparah, Tatenyu!*

R' Yeruchom Fishl Dan was a Gerrer *chassid* who learned in the Lomzah Yeshivah. He married my father's sister, Chavah, and joined the *kollel* of R' Archik (R' Aron Baksht, the Rav of Lomza).

R' Fishl later became *Rav* of the chassidic town of Kosowo-Lacki, located near Sokolov and Siedlce. When traveling home from the *yeshivah* in Baranowitz, I would make a point of visiting them, even if it meant changing trains in three cities.

On one such visit, I noticed people bringing money to the *Rav,* while the women brought jewelry, gold and diamonds to the *Rebbetzin.* My aunt, the *Rebbetzin,* muttered constantly to herself all the while. I overheard the words, "Just like in the days of the *Mishkan* (Tabernacle in the desert)!" Finally, I asked her what she was talking about. She explained: The community was building a new *mikveh.* The men were contributing money and the women were donating their jewelry, just as they did in the days when the *Mishkan* was built.

She took me for a walk to show me the new *mikveh* under construction. I was astonished to see *chassidim* carrying bricks on their backs and delivering them to the bricklayers waiting on the scaffolding. "Can't they hire someone to do that?" I asked *Tante* Chavah. She replied, "*Nareleh* (Silly one), they wouldn't give away this *mitzvah* for all the money in the world."

No sooner had she uttered these words than I had an even greater shock. The *fetter* (my uncle), the *Rav*, *kapote* tucked into his *gartel* (belt), was pushing a wheelbarrow full of cement. As though reading my mind, the *Rebbetzin* added, "If your uncle knew how to lay bricks, they wouldn't hire bricklayers either!"

Back home, I described to my father what I had seen. "That," he remarked, "is what you call chassidic fire." When I voiced a doubt as to whether it befit a *rav* to push a wheelbarrow, he looked at me as if I'd asked the stupidest question in the world and exclaimed, "That wheelbarrow full of cement is the greatest *kavod* (honor) for a *rav!*"

In fact, among *chassidim*, almost nobody but the *rebbe* receives extra honor. The Lomza *Rosh Yeshivah*, R' Yehoshua Zelig Ruch, was born in Rokishok, an island of *Chassidus* in the heart of Lithuania. Though *Chassidus* had generally been unable to penetrate deep into Lithuania, Lubavitch had managed to conquer this particular little town. The entire place, including the *Rav*, were Lubavitcher *chassidim*. The *Rav* of Rokishok was a great scholar by the name of R' Bezalel HaCohen. He was referred to familiarly by his fellow townsmen as "Tzali the *Rav*" — just as they might say "Yankel the Blacksmith" or "Shmerel the Tailor"!

When, as a young teenager, R' Yehoshua Zelig Ruch left town for the first time in his life, he traveled to the *yeshivah* in Slobodka bearing a letter of introduction from his *Rav*, Reb Bezalel. (In those days, no one was accepted into a *yeshivah* without a letter of introduction, testifying to the bearer's level of learning and *hashkafah*.) He presented the letter to the *mashgiach*, the Alter of Slobodka. It was the Alter's practice to read the letters of introduction and personally interview every applicant to the *yeshivah*.

"From whom is this letter?" the Alter asked.

The boy replied, "From Tzali the *Rav*."

The Alter, who had labored to make *mussar*, *kavod haTorah* and *kavod bnei Torah* (ethics, respect for Torah and respect for Torah scholars) the very foundation of the *yeshivah*, was shocked. "From whom?" he asked again. And again, the youngster innocently answered, "From Tzali, the *Rav* in our town."

The Alter raised his eyes to Heaven. "*Ribbono Shel Olam* — if Tzali is a *Rav*, and boys are still coming to the *yeshivah* to study Your Torah, then things are not so bad after all!"

As a general rule, however, Eastern European Jewry treated their *rabbanim* like royalty. In some communities the *rav* was not permitted to walk alone. He was always accompanied by the

R' Nosson Tzvi Finkel,
"The Alter" of Slobodka

local *shammas*. In Luban, the *shammas* would call for the *rav* every morning and escort him to *shul* for *Shacharis*. When R' Moshe Feinstein became *Rav* of Luban at the age of 22, he could not tolerate the fact that the *shammas*, who was in his late 70s, would come to his house to bring him to *shul*.

He explained to the *shammas* that, as *Rav*, he was prepared to pass up this honor. He ordered the elderly man to stop the practice — to no avail. The *shammas* refused, insisting that this was the faithful tradition he had clung to all his life. But when R' Moshe remarked that he was prepared to discuss the matter with community leaders, the *shammas* became alarmed.

"*Rebbi*," he pleaded, "I'll lose my job. I'll lose my livelihood! Please, let's continue the way I've been doing it for the past 50 years."

The argument disarmed Reb Moshe totally. The two finally reached an agreement: Instead of the *shammas* coming to the *Rav's* house every morning, the *Rav* would come to the *shammas's* house instead. Together, the two marched off to *shul* each day. No one in the community ever noticed that the *Rav* was escorting the *shammas* instead of the other way around![1]

The Office of Rabbi

A *rav* rarely, if ever, allowed political considerations to color his decisions. This point is illustrated by a story told of the *Rav* of Kalish who spurned the patronage of no less a personage than the Crown Prince of Germany.

One Yom Kippur, the *Rav* found himself in Berlin, where he attended the central synagogue for the *Kol Nidrei* service. Also present was the Crown Prince of Germany, who loved Jewish music, and especially the haunting *Kol Nidrei* melodies. When the prince noticed the silvery-white beard and dignified mien of the *Rav* of Kalish, he decided that this was the man he wanted as the *Rabbiner* of Berlin. Next night, immediately after the conclusion of Yom Kippur, a delegation came to the hotel where the *Rav* was staying and presented him with a *ksav rabbanus* from the Berlin *kehillah*.

The *Rav* jumped to his feet. "What! I should become *Rav* because the Crown Prince wants me? To please the *goyim*? The Midrash states, 'For you — not for the *goyim*.' "

He left Berlin that same night.

The city of Lodz, second largest city in all of Poland, was seeking a rav. At that time, R' Archik Baksht held the position of *Rav* of Lomza. Two *talmidim* who studied in his *kollel* — my uncle, Rabbi Hirsch Yitzchak Margolis, *zt"l* (who later became director of the Orthodox Teachers Seminary in Grodno), and Rabbi Joseph Feldman, *zt"l* (later of Baltimore and Jerusalem) — came up with the notion that R' Archik would be the perfect *Rav* for Lodz. Although Lodz's Jewish community was largely chas-

---

1. The exception was on the days when *Selichos* were said. Then, as was the custom in every town, the *shammas* would rap on the shutters of each house, calling the people to wake up to the service of their Creator!

sidic in character and R' Archik was a Litvak and *ba'al mussar,* the two did have some grounds on which to pin their hopes.

First, the Chortkov *chassidim* had a large presence in Lodz, and Rabbi Feldman — a native of Warsaw and himself a Chortkover *chassid* — had received his *Rebbi's* blessing in going to Lomza to learn Torah and *mussar* with R' Archik. Second, the Gerrer *Rebbe* knew R' Archik from their Agudah activities, and a *haskamah* (approval) from him would carry tremendous weight.

R' Aharon (Reb Archik) Baksht

Finally, the personality of R' Baksht — his genius, his Torah knowledge, his *mussar, chassidus,* and oratory — would appeal to even a *chassidic* community.

The pair nearly succeeded in making the match — until the government came along and threw a monkey wrench into the works. It did not approve of the *shidduch* (match). R' Baksht was a Lithuanian citizen, the government argued, and Poland was presently in a state of war with Lithuania over possession of Vilna. Also, it rejected the idea of having the second-largest city in the country officiated by a *rav* who did not even speak Polish.

When he heard this, Reb Archik exclaimed, "What? We need the approval of the *goyim*? It says '*Lecha*' — to you. Not to the *goyim*!"

Reb Archik subsequently left Lomza for Shavl in Lithuania.

Mara D'Asra

While studying the *sefer Devar Avraham* by the *Rav* of Kovno, I was astonished to see him refer to his brother-in-law, the *Rav* of Minsk, as "my dear brother-in-law, the *Mara D'Asra* of Minsk."

This title is inferior to those of *Rosh Bais Din* and *Av Bais Din*. How was it, I wondered, that an illustrious Jewish city such as Minsk had no *Rav* with a title higher than *Mara D'Asra* (literally, "Master of the Place")?[1]

When I had a historical question I usually consulted the encyclopedic minds of the *Rosh Yeshivah*, Rav Ruderman, and Rav Yaakov Kamenetsky. In this case, the *Rosh Yeshivah* was amazed. "How did you ever come to notice that? Why has no one else ever asked me that question?" He then related the following tale.

Some 200 years ago, the *gubernator* (governor) of Minsk imposed a heavy tax on the *Rav* of Minsk. As no *Rav* ever possessed so much money, it was the *kehillah* which would have to come up with the staggering sum.

Had the tax been imposed on the Christian clergy as well, the *kehillah* would have had no choice but to pay, as the Torah requires us (*dina d'malchusa dina*) to obey the laws of the governments under which we live in exile. However, since it was imposed only on the rabbi, the dictate of *dina d'malchusa dina* was not applicable. The wise men of the *kehillah* put their heads together and came up with a plan. They informed the governor that the city of Minsk has no *Rav* — only a *Mara D'Asra*!

"And that," concluded the *Rosh Yeshivah*, "is why the city of Minsk has no *Rav*."

I had another question. "The *Gemara* tells us, *gezeirah avidah d'batlah* — it's the nature of a decree to eventually disappear. The governor did not live forever. No doubt he died, or was transferred, or promoted, and the problem of the tax vanished. Why not give the next *Rav* a higher title?"

---

1. The story goes that a young scholar once came to the *Rav* of Minsk for *semichah*. During their discussion, the *Rav* asked the applicant where the gall bladder is located. The Aramaic word for gall bladder is "*mara*," meaning bitterness or gall; the word for "place" is *asra*. The applicant did not know the answer, whereupon the *Rav* chided him, in a play on words: "If you don't know the *asra d'mara* (location of the gall), how can you hope to be a *Mara D'Asra* (Master of the Place)?"

The *Rosh Yeshivah* explained, "Once the *Rav* was *niftar* (died), respect for his memory did not allow the town to give the new *Rav* a higher title than he had had. So, for 200 years, the title remained *Mara D'Asra!*" A short time later, I began telling R' Yaakov Kamenetzky this interesting tidbit — but he already knew why Minsk had no *Rav*.

Rav-Mita'am

In its drive to make Russians of the Jews, the czarist government issued a new edict. Every *rav*, it insisted, must be educated in the Russian language and in secular studies. Whether the idea originated with the government itself or with the *maskilim* (proponents of the Enlightenment), the plan delighted them both.

The government established and funded rabbinical seminaries aimed at "training" rabbis to serve across the length and breadth of the huge Russian Empire. When the Jews refused to recognize these "rabbis," the government — with help from the *maskilim* — forced the *kehillos* to accept them. Matters reached the point of absurdity, where each town had two rabbis: one that the Jewish populace recognized, and a second one, recognized only by the government. The latter individual was known as the "*Rav-mita'am*" — i.e., the *Rav mita'am hamemshalah*, or the government-appointed rabbi. Occasionally, when a Jew disliked some dish that his wife had prepared, he would say sarcastically, "*Es hut ah ta'am vee ah rav-mita'am!*" (A play on words; literally, "It has the taste of a government-appointed *rav!*")

The *maskilim* wholeheartedly approved of the government-operated seminaries. They even had the audacity to approach the Warsaw *Rav* (known for his work, *Chemdas Shlomo*) with the following proposition. The government wanted to open a rabbinical seminary in Warsaw. To ensure the spiritual qualifications of the students, he, the *Rav* of Warsaw, would be hired to lecture the students in Torah and Talmud. (Their aim, of course, was to get the *Rav's* "*hechsher,*" or seal of approval, for the seminary —and the bribe was a nice, fat salary for the *Rav.*)

The *Rav* felt ashamed to have even listened to the suggestion. His *mechutan,* R' Lando, who was present in the room, turned to the delegation and told them, "In *Avodah Zarah* [2a], *Chazal* tell us that, in the future, the nations of the world will defend themselves for all their wrongdoing by claiming credit for the large amounts of money they spent on improvements such as roads and public baths for the Jews' convenience, thus enabling them to study Torah. Now, why do you suppose that only indirect benefits are mentioned? Wouldn't it strengthen their case to speak directly of Torah studies in rabbinical seminaries financed by the government, such as the one you propose?

"Apparently," he concluded, "the kind of rabbis that will be 'manufactured' in those seminaries! even the *goyim* will be ashamed to mention!"

Chapter 3:
Shuls, Schools,
and Books

In the Shul — The Shtut

"And Rav Huna said: Whoever establishes a place of prayer for himself, the G-d of Abraham will come to his aid" (*Berachos* 6:2).

The word *shtut* means a city or town. (A *shtetl* was a small town or village.) However, it had another meaning as well: a pew, or seat, in the *bais hamidrash* (house of study). When a new *shul* was built, pews were sold to finance the building and these seats became, for their owners, permanent places of prayer. As such, they were considered personal property. Men would indicate in their wills which of their sons would inherit their seat in

The interior of Lomza's
main Bais Knesses

the event of their death; in the women's section, seats passed likewise from mother to daughter. These pews — drenched as they were in the tears and prayers of many, many years — had special meaning for the children. Often, if a father died without leaving a will, it would be up to the *rav* to settle the subsequent litigation and decide which son or daughter received the parent's pew in *shul*.

The most desirable, and thus the most expensive, pews were to be found at the *mizrach vant*, the eastern wall. The Holy Ark stood against this wall. To the right of the Ark was the *Rav's* pew, and to the left, that of the *dayan*. The pew adjoining the *Rav's* was naturally considered the most distinguished and was the most costly. In general, the eastern wall was reserved for Torah scholars and community leaders.

The Shtut that Moved

In a certain *shtetl*, there was once a strange *din Torah* involving the pews of a particular *shul* that was undergoing renovations. In order to enlarge the building, one of the walls had to be moved. Space in the rear did not permit the moving of the western wall, and so it was the eastern one, the prestigious *mizrach vant*, that was moved. When the renovation was completed, the pews on the former eastern wall were now five rows away from their original place.

The outcry was intense: "Our forefathers paid for pews on the *mizrach* wall, not in the fifth row!" It was up to the *Rav* to settle the dispute.

He had a hard time finding a source on which to base his *psak* (judgment). Finally, he discovered a *midrash* that could be applied to the case:

When Moshe *Rabbeinu* changed Joshua's name from Hoshea bin Nun to Yehoshua (*Bamidbar* 13:16), the *midrash* tells us that the letter *hei* complained to G-d that its place at the beginning of the name had been moved to the less distinguished second place. The complaint was rejected. The *hei*, after all, had not actually been moved from its previous place: There had merely been an addition which had displaced it. So, too, said the *Rav,* with the *mizrach vant* in the renovated *shul.* An addition had displaced it.

With this, the erstwhile eastern-wall *shul*-goers had to be content.

The Poloosh

The *shul* or *bais midrash* was usually not built with its entrance leading directly into the sanctuary. From the street, one stepped into a small room, or *poloosh*, from which he could then enter the sanctuary. The *poloosh* served a dual purpose. It was a place where people could talk to each other without disturbing those who were *davening* inside. (The doors to the sanctuary remained wide open, so that the talkers would not miss a *Borchu* or an *Amen.*) Secondly, in the absence of book stores the *poloosh* provided itinerant booksellers with a place to lay out their wares. Like the Chofetz Chaim, who used to travel incognito to spread his master work, *Shemiras HaLashon*, sellers of holy books were loath to turn the body of the *shul* into a place of business, G-d forbid. Instead, they found that the *poloosh* served their purpose admirably.

The small entrance room was also used as a meeting place for the *rav* and the *gabbaim* (*shul* officers). Officials of the various charitable societies met there as well.

Many a sage discussion was held in the *poloosh*. The story is told of the *Rosh Yeshivah* of Slonim, Reb Shabsi Yogel, a Torah genius and great *tzaddik*, who had a wife named Libby — known as Libby the Rebbetzin. Libby was blessed with a gift from heaven: a mind full of great native wisdom. Whenever a problem arose in the *yeshivah*, the *Rosh Yeshivah* would consult with his *Rebbetzin,* and she would invariably come up with the answer. However, if a problem arose in the town, it fell to the *Rav*, Reb Yehuda Leib Fine,[1] to solve it. Reb Yehuda Leib was a giant of a man both physically and in Torah scholarship, and a close personal friend of the *Rosh Yeshivah* from their own *yeshivah* days. It was natural for the *Rav* to consult with his friend, Reb Shabsi.

Where would they meet to discuss the problem? There were no telephones in the *shtetl*, and no modern offices. They met in the *poloosh* after *davening*, of course.

The *Rav* would explain the situation, and the *Rosh Yeshivah* would say, "Let me think it over." At home, he'd discuss the problem with his *Rebbetzin*, and the next morning present the *Rav* with the solution.

The *Rav* was amazed at the wisdom of the *Rosh Yeshivah's* advice. However, it didn't take him long to discover where all this

---

1. During the war, this same R' Yehuda Leib Fine of Slonim stood up to a German officer to defend his *kehillah*, and was shot in cold blood in the presence of all the other Jews. May Hashem avenge his memory!

wise advice was coming from. One day, as the *Rav* was outlining a difficult case, the *Rosh Yeshivah* answered, as usual, "Let me think it over." The *Rav* already knew what that meant.

"Yogel," he asked his friend, "did you hear what the *chazan* just said?"

"No, what?" replied Reb Shabsi.

The *chazan* of the next *minyan* had finished reciting the last line of *Hodu*. Said the *Rav* to the *Rosh Yeshivah*, "The *chazan* just said the words, *Yagel libbi biyeshuosechah* ('My heart will rejoice in Your salvation'). You, Yogel, are a wise man because Libby *beyeshuosecha* — she is your salvation! Praised be the L-rd, Who gave you a Rebbetzin Libby, blessed with abundant wisdom and reason!"

Stop the Reading!

Occasionally, the *shul* became the scene of unexpected drama. Suppose a person had a claim against an individual or the community, and was for some reason unable to bring the individual to court or persuade the community to heed his claims. What recourse did he have? He had two options.

First, he could hand over his case to Heaven for judgment — *moser dino lashamayim* — in accordance with the Biblical statement, "The L-rd shall judge between me and you" (*Bereishis* 16:5). However, this method is not without its own dangers. The Talmud says, "Whoever hands over his case to Heaven, he gets punished first" (*Rosh Hashanah* 16b). *Rashi* explains, "Does he merit that his opponent should be punished because of his complaint?" And *Tosafos* adds, "This is because he is so sure that his opponent will be punished because of his complaint." In other words, Heaven may in fact decide the case in favor of his opponent!

There is a second method. The claimant would call a halt to the *davening* in *shul*, before *Borchu*, or call a halt to the reading of the Torah, forcing the community to listen to his complaint. That is, he can either refuse to permit the Torah to be removed from the Ark, or, if it is already out, he may stop the reading.

I must have been 10 years old when I witnessed this very thing, and it is inscribed in my memory as vividly as if it happened yesterday. The background of the case was as follows:

For the past decade, the government of independent Poland had enforced a policy of driving the Jews out of every segment of the economy. For example, the intercity bus service, which provided a living to thousands of Jewish souls, was abruptly nationalized. The transportation industry now belonged to the government — who placed it entirely in the hands of the Poles. No Jew was permitted to hold a government job. (In the entire country, there wasn't a single Jew on the government payroll, except for soldiers and members of the parliament, the *Sejm*.)

Under the new system prices soared. The newly appointed bus drivers and conductors took bribes, allowing passengers to travel at half price and pocketing the rest of the fares themselves. But inefficiency and loss of revenue were apparently acceptable to the government — as long as the Jews were out.

Next, the Prime Minister of Poland declared an economic boycott against the Jews. Suddenly, pickets appeared in front of every Jewish store, as well as signs warning Poles not to buy from Jews. Their slogan was *"Swoj do swego za swojego"* ("A Pole should buy from Poles products made in Poland by Poles.") In a single stroke, Jewish shopkeepers lost their means of earning an income.

In consequence, many Jews tried to earn a living by setting up tables in the *stragan*, a rent-free open-air market. They would bring their wares in the morning, lay them out on the tables, and pack them up again to take home in the evening. The merchandise was brand new and sold for less than the store prices.

Then, one day, the first Polish *stragans* appeared on the scene to compete with the Jews. The Church and *Endekes* — a fascist, Nazi-like political party — had furnished Poles with the funds to open up these *stragans* for the sole purpose of taking away Jewish business. The strange twist in the affair was that the person who

The open-air market in Lomza

sold these Polish marketeers their wares was none other than a Jewish wholesaler!

The original wholesaler was a man by the name of Reb Zalman. He built up the business, passing it to his son upon his retirement. The Jewish *stragan* sellers appealed to the son to stop selling to their Polish competitors, but he had one answer: He was required by law to sell to the Poles.

Reb Zalman and his son *davened* in the *Bais Midrash HaGadol,* the very *shul* attended by the *Rav* and my own father. One Shabbos morning, two strange men suddenly ascended the *bimah* and stopped the Torah reading. In ringing tones they called out the names of Reb Zalman and his son. When Reb Zalman heard this, he smacked his son's face and burst into tears. He had not known what was going on; he himself would never have done such a thing to his Jewish brethren.

Reb Zalman sat down, head covered with his *tallis,* and wept bitterly. The two *stragan* men cited their grievance. I looked up at the *Rav,* R' Moshe Shatzkes, and saw that his face was constricted in pain. There were tears in his eyes — tears that he was making a valiant effort to hold back because it was Shabbos. The *Rav* turned to face the *Aron HaKodesh*, the Holy Ark, and he, too, covered his head with his *tallis*. His shoulders shook; he was crying, but didn't want his tears to be seen in public. He wept for the fate of his *kehillah*. People were losing their means of livelihood, Jewish life was being destroyed by the Poles, and he was helpless.

Finally, he turned around, eyes red, and walked over to the weeping Reb Zalman. They embraced, and the *Rav* said, "Reb Zalman, I want to see you and your son and these two poor *Yidden* in my *bais din shtub* tomorrow at 10."

The two men thanked the *Rav*, apologized to the congregation, and the reading was resumed.

Books and the Shtetl

Today, most printing is done by the offset method (a photographic process). In *shtetl* days, printing was a much more primitive procedure. The printer would set little pieces of lead, letter by letter, and compose them into words and lines of type. Because it was humanly impossible to avoid making mistakes, the proofs required constant checking and correcting by a proofreader. These men were known as *zetzers* (setters); after a number of years of this meticulous work, they were apt to go blind. Printing was a very expensive, time-consuming and tedious business, which made the price of a *Shas* or a set of *Chumashim* astronomical. Hence, every *shul* had an organization called *Chevrah Kinyan Sefarim* (Society for the Purchase of Books). Dues were 5 or 10 cents a week. From these modest sums the Society would buy holy books for the *shul*.

Books have a habit of getting worn and torn from constant use. To repair ripped pages and dislocated covers, there was another Society: *Chevrah Tikun Sefarim* (the Society for Repairing Books). The use of *sefarim* in the *shuls* was so great that every town was capable of supporting a professional bookbinder.

...And Without Books: The Zogerke

With sacred books so expensive — and also as a result of some Hebrew illiteracy among the women — the institution of the *zogerke* was born. This was a woman who would read aloud to the other women in the section allotted to them in *shul*. (The term derives from the Yiddish word *zog*, to tell or say.) Needless to say, this was an unpaid position. Every Shabbos, the *zogerke* would read from the *siddur, machzor*, or the *Tz'enah Ur'enah*. She also recited various pleas and prayers. It seemed as though the women listened with their eyes rather than their ears; they focused intently on her mouth, so as not to miss a word. Some women would merely listen very attentively, while others quietly repeated to themselves every word the *zogerke* said.

The Zogerke and her audience

My *Bobbe* Faigl was a *zogerke* in Tiktin. To qualify for the job, she was required not only to read loudly and clearly, but also had to be able to explain what she was reading. Above all, it was essential that she have a pair of glasses perched on the tip of her nose! I always suspected that my *Bobbe* did not read through the glasses, but over them. It was her habit to close her eyes when talking to someone, and open them to listen. I once asked her, "*Bobbe*, why do you wear glasses when you read?" Jokingly, she replied, "To make my nose useful." I later learned that she had functioned without them for years, until she discovered that, on one occasion, she had missed a few words while reading aloud the story of *mechiras Yosef* (the selling into slavery of Joseph). She was aghast at the thought of having robbed her listeners of irreplaceable words! On her next business trip to the big city, she purchased a pair of glasses.

It was most likely the tears in her eyes that had made her miss the words, for the sale of Yosef was a very emotional topic for the women. Listening to *Bobbe's* description, they would shed sorrowful tears. Faigl the *Tzaddeikes* (righteous one), as she was called, was never satisfied with merely reciting the story; she always added a little something of her own. She "knew" the color of Yosef's jacket, which, she asserted, had a pocket on the left side for a handkerchief. [Can you imagine Yaakov *Avinu* (our Patriarch Jacob)'s son without a handkerchief?] The material was as soft as velvet and as smooth as silk. On which side were the buttons sewn? On the left side, of course — everyone knows that a Jew buttons his coat right over left!

The circle of women was transported by Faigl's performance. When she reached the verse, "And there was no water in the pit," she described the dreadful, hot weather in the desert, followed by a graphic account of the effects of dehydration on the human system. Next, at the words, "But there were snakes and scorpions in the pit," she would deliver a report on the venom each snake delivers and the effect it had on people. "But not to Yosef *HaTzaddik*, of course," she would add with authority.

The tears in Yosef's eyes as he pleaded with his brothers

were reflected in the storm of weeping among the good women of Tiktin. On one occasion, they say, a woman burst out, "*Gut azoy*! Good for him, he deserves it. He knew what they did to him last year. *Far vos is ehr noch gekrochen*? Why did he crawl in again?" This, of course, is just an old joke circulated by the *shtetl* menfolk about the women and their *zogerke*, but it illustrates the faithfulness and sincerity of the listeners, their close attention and retentive memory, and their identification with Yosef's suffering.[1]

Censorship

One of the tactics the czars used to subdue the numerous nationalities living in the Russian Empire was the strict enforcement of censorship. Absolutely nothing — no book or newspaper — could be published without the government's stamp of approval.

The Jews were in the worst position of all. They were essentially outside the law. In legal terms, they did not exist as citizens of Russia. The 18th century, when the Russian Empire incorporated the Baltic states plus half of Poland, saw the Jewish population rise to nearly four million people (as compared to the Jewish population in America at that time, which numbered some 50,000). Yet the Jews were not permitted to publish a single newspaper or magazine, not even in the Russian language. In Lik, a little town on the Prussian-Russian border, a small Hebrew weekly was printed under the name of *Hamagid* and smuggled into Russia.

In the year 1855 Czar Alexander ascended the throne. In the aftermath of the Crimean War debacle, he loosened the reins a

---

1. I know for a fact that here in America there were *shuls* where *zogerkes* practiced their talents every Shabbos. At every *shul*, at the entrance, there were *siddurim*, *Chumashim* — and a box of glasses. Those in need would pick the pair that fit best, to be returned after *davening*.

little, and the first Jewish-Russian paper was printed in 1860. The same year, a permit was issued for a Yiddish paper in Odessa and a Hebrew weekly in Warsaw. There were at that time only two printers who used Hebrew letters: one in Vilna and the other in Zytomir. Hence, the Hebrew weekly *Hameilitz* and the Yiddish *Kol Mevaser* were published in Odessa, near Zytomir.

Permission to print might have been granted, but freedom of expression was virtually nonexistent. The censorship was overwhelming. Legal rights for the Jews was a forbidden subject; pogroms, the daily diet of the Jews, was also taboo. One outspoken article, and the paper was confiscated, its license revoked, and sometimes the editor sent to prison.

But the Jewish editors found ways to fool the censors. If there was a pogrom somewhere in Russia, they would leave half a page blank. On the other half, the paper would announce in huge letters, "CANDLE-LIGHTING TIME IN YEKOTARINOSLAV IS AT 5:30." The censors never figured out why a Jew in Minsk would be interested in the time candles were lit in a city 2,000 miles away — and the Jewish readers knew that a pogrom had taken place in that city, with 53 dead.

The government had a hard time finding Russians with enough Hebrew or Yiddish knowledge to qualify for the position of censor. Most of the censors, consequently, were *maskilim* — the so-called "enlightened" Jews.

Ben-Zion Katz, editor of *Hazman* and other publications, tells of one censor by the name of Israel Landau. He served as assistant to the senior censor, Zusman, a convert to the Russian church.[1] Zusman was a drunkard. Constantly under the influence of alcohol, he was unable to read all the handwritten material (typewriters were yet unknown) that arrived in his office each week. Landau had to do his work for him.

As a Jew, Landau had no right to live in St. Petersburg, the capital. Although the police never stopped people in the streets

---

1. Certain *maskilim* would convert to the Russian Orthodox church. However, their conversion was merely a formality to win them a well-paying job. If they didn't believe in Judaism, they certainly didn't believe in Christianity!

to check for legal residence papers, they would raid Jewish homes at night searching for illegal Jews. Therefore, Landau used to roam the streets all night, avoiding the police. During the day he caught a few hours' sleep at the homes of various "legal" Jewish friends. He finally got tired of the arrangement and "converted" at the age of 48. When his friends met him on the following day and asked why he hadn't been at their house for his customary sleep, he told them, "I converted!" His announcement caused great shock. No one believed him. He continued to pray every day wearing *tallis* and *tefillin*, ate only kosher food, and donated money in his daughter's name for charities in *Eretz Yisrael*. (He sent his wife and daughter to Switzerland to study medicine; as a Jew, his daughter could not enter a Russian university.)

Landau rose to the position of chief censor, all the while living as a Jew and faithful to Lubavitch. He advised Jewish editors about all sorts of tricks aimed at "kosherizing" their writings for the Russian government. Thus, when one of the most vicious pogroms took place in Kishinev, the Hebrew poet Bialik visited the city and composed a long, heartrending poem entitled, "In the City of Slaughter." Since it was illegal to print anything about a pogrom, editor Katz went to Landau for advice. How might he publish the poem?

Landau suggested that he rename the poem *"Ma'aseh Nemirov"* (The Tragedy of Nemirov), because the pogrom in Nemirov had taken place many years earlier. The title would pass the censor, while the reading public would know that Bialik was writing about Kishinev. Then Landau discovered one line in the poem that he would not let pass because it smacked of *apikorsus* (heresy). Bialik wrote him a letter in which he asserted that the line was found in the *Zohar*.

Retorted Landau, "Bialik cannot tell me about the *Zohar*, because I am the one who permitted the publication of the *Zohar*, and I am a bigger expert on the *Zohar* than he is. I am not afraid for my sins against the czar; for them I can always find an excuse. But I am afraid of my sins against Hashem. For such a sin I'll not have any excuses. I don't want to lose my share in the World to Come."

I was once reading the two-page introduction to *Aruch HaShulchan*, a monumental 12-volume work compiled by R' Yechiel Michel Epstein, the *Rav* of Novarodok (Novogrudek in Russian and Polish), a major city in Russia. Under the heading, "Honor of a King," he writes the following:

> It is our duty to love our master the czar, His Majesty. Hence, in every synagogue, on every Saturday and holiday, we pray with a pure heart for peace for our master, His Majesty the czar, and for the queen and their children and the entire royal family. In our long history of living under the protection of the Russian kings, we cannot find one Jew, living by Torah law, who was involved in any revolts against the Russian kings. On the contrary, Jews gave their lives for Russia in the war against the French (1811) and during the revolt of 1830. Czar Alexander the First, of blessed memory, and Nikolai the First, of blessed memory, rewarded the Jews for their loyalty to their king.

These lines shocked me. Had they been written by one of the *maskilim*, sycophants and hangers-on of the Russian "doctors" and "literati," I would have understood. But how could they possibly have been penned by a giant in Torah who well knew the animosity of the czars toward the Jews, and the vicious pogroms they'd initiated? How could he bless their memory?

After a good deal of thought, a possible answer came to me. I marveled at the wisdom and diplomacy of the brilliant author. He had handwritten 12 volumes — a total of 7,278 pages. It would have taken the censor years to read through it all. The *Rav* was getting on in years and wanted to see the work published in his lifetime. After reading the first two pages, the censor was so impressed by the loyalty and patriotism of the author that he felt no compunction about passing on the remaining pages. Permission to print granted! What a clever ploy![1]

In fact, that two-page introduction opened doors for R' Yechiel Michel to government officials, from the local police chief to cabinet ministers. He became known as a super loyalist and Russian patriot. Often, with the Jews existing, as it were, outside the law, the rabbis of Russia had to plead before government officials. Whenever a delegation was organized to visit a governor, cabinet minister, or adviser to the czar, the spokesman was always the Rabbi of Novarodok — the only one among them who spoke a perfect literary Russian. The way he gained his proficiency in the language tells the story of the *Rav's* life:

Rabbi Epstein's father was a *podryachik*, a contractor for the government, and he had hoped to bring his son into his business. To this end, he hired tutors to teach him Russian in preparation for a business career. The son learned the language, but rebelled at the prospect of becoming a businessman. Instead of business, he joined the rabbinate. Instead of building railroads, he wrote 12 magnificent volumes of Torah!

R' Yechiel Michel ends his "patriotic" outpouring with the following lines:

> Long live our king, Czar Alexander the Third, and the queen, the daughter of a king, and their son, the crown prince, and the entire royal family. His majesty should reign for many years to come.

May our people be blessed with many more such loyal patriots!

In my hometown of Lomza, a weekly Yiddish magazine was published under the name *Lomzer Shtimme* ("The Voice of

---

1. Most *siddurim* included a *mishebeirach* for the czar's welfare. In many communities it was recited weekly, in others on special occasions.

A simple Jew once asked the Chofetz Chaim, "How can we pray for the welfare of the czar, who hates and persecutes us so?!"

The Chofetz Chaim replied, "The prayer for the czar is immediately followed by the *Av Harachamim* prayer, in which we ask Hashem to avenge Jewish persecution. The reason that one follows the other is clear."

Lomza"). My father wrote a regular weekly column for it. When I mentioned this fact to my children, they set off for YIVO in New York to search for copies of that magazine. Indeed, they found a number of copies that carried my father's column.

The Cheder

Wherever the Jew went, the *cheder* went with him — and this, in a time and a place when his non-Jewish neighbors did not even dream of a regular school. In czarist Russia, where education was not available to the masses, a large percentage of the populace was illiterate. Real schools existed only among the upper class. In contrast, where there lived even half a dozen Jewish families, a *cheder* was opened.

The custom was (and still is: as my father did to me, so I did to my own children) for the father to wrap his son in a *tallis* on the first day of school and carry him to the *rebbi*, in commemoration of the giving of the Torah to the Jewish nation at Mount Sinai, as described by the *Gemara: Kaffa aleihem har kegigis,* ("Hashem held the mountain over their heads").

The *rebbi* would pick up the child, calling to mind the verse (*Bamidbar* 11:12), "Carry them as the nursing father carries the suckling child," and begin to teach him the *alef bais,* while the father dropped candy, honey, and other sweets into the child's mouth — to teach him from the very first how sweet the Torah is!

The *maskilim* (proponents of the Enlightenment), in their fanatic crusade against tradition, have painted the *cheder* as a prison, with the *rebbi* (teacher) as the brutal warden. They claimed he was uneducated, unqualified, and unprepared, armed with a *kanchick* (a whip made of leather, or sometimes a calf's foot, with four straps) without which he could not maintain order in the classroom. The greatest portion of their claims are lies, and the small percentage that is true was a product of the circumstances.

Cheder children with their rebbi

It is true that the *cheder rebbeim* never heard of pedagogy or child psychology. Many were primitive; many depended on the *kanchick,* and some took the job only because they couldn't do anything else. But these were only the "beginner" *rebbeim* — those who taught the *alef bais, davening,* and introduced the children to *Chumash* — and even they were checked by the *rav* and the boys' parents. No *rebbi* would dare raise his hand against a student unless he had permission from the parents. On the first day of school, the parents voluntarily told the *rebbi,* "Use the whip!" for they themselves used it at home. They believed in King Solomon's dictum, "Spare the rod and hate your son" (*Proverbs* 13:24). No one accused the *rebbeim* of child harassment, and the school doors did not need metal detectors.

The more advanced *rebbeim,* those who taught *Chumash* and *Rashi,* then *Tanach,* then *Gemara* and *Tosafos,* surely disproved the *maskilim's* lies. These men were true *talmidei chachamim.* In many towns they exceeded even the *rav* in Torah learning, but their expertise did not lie in halachic decisions; their learning was scholarly in nature.

The Talmud Torah and the Cheder

There were two kinds of schools. In the bigger cities, a Talmud Torah was established by the *kehillah* and owned by the community. The school employed a principal and various teachers who provided instruction on all levels, from beginners through *Gemara* students.

Such community schools did not exist in the smaller towns and villages. There, each *rebbi* opened a class in his own home. The Talmud tells of R' Yehoshua ben Gamla, who established schools in every town (*Bava Basra* 21a). Ever since that time, the rule was a maximum of 25 children per class, with a *rebbi's* private *cheder* being limited to 10 children per class. Parents would select the *rebbi* that was most fit for their child, and bargain privately about the tuition. (Actually, one is not permitted to charge money for teaching Torah. As the Talmud states, "Just as I [Hashem] teach Torah free of charge, so you, too, teach free of charge" [*Chagigah* 7a]. A *rebbi* was paid, therefore, not for his teaching but for his time.)

The official contract between *rebbi* and parents covered one *z'man*, i.e., a six-month semester, from Pesach to Rosh Hashanah and from Succos to Pesach. Woe to the *rebbi* whose students failed their tests: He had a hard time getting new pupils for the next *z'man*.

Thursday was *chazarah* (review) day. Teacher and students would go over the material learned during the course of that week. On Shabbos, the children were tested, either by their parents or by the *rav*. In some places the *rebbi* had an assistant to bring the children to and from *cheder* each day. The assistant also helped with the discipline, eventually "graduating" to becoming a *rebbi* himself. The Ba'al Shem Tov began his illustrious career

A class in the Lomza Talmud Torah

first as a *cheder* helper and later as a *rebbi,* before he established his *Chassidus* movement.

Another sort of *rebbi* was the one who accepted a position teaching farmers' children. The farmers, known as *yeshuvniks,* though immersed in their lands and livestock rather than Torah learning, knew the importance of a sound Torah education for their offspring. They would hire a *rebbi* and pay him room and board, plus a salary and a set of clothes every year.

The *rebbi* had a hard time enforcing discipline, even with a *kanchick.* He had to teach not one class, but a variety of classes made up of students of various different ages — and dispense with their attendance at the end of each summer, when the children were called upon to help with the harvest.

From these "primitive" classrooms and "ignorant" *rebbis* emerged generations of great Torah scholars, rabbis and *roshei yeshivah* — and even those very same *maskilim* who were so eager to spit in the well from which they'd drunk.

Essen Teg

The Talmud states, "Be extra careful with the children of the poor; Torah will come from them" (*Nedarim* 81a).

Many poor folk would send their boys to *yeshivos* in other towns. These families were unable to afford room and board for their sons. In towns that had no dormitory, a *gabbai* would be responsible for placing these out-of-town boys in homes, where they slept free of charge. He also arranged *essen teg* (literally, "eating days") for them. This was a system whereby the boys ate their meals in a different house every day. In our home, two boys ate with us every Shabbos, and another ate every Sunday for three years. (He is now a *rav* in New York.)

It became part of Jewish life for hundreds of years, even in homes of moderate means, to provide a *yeshivah* boy with meals one day a week. This was a higher form of charity than just donating money, because it involved the personal, physical effort of cooking, baking and serving a meal three times each day. Has any other nation ever voluntarily fed its students the way we Jews do? This willingness to cater to the needs of Torah students is unique among our people.

It was customary for the woman of the house to have a set menu for each day of the week. For example, Sunday she served rice; Monday, potatoes; Tuesday, kasha. The story goes that one boy complained to his friend, "Just my luck — every day I eat in a different house, and every day I get fed kasha. It's coming out of my ears!"

Replied the other, "You're complaining? At least you get to eat kasha. Me they feed every day with a different *terutz*. (In the vocabulary of the Talmud, a *kasha* is a question and a *terutz* means an answer or excuse.) Here, Mother went out of town. There, Mother is sick. I'd rather have kasha than a *terutz*!"

Reb Chaim Velvl, the former *poretz* of Kollaki, insisted that his own sons eat *teg*. Although Lomza had its own big *yeshivah*, he maintained that a boy must study out of town. "You should wander off to learn Torah," he would quote from *Pirkei Avos*. He sent his son to Kharkov. Lazer, however, refused to eat *teg*.

"Father, *teg* were invented for poor kids. You can afford to pay for my room and board."

"My dear son, you miss the point," replied the father. "*Essen teg* develops a boy. It teaches him good *middos* and appreciation to others for the favors they do. Do you know what it takes for a woman to cook a meal, and for a total stranger? Besides, it gives a boy a chance to meet *balebatim*. You could spend 10 years in *yeshivah* and never meet a homeowner or his family."

Some *roshei yeshivah* had abolished the custom of *essen teg* in their cities. They claimed it was degrading, and insisted that, if people wanted to give charity, they could donate money to the *yeshivah* instead of offering a "day." Reb Chaim Velvl disagreed.

"I, too, was a rich man's son," he told his own Lazer, "yet I ate *teg*. My father made me do it. Those who have abolished the custom have deprived the local people of the *mitzvah* of *gemilas chasadim* (lovingkindness) — the highest level of charity." Reb Chaim Velvl smiled in recollection. "If I ever didn't feel like eating, the lady of the house would say, 'That means you're not learning. If one studies, he is hungry. You have to eat like a *goy* and learn like a Jew!'

"And so, my dear Lazer, I will not send you a kopek if you refuse to eat *teg*!"

Shmuel Leib the Wise

My other *zeide*, who lived in Tiktin (Tykocin), was known as Shmuel Leib the *Pikei'ach* (Wise Man) because of his great wisdom and his photographic memory. Even during his lifetime, people would add the words *zichrono liv'rachah* to his name, meaning that his memory was such a blessing. He was a great *talmid chacham* (Torah scholar). Being a Cohen, he joined the *kollel* that the Chofetz Chaim established in Eishishok, to study *Seder Kodashim* (the portions of the Talmud which deal with the

Temple service). He knew half of *Shas* by heart. In his old age he became blind, but still recited the daily *blatt* (page) in the *Chevrah Shas* (Talmudic Society) from memory.

Reb Shmuel Leib was also an important businessman who had dealings with the Polish *pritzim*. Once, during World War I, he visited a village in the vicinity of Tiktin to talk business with the local *poretz*. As was his habit whenever visiting a village, he dropped in on the *cheder*. Entering the classroom, he noticed something unusual. Ordinarily the *rebbi* always carried his *kanchick* at the ready, this being the popular method of enforcing discipline on the wild farm boys. This time, however, my *zeide* noticed that the *kanchick* was hanging on the wall. Apparently the new *rebbi* was capable of maintaining order without resorting to the whip.[1] Reb Shmuel Leib began talking to the young teacher, and was amazed and impressed by his knowledge and quick grasp.

Gradually, the young man's story emerged. It seemed that he was from Minsk (actually, Dolinov, a village near Minsk), and when all the *yeshivos* were evacuated by order of the czarist government, he'd begun to wander from place to place, hungry and destitute. He had finally found a secure place in this little village, where he could earn a modest living free from the twin horrors of homelessness and poverty.

My grandfather began to shout at him, "You — a scholar, a genius — you're wasting your time here! Go at once and join a *yeshivah*! The *yeshivah* at Lomza hasn't been evacuated. Go to Lomza and learn!" Reb Shmuel Leib handed the befuddled young man a bundle of rubles and saw him out of the village that same day.

---

1. Interestingly, the parents in the town didn't know how to deal with this *melamed's* gentle touch. They approached the town *Rav* and demanded that he order the *melamed* to use the *kanchick*. The *Rav* met with the young man and spoke with him for a long time. When the villagers returned to the *Rav* he asked them, "Do you have pictures of the Kovno *Tzaddik* (R' Yitzchak Elchonon Spektor) hanging in your homes?" "Certainly!" they replied. "One day," the *Rav* continued, "this young man's picture will be hanging on walls."

The young scholar accordingly made his way to Lomza, which was situated some 50 or 60 kilometers from Tiktin. The Jewish community there had become poor again because of the war, and R' Yechiel Mordechai Gordon, the *Rosh Yeshivah* of Lomza, refused to accept the new arrival. He explained, "I have to feed 400 boys, plus a faculty with wives and children. We are cut off from America because of the war. I'm sorry, but I cannot accept any new *talmidim* (students)."

The next day, someone mentioned to the *Rosh Yeshivah* that a boy from Minsk, an *iluy* (genius) with a brilliant mind, had come to the *yeshivah* the day before. R' Gordon asked, "Where is he?"

"He was told that he was not accepted, so he left."

The *Rosh Yeshivah* immediately sent boys out to search for him, and the *iluy* was discovered. He was brought to the *yeshivah*, where he studied for three years and became one of the best *talmidim*. It was many years later, when R' Gordon traveled to America and met his former *talmid*, that he told him, "Because of you, I made a vow never to refuse anyone entrance to the *yeshivah*, no matter what the circumstances. One can never tell how a *talmid* will turn out."

That boy later became known throughout the world. His name was R' Yaakov Kamenetzky.

Chapter 4: Shtetl Personalities

At the River's Edge

In every *shtetl*, the well-to-do Jews lived in the center of town where their homes and businesses were located, while non-Jews lived on the outskirts. There were also sections for the poor, Jew and Pole alike. But what a difference there was between them! The average Pole, in his poverty, was perpetually drunk and did not hesitate to treat his family to oaths and blows. His behavior was particularly appalling on Sundays and after one of his Christian festivals. I remember as a boy witnessing police wagons come to pick the drunken, brawling figures off the streets. In stark contrast, there were no Jewish drunkards. In a thousand years of Russian, Polish and Lithuanian history no Jew was ever convicted of murder.

Lomza was built on a mountain, with the Narew River running along its foot. At the river's edge was the poor neighborhood known as Rybbakes. (In Polish, *ryba* means fish;

Homes in the Rybbakes neighborhood

rybaki means fishermen.) The wagon drivers, known as *balegolas*, lived there, and led their horses down to the nearby river to drink. There were also, of course, the *vasser treggers*, or water carriers. Each day these men filled their barrels with river water. The barrels were then loaded on horses and carried up the hill to the center of town, and the water was delivered to various homes by the bucketful. In winter, the water carriers cut holes in the ice that covered the river. They made sure never to leave their buckets outside overnight, lest pranksters fill them with water, which would freeze and leave the buckets unusable.

The town's *shnorrers* (beggars) had their homes in Rybbakes as well. On Mondays and Thursdays they would beg in the city, and spend the rest of the week in the neighboring villages.

And then there were Lomza's *treggers* (stevedores).

These men — many of them advanced in years — could carry incredibly heavy loads on their backs. Though they lived beside the river, their station was in the center of town, in front of our store. There they sat, day after day, waiting for jobs.[1] Because they

---

1. Their willingness to work transcended their own borders. In 1935, the first Jewish port opened in Tel Aviv (Jaffa was an Arab port and Haifa a British one), and the Jewish stevedores of Salonika came to Palestine to help in its operation. Upon hearing of this, the *treggers* of Lomza immediately fired off a telegram: "We are just as strong and willing as the stevedores of Salonika."

The Lomza treggers sitting on the bench in front of my father's shop.
Seated, L-R: Noshkeh, unknown, Avrohom, "Mashiach" (the foreman), unknown.
Standing L-R: unknown, Feivel, unknown, "Mashiach's" son, Dovid.

blocked the entrance to the store, my father had two benches built
for them on either side of the store's steps. My little brothers and
I practically grew up on the *treggers'* knees. They loved us because
they loved our father and mother, and also because we were the
Kollaker *Poretz's einiklach* (grandchildren). Among them were Reb
Avrohom (the *treggers* were often addressed as "Reb"); Reb
Yehudah, whose son would come by every morning and roll up
his sleeve to show his father he'd put on *tefillin*, Reb Noski, Reb
Feivel, Reb Mendel, Reb Zavel, Meshuganeh Dvora (called thus,
apparently, because of his wife), and their leader, Mashiach.

The *treggers* had their own shul, *Poalei Tzedek*, and hired a
rebbi to instruct them in the *Chaye Odom* and *Ein Yaakov.*
Mashiach made sure that the *rebbi* was paid every week from
the stevedores' meager income. "We carry loads on our back
and want to get paid for it," he would remind his fellow workers. "The *rebbi* carries the Torah in his head and tries to teach it
to us *grobbe kep* (lunkheads). Why shouldn't he get paid too?"
No one dared contradict him.

Meshuganeh Dvora disliked children, but he had to tolerate us four Shapiro boys. We, in turn, tried our best to steer clear of him. I remember a curious incident, though, that happened one day — I must have been 9 or 10 — when I stepped inside the *Chevrah Tehillim shul* to *daven Minchah*. (*Chevrah Tehillim* was known for its nonstop *minyanim*, from sunrise to midnight. The beggars who plied their trade there were called "millionaires," for in a single day they would acquire a wealth of *"amens,"* *"borchus,"* and *kedushahs*. Between *minyanim*, people would recite *tehillim*.) There sat Meshuganeh Dvora, saying *Tehillim*. He

At the Chevrah Tehillim

looked up, saw me, and motioned for me to come closer. Hesitantly, I approached him. The huge, strong arms reached out to encircle me, and the *tregger* asked me to join him in saying *Tehillim*.

He must have just unloaded a wagon of flour, because he was white all over. When I got home, my mother exclaimed, "What have you done to your clothes? They're covered with flour dust!"

But I had the best excuse. "You won't believe it! Meshuganeh Dvora put his arms around me and made me say *Tehillim*."

"You mean Reb Shloime said *Tehillim* with you?" My mother was as amazed as I had been.

The tallest and strongest of the *treggers*, and their leader, was called "Mashiach." Mashiach had six sons and three daughters, all of them strong and tall, like him. At the birth of the *muzinikl*, the youngest (who was also a *ben zekunim*, a child of their old age), Mashiach and his wife decided that he should be a *rav*, no less. Little Yudele was sent to Talmud Torah through all 10 grades. He was my brother Lazer's classmate, and both of them graduated with honors. Together they were admitted to the Lomzer *Yeshivah*, where they became *shutfim* (Lomza was the only *yeshivah* where a *chavrusah* was called a *shutef* [partner]).

Mashiach would glow with pride when he spoke of his Yudele. Every so often he would nonchalantly address my father, "Reb Alter, your Lazerke and my Yudele are *shutfim*. Please test him to see how he's doing in *Gemara*." The simple laborer could often be heard boasting, "My *muzinikl* is a friend of the Kollaker's *einikl*. Can you believe it?"

Then, one summer day, the two 15-year-old boys, both excellent swimmers, rented a rowboat and went out on the Narew River. Unexpectedly, the boat ran into a strong current and tipped over. My brother Lazer made it back to the shore, but "Little Mashiach" (as we boys called him) did not. What a tragedy! The town was devastated. The funeral was heartrending.

My brother knew that Yudele had been recording the *rebbe's shiurim*, and had also written down Torah thoughts of his own.

Talmidim in the Lomza Yeshivah.
R' Moshe Rosenstain is in the front row, center. My brother Lazer is back row, center.

He found the notebook in Yudele's *shtender* at the *yeshivah*, but didn't have the heart to deliver it personally to the grieving parents. I was appointed Lazer's messenger.

When I handed the notebook to Mashiach, he pressed it to his heart. "This is our Yudele's Torah," he told his wife, "written with his own hands." Soon afterward, the *Rosh Yeshivah*, Reb Yehoshua Zelig Ruch, came to visit the mourners. The giant *tregger* fell to the floor, seized the *Rosh Yeshivah's* feet and sobbed, "*Rebbe, ich bin an erlicher Yid. Farvos hob ich nisht zoche geven zu a zun a rav?* (*Rebbe*, I'm a sincere Jew. Why wasn't I worthy of seeing my son become a *rav*?*")

Rich or poor, lofty or humble, the hopes and griefs of a Jewish father are ever the same.

At the other end of Lomza's hill was the section known as Kulkin's *hoif* (estate). Kulkin was a Jewish lawyer who owned an ancient block of houses. These were divided into apartments that housed numerous families, many of them Jewish. (I would never have set foot in the place except for the fact that two of my *rebbeim* lived there, and my father had the custom of sending a lavish *shalach manos* to his children's teachers each Purim.) While the residents of Kulkin's *hoif* were not as poor as the ones in Rybbakes, one could see bedbugs crawling on the walls there. Neighbors often communicated in shouts through the windows:

"Let me have some of your cobwebs, I cut my finger!" (Cobwebs were supposed to stop the bleeding and protect against infection.)

R' Yehoshua Zelig Ruch

"Rochel, lend me your cat for the night, I have a few mice in my kitchen."

"Reb Shmerel, what time is it? My mother just salted the meat and she has to know."

"Reb Zavel, can I borrow a cigarette? With a match, please."

Kulkin insisted on receiving his rent on time. Upon request, he'd agree to defer payment for one month. After that — eviction! The anxious tenants would run to the *kehillah* office to plead for rent money. If all else failed, the last resort was Reb Yisrael Yaffe (See Chapter 9, below: *The Winds of Change*). Reb Yisrael would pay the rent — while berating Kulkin for his hardheartedness — and then personally help the grateful tenants carry their furniture back into the house.

Opposite the Kulkin estate stood the Capuchin monastery. Between the two was the tall hill that ran all the way down to the river's edge. In the winter the hill was covered with thick snow, as was the frozen Narew River. Youngsters would ride their sleds down the length of the mountain and all the way across the river — a considerable distance — while the monks watched this "forbidden" pleasure enviously from their windows. However, the pleasure had its flip side: Once the rider reached the other side of the river he had the long climb back up the hill, dragging his heavy sled behind him. A wry Russian proverb was often

Some prominent members of the Lomza community. Seated second from left is R' Yisrael Yaffe. Seated at the far right is R' Yisrael Rabinovitz, who was known as Yisrael Zembrover.

quoted by Jews and Poles alike: *"Lubish katatsa lubish sanoka vozits!"* ("If you enjoy sledding down, then enjoy dragging the sled back up!")

Even for the children, however, all was not fun and games — especially on a Friday. Young as well as old had to pitch in and prepare for Shabbos. It was a tense day filled with washing, cooking, and cleaning, with no electricity or gas ovens to help them along. The *cholent* and *kugel* for the next day's Shabbos meal had to be sent to the baker's oven to keep warm (sometimes resulting in mix-ups, such as a rich man's pot accidentally being taken by a poor one!). But with the lighting of the Shabbos candles, all was peaceful. Fathers and sons marched off to *shul*. The women finally caught their breaths and were able to rest. The homes were clean and filled with the aroma of gefilte fish. Shabbos chased away the week's drudgery and its never-ending worries. For over 24 hours, rich and poor alike enjoyed peace, rest, beauty, and happiness.

The same gift belonged to Rybbakes. The river that provided a livelihood for so many of its inhabitants also helped in their Shabbos preparations. While men, women, and *yeshivah* students swam there in summer (each in a separate section of the river), on Fridays everybody was in a hurry to bathe their children and themselves before the onset of Shabbos. Earlier, laundry had been done in the same waters, and bucketsful hauled up to the houses to wash floors and provide a base for the Shabbos soup.

Finally, with the sinking of the sun, the residents of Rybbakes were no longer poverty stricken. They were princes and princesses, the girls in their long braids with ribbons at the ends, the men's boots polished to a high gloss with axle-grease. Every father held his head up in pride and joy as he led his children off to *shul*. Shabbos gave the ragged neighborhood a lift in the midst of a struggling existence. Rybbakes, for this one day out of seven, was imbued with a special dignity.

The Meshuganer

A town could get along temporarily without its *rav*, without a *dayan*, without a *chazan*, but never without a *meshuganer*. The medical personnel of the time simply had no idea what to do with cases of mental illness — although the Russians, inexplicably, had a mysterious respect for the mad. If a person became violent and uncontrollable, a danger to people and property, he was locked up for life. Every hospital had a separate facility with iron-barred windows, similar to a prison. At a loss for a cure, the hospital kept the violently insane on starvation rations until they died.

If the mentally ill were not violent, they were permitted to roam the streets, talking to themselves, to the walls, to the moon. They were recognizable from the moment they opened their mouths. Some of these *meshuganers* were amazingly wise; some were "philosophers" and thinkers. Eventually, these smart ones came to fill the role the court jester had had in previous times; and, as such, served a purpose in the community. If someone had to be "told off" but nobody dared tell him to mend his ways, the *meshuganer* would deliver the message. The recipient of the chiding would not feel insulted; after all, the criticism had come from a madman. On the other hand, the crazy one must have heard it somewhere . . . The offender got the message.

Some of the *meshuganers* did not speak at all. A strange look in the eyes told of a profound sorrow that dwelt within. It seemed as though his very soul was crying out for help in silence. They were also characterized by their peculiar way of laughing — an abnormal "Hee! Hee! Hee!"

Many of the mentally ill in the Jewish community claimed to be *Mashiach*. Seeing a stranger in town, one of these madmen would approach. Pointing to a passer-by, he'd whisper, "See that fellow? He's crazy!"

"Crazy? Why?" the stranger would ask.

"Because he thinks he is *Mashiach*!"

"Well, how do you know he's not?" the stranger would smile.

"Because *I* am *Mashiach*! There can't be two of us!"

The stranger had never even suspected that he'd been talking to a *meshuganer*.

Then there was the glazier who found himself without work for weeks on end; no one in town had suffered any broken windows. As a last resort, he approached the town *meshuganer*: "Do me a favor. Go break some windows. I haven't had a job in weeks."

Next morning, the madman began breaking every window in the glazier's house. The glazier rushed out, screaming, "*Meshuganer*! *My* windows you're breaking? You're supposed to break other people's windows, not mine!"

Serenely, the madman replied, "You see, if I break other windows, I can't be sure you'll get the job of replacing them. But in your house, I'm sure you'll get the job!"

During World War I, when the Russian Army was in retreat, a unit of Cossacks passed through town. Any army in retreat is an army defeated, and angry at the whole world. This was especially true of the Cossacks. They were vicious in peacetime and all the more brutal in battle. When they passed through a town, all the civilians went into hiding. That day, as the people of Tiktin peeped through cracks in their places of concealment to see if the unit had passed, they were shocked to see Reb Binyamin out in the street. He was a fine Jew who had tragically had a nervous breakdown, and thought he was *Mashiach*.

"He's really crazy. He's committing suicide!" they cried.

Suddenly, Binyamin grabbed the bridle of a Cossack's horse and ordered the rider to get off. No soldier ever took orders from a civilian, even in times of peace. This was war, and the Cossacks were in retreat, and the civilian was a Jew. The Cossacks were notorious Jew-haters. This one whipped out his sword and raised it over Binyamin's head. The hidden observers were sure he would lower the weapon with all his strength on the crazy man's neck. They all knew that the Cossacks had their rule: Once a soldier pulled out his sword, he had to use it. He could not return the sabre to its sheath without wetting it with blood!

Holding aloft the sword, the Cossack looked into Binyamin's eyes. Smiling, he asked, "And why should I get off the horse?"

"Because I order you to! I am the *Mashiach*!"

Still the Cossack stared into the crazy man's eyes, apparently bewitched. The old Russian respect for the insane took over. With his sword, the Cossack politely touched Binyamin's finger, drawing a little blood. Then he gently pushed Binyamin aside, replaced his sword, and rode away after his fellow soldiers.

Nochumke Pietrushke

Why they called him Pietrushke ("parsnip" in Polish) is something I never discovered, but he was one of the two *meshugoyim* of Lomza. In his younger days he had worked for a butcher and sausage maker. Apparently, the sight of killed animals affected his delicate *neshamah* (soul). He became filled with compassion toward animals and the earth. "*Baruch Merachem al ha'aretz!*" he would proclaim. "Blessed is He Who has compassion on the earth!" He thought it outrageous that people constantly stepped on the ground with both feet. Therefore, he never walked, but always ran. That way, only one foot at a time came into contact with the earth. When he grew tired of running he would lean against a wall while standing on one foot. He never put both feet on the ground at the same time.

Nochumke also had a tremendous feeling for music. Whenever a famous *chazan* arrived in town to give a concert, Nochumke was admitted free of charge. We kids, not so fortunate, would climb through the open windows and watch *Nochumke*. He stood behind the *bimah*, on one foot as usual, eyes closed in rapture, waving his little stick in time to the *chazan's* melody like an orchestra conductor. We could tell the quality of the *chazan's* singing by Nochumke's facial expressions and the way he moved his stick.

Moishe Chetz

Our second *meshuganer* was Moishe Chetz. No one was sure of the name's origin; perhaps it came from the word *chetz*, the Hebrew for "arrow," for he could run with the speed of a flying arrow. He was one of the "mad philosopher" types, the well-known "court jester" of the town. Physically, he was extremely strong; equally strong was his love for Jews. If a gentile dared raise his hand to a Jew, Moishe would break his arms. When we children, on our way to *cheder*, would occasionally come under attack by non-Jewish kids, all we had to do was tell Moishe Chetz. For the next two weeks he would skulk at the corner every day, waiting for those bullies to make a return appearance. Seeing him there, they ran away — but not fast enough for Moishe. He caught them and twisted their arms. Never again did they repeat their hooliganism.

A new policeman once arrived in Lomza. He had never heard of Moishe Chetz. Walking his beat, he paused outside the largest church in town. In front of the church stood a monument to the "holy son, the Nazarite," surrounded by tall trees filled with birds' nests. The crazy man walked up to the officer and declared, *"Panie Policjancie, przekonowalem sie ze wasza wiare prawdziwa wiara!"* ("Sir Policeman, I've become convinced that your faith is the true faith.") The Pole was filled with joy; here was his chance to save a Jewish soul. Taking out a package of cigarettes, the policeman offered one to Moishe. As the two stood smoking, the officer asked, "Tell me, sir, how is it that you suddenly became convinced that our faith is the true faith?"

Moishe replied, "All the *tzores* (troubles) in this world come from the Jewish G-d. Take your god, for instance. He stands there, so still, and doesn't bother anyone. The birds deposit their droppings on his head and not a word out of him!"

The constable took out his wooden club and advanced on Moishe, swinging it threateningly. Little did he know how fast Moishe could run! He began chasing Moishe, but couldn't catch him. He had pulled a gun and was ready to use it, when he ran into another policeman — who began laughing. "Him you want to catch? The crazy man? Never!"

The police tolerated Moishe Chetz because he hated Communists. In Poland, the Communist party was illegal. Active members were routinely arrested, convicted, and sentenced to ten years in prison. Moishe Chetz used to roam the streets, shouting, *"Communisci Hitler przyjdzie na was!"* ("Communists, Hitler will fall upon you!")

But trouble was waiting for Moishe when the Russians entered Poland in September, 1939. He was still roving the streets, shouting the same slogan. At first, the Russians thought he was welcoming them. Then a Pole explained what he was really saying. Moishe Chetz was arrested. When they learned that he was insane they let him go, making him promise never to repeat those words again. He kept his promise by not saying it in Russian, but (as he later explained) he never promised not to say it in Polish!

Crazy as he was, Moishe Chetz had his eyes and ears wide open. He noticed everything, and everything was his business.

Once, while roaming the park, he noticed a Jewish girl reading a book. Thereafter he saw her there nearly every day; she was an avid reader. One day he spotted a Capuchin monk sitting beside her, engaging her in conversation. The Capuchins had their monastery next to Kulkin's estate, where the poorer element among the Jewish community lived. These monks never shaved or wore shoes; even in wintertime they wore only sandals. Their garb was a long brown skirt, a hood over the shoulders, and brown skullcaps on their heads. A crucifix hung at the waist.

Moishe was suspicious of the closeness between the monk and the Jewish girl, especially when he saw that their discussions continued daily. He made a point of taking a seat on a bench behind them in order to eavesdrop on their conversation. He discovered that the young monk knew the girl from the Kulkin section, and was trying to convert her. Better yet, he wanted her to become a nun.

Moishe knew he should not start a fight with a monk, yet he could not permit him to snatch away a Jewish soul. One day, he overheard the monk glorify "marriage" to his "savior." He told the girl that when she was a nun she would wear the Nazarite's ring on her finger. The monk picked up his crucifix, explained its symbolism to the girl, and asked her to kiss it.

This was too much for Moishe Chetz. He lunged over to the monk and, with his powerful hand, grabbed him. "With us Jews," he shouted, "the groom kisses the bride first. Let me see *him* kissing her first. Then she'll *kiss* him!" He twisted the monk's arm until he cried out in pain, after which he pushed him off the bench to the ground. Then he seized the girl's long hair and cried, "Take me to your home!" The girl resisted, protested, and tried to fight him off, but he held onto her long hair until she brought him to her apartment. It emerged that her father had died and her mother worked day and night, neglecting the daughter. The townsfolk praised Moishe for his action, though it had carried the real risk of a pogrom.

1939: "Why?"

When the Germans arrived, they would grab people in the street to dig trenches. Moishe was one of them. While at work one day he saw a German soldier strike a Jew with his rifle. As usual, Moishe could not let this pass. He picked up his pickax — the sharp, pointed tool he was using to loosen the earth — and brought it down on the German's neck, killing him. He began to run, but bullets are faster than the fastest human legs. He was found dead later, lying face to the sky, with his eyes and mouth wide open. He must have had a lot of questions to ask of Heaven: "Why, why, and a thousand times why?"

Genius or Madness?

A thin line separates genius from insanity. Almost every *shtetl* had its "genius" whose talent was wasted because it was never developed. Self-educated youngsters could be found, fluent in Latin, French, or German. They'd picked up the languages from books. In Vilna there was a Jewish boy who was blessed with a photographic memory. Whatever he read remained in his mind forever. The Poles refused to develop such a talent; they would not make use of a Jewish brain. The Lithuanians likewise declined. But the Russians, when they took over the city, assigned this lad to the "information" service of the telephone system. He could rattle off every number in the book without even checking.

In Baranowitz, there was a teenager who, unfortunately, crossed the fine line from genius to madness. He used to roam the streets singing and playing. When asked the name of the weekly Torah portion, he would begin reciting it from memory, complete with the proper *trop* (cantillation). If someone scoffed, "I can do that too," he would ask, "Backwards?" whereupon he would proceed to recite the entire portion — backwards!

Whenever I ran into that boy I felt inferior. Here I said *Ashrei* three times a day, but I couldn't repeat even one line backwards, while that unfortunate youngster could recite practically every portion in the Torah in reverse!

We had one such genius in our town of Lomza, who became an expert on Karl Marx and his writings. He taught himself German from a book so that he could read *Das Kapital* in the original. Berele, as he was affectionately known, would constantly pepper my father with his thoughts on Marxism, Communism, and Socialism. My father listened to him out of pity; such a fine mind was going to waste. Berele's ideas were brilliant indeed, but also utopian — way out of touch with reality.

"Berele," my father said once, trying to bring him down to earth, "you once learned in a *yeshivah*. Remember what the Torah says: 'Although indeed there shall be no needy man among you, for the L-rd will greatly bless you' (*Devarim* 15:4). Then there comes a contradiction. Verse 11 there states, 'For the needy will not cease from the land.'

"We Jews try to shorten the distance between these two statements by insisting on living according to the Torah and being blessed — and by giving charity to help the poor in their misery. Humanity is also trying to help the poor through socialism and social welfare legislation. Then along comes your Marx, an impatient man, and proclaims a revolution to eradicate poverty all at once by abolishing money and doing away with private ownership. In your Marxist dream, you think that by confiscating the wealth of the rich and dividing it among the poor, we will all be rich. Well, the Russians are trying to do just that, and it turns out that everyone winds up with 39 kopeks in his pocket. So far they've only succeeded in making everyone equally poor!"

My father went on, "The terrible notion that the government must take care of the people from the cradle to the grave takes away any sense of charity among the populace. In the entire Soviet Union, there is not a single charitable institution — for charity is contradictory to Marxism. Isn't that right, Berele?"

But Berele was quick to defend his hero's ideas. "Don't talk to me about the Russians. Marx said that the revolution can take place only in the developed, industrialized nations: German, England, and America. Marx looked down on the Russians. He called them a backward, unenlightened country. But just you watch, Reb Alter — the nations who ignore or laugh at Marx will eventually come to accept his ideas: ideas like free education, a ban on child labor, a progressive and graduated income tax, centralization of credit in the hands of a state bank, centralization of communication and transportation in the hands of the state, and many others. They may fight Marxism, but sooner or later they will join him!"

In 1939, when the Russians marched in and grabbed half of Poland, one of their first moves was to confiscate all businesses and factories. All movable merchandise was loaded onto trains and shipped to Russia. Overnight, everybody became an employee of the government. The Communist Party, up until that time illegal in Poland, suddenly emerged triumphant. Every town and village had its secret nest of party men, who rose up now in victory. Propaganda meetings were called everywhere, to praise Communism and its idol, Stalin. And, since everyone was now employed by the government, all were forced to attend these meetings and demonstrations. The direst consequences awaited anyone who dared to appear less than enthusiastic as the speakers presented the rosiest of pictures about life in Russia.

Resolutions would then be presented, with greetings to be sent to the "father of all proletarians, the sunshine of the human race, Comrade Stalin." The speaker never asked, "Is anyone for the resolution?" Instead, he asked, "Who is against?" Not a peep would be heard in the audience, for to speak up would be to vanish forever. "It's unanimous!" he would declare. Not surprisingly, every vote on any subject was invariably "unanimous."

On one memorable day, a *politrook* (political officer) stood atop an army tank, lecturing the people.

"You see all those houses," he said, pointing at the buildings demolished by German bombs. "Who lived on the first and second floors? The capitalists! The bourgeoisie! Who lived in the basement? The proletariat — the working class!"

Suddenly, a voice called out from the crowd, "Comrade Captain, do you have basements in Moscow?"

This was a dangerous question, for the Russians were very intent on proving to their newly absorbed citizens that Russia had everything that a capitalist country had. The *politrook* retorted, "Of course we have basements in Moscow."

"Do people live in them?"

"Why, certainly!" sputtered the captain.

"Then what's the difference?" demanded the questioner. "Here, capitalists exploit the proletariat. In Moscow, the exploitation is practiced in reverse."

Berele, that poor genius, quickly disappeared from sight, never to reappear. He had dared to ask the wrong question.

Chassid versus Misnaged

The *shtetl* saw *chassidim* and *misnagdim* (the collective term for early opponents of the Chassidic movement) living side by side in peace. But that didn't mean there weren't lively debates on the subject of their different outlooks and practices.

Reb Ely Mayer Rosenblum was a Gerrer *chassid* who lived across the street from us. He had ten children; the youngest, Yudele, was my classmate. Reb Ely Mayer was a *heisser* (fiery) *chassid* who enjoyed his heated Talmudic discussions with my father. But the supreme fire was reserved for defending his beloved *Chassidus*. As he debated with my father — the archetypical *misnaged* — Reb Ely Mayer's long beard would shake right and left. Yudele and I enjoyed watching them raise their voices in the never-ending debate.

"Show me," my father, a *Litvak-misnaged* from generations back, would demand, "where the term *shtibl* is mentioned even once in the *Tanach,* Talmud, or *Midrash!"* (The place where *chassidim* gather to pray is always called a *shtibl.* The term originated when the first *chassidim* separated themselves from the *misnagdim,* their opponents, because they had changed the *nusach hatefillah* [text of the prayers] and also because they liked to sing more. Small in number, they would rent a room or other modest location in which to pray, known as a *shtibl* — literally, a "small house.")

My father went on: "*Chazal* (our Sages) always use the term *bais hamidrash* or *bais haknesses.* They never mention a *shtibl!"* And he would quote the statement in the Talmud, "If you run into the despicable one (i.e., the *yetzer hara,* the evil inclination), drag him into the *bais hamidrash"* (*Kedushin* 30b).

Reb Ely Mayer, beard shaking and eyes sending out sparks, replied passionately, "Reb Alter, my dear friend, I hate to tell you this, but you don't know the true meaning of that *Gemara.* What it actually says is, 'drag him into the *bais midrash* — of the *misnagdim.* Then you yourself run off to the *shtibl!"*

The Maggid: Words From the Heart

The prophets were called *maggidim* — literally, "those who tell," for they used their power of speech both to foretell the future and to chastise the people and guide them to improvement. It was this title, apparently, that was borrowed centuries later to describe the men who roamed Eastern Europe preaching, chastising and reproving the people.

While every Jew is obliged to give *tochachah* — to reprove his fellow Jew — on an individual basis, it was generally left to the *rav* to chastise the community as a whole. However, as the *rav* was primarily occupied with Torah study and community affairs and would only speak publicly twice a year (on *Shabbos Shuvah* and *Shabbos HaGadol*), the area of *tochachah* was left largely to the itinerant *maggid*. In chassidic communities, on the other hand, it was the *Rebbe* who traditionally gave *tochachah*, leaving little opening for the *maggidim* to ply their trade.[1]

Officially, these speakers bore the title *Maggid d'Massa* (Town Maggid) or *Maggid Meisharim* (Speaker of Righteousness). An *MDM* or *MM* preceding a name identified the man as a *maggid*.[2]

Except for the city of Vilna, where the *maggid* was salaried by the *kehillah*, a *maggid* earned his living by wandering the countryside. Upon his arrival in a town, announcements were made in all the *shuls* that the *maggid* from such-and-such a place would be speaking at such-and-such a time and location. These men were never known by their names, but rather by their native town or residence; thus, the "Dubner *Maggid*" and the "Bialystoker *Maggid*" hailed, respectively, from Dubno and Bialystok. A *k'arah* (collection plate) was placed at the door of the *shul* in which the *maggid* was speaking, and people would drop in their donations after his speech.

The Makings of a Maggid

Needless to say, these men were all gifted orators with a vast knowledge of *Tanach* (Scriptures), *Chazal* (rabbinic writings), *midrashim* (homiletic interpretations), *mussar* (ethics), and *meshalim* (parables) — veritable treasurehouses of knowledge and wisdom! Moreover, their delivery reflected the attitude that "Whoever says a *dvar Torah* in public that is not as sweet to the listeners' ears as milk mixed with honey had better not speak" (*Shir HaShirim Rabbah*). An excellent delivery was combined with incisive content, for these orators were interested in more than just entertaining their audience for a few moments. They wanted something to remain in the listeners' minds long after the speech was finished.

---

1. Notable exceptions were the *Rebbe* Reb Dov Ber, the "Mezeritcher *Maggid*," and Reb Yisrael, the "Kozenitcher *Maggid*" — both of whom were chassidic giants.

2. Sometimes, it was "*Moreh Tzeddek MM*," meaning one who was both *dayan* and *maggid*.

Masters of psychology (though they may never have heard of the word), they knew how to manipulate the public mood. Their words inspired tears or laughter, happiness or sorrow, in quick succession. Some had unusual powers of description. The Kelmer *Maggid* would describe *Gehinnom* in such detail that the people would actually feel their toes burning! R' Zundl Kamenitzer, who was known to speak for up to six full hours at a stretch, used to relate the story of the plague of frogs in Egypt so that his audience heard frogs croaking in their ears.

Ready When You Are

Some *maggidim* were so full of ideas, parables and *midrashim* that they functioned like a computer's memory bank, able to retrieve at will the appropriate sermon for any topic.

The Minsker *Maggid*, R' Binyamin Shakovitsky,[1] was once invited to nearby Novarodok to speak at the funeral of R' Yechiel Michel Epstein, revered author of the *Aruch HaShulchan*, the outstanding *halachah* authority of his time and *Rav* of Novarodok. The *Maggid* had naturally prepared an appropriate eulogy. But before he ascended the lectern, a delegation of *yeshivah* students approached him with a problem of their own.

Because *sefarim* were prohibitively expensive, very few people owned so much as a *Shas*. As was mentioned, every *shul* had its *Chevrah Kinyan Sefarim* and a *Chevrah Tikkun Sefarim* (societies for the purchasing and repair of books).[2] The Novarodok *gabbaim* (Society officers) were impatient with the *yeshivah* boys who, they claimed, were careless with the *sefarim* and never seemed to return a book to its proper place, or else returned them with ripped pages. Finally, the *gabbaim* ordered the *shammas* of the *shul* to lock up the *sefarim* and only hand them out to the town's *balebatim*.

---

1. As related to me by Reb Binyamin Shakovitsky of Bnei Brak, grandson and namesake of the Minsker *Maggid*.

2. For more on *sefarim* in the *shtetl*, see Chap. 3.

The boys had never complained to the *Rav* — perhaps because he was old and ill — but they now approached the Minsker *Maggid* with their problem. The *Maggid* didn't let them down. He ascended the podium and opened his eulogy with a story.

> There was once a widow whose one and only son had died. As one can well imagine, she felt that her life was over; the future held nothing for her except memories.
>
> Before every Pesach, like all other Jewish housewives, she would clean her house, removing the clothing from the closets to give them an airing. As she carried each suit from the house, tears rolled from her eyes. More suits, more tears. A passer-by stopped and said, 'Lady, you own all these beautiful suits, and you're crying? I'm the one who should cry! I wear these same *shmattes* all year long.'
>
> The woman replied, 'My dear man, don't you understand? When you see a suit hanging in a closet, with not a button missing or a wrinkle in the pants, what does it mean? It means that the one who should be wearing the suit is no longer here. He died! That's why I'm crying!'

The *Maggid* continued: "*Hakadosh Baruch Hu* has just one daughter: the Torah. Her beautiful clothes are the holy *sefarim*. And when one sees *sefarim* with no pages missing, no covers torn, what does it mean? It means that the Torah has died in Novarodok! The *Rav* of Novarodok, the *Aruch HaShulchan*, has also died!"

Needless to say, all the bookcases were opened that very same day.

Askanus (Public Service)

With the power of their speech, *maggidim* influenced countless individuals to perfect their *middos* (character traits) and engage themselves in Torah study. This same mastery could similarly be used to mobilize entire communities.

The Kelmer *Maggid* once visited a town and discovered that the Jewish hospital there was about to close its doors. In those days of primitive medical knowledge, the ill only entered the hospital as a last resort. Nonetheless, for the poor, a hospital stay was advantageous. It guaranteed the destitute patient daily visits by a physician, around-the-clock nursing care, a clean bed, and proper nourishment — things that the prosperous could well afford to have in their own homes. The Kelmer attacked the subject from the pulpit:

> *Chazal* tell us that the *Shechinah* (Divine Presence) rests at the head of an ill person's bed. I can picture the *Shechinah* bringing a complaint before the *Kisei HaKavod* (G-d's Throne). 'Why am I always in the homes of the poor? I find it absolute intolerable! Hunger, poverty, children running around barefoot, no doctors or medication! Why not permit me to dwell in the homes of the wealthy, where a clean bed, comfortable rooms, food and medicine are to be found — much more in keeping with my dignity!'

The *Ribbono Shel Olam* agreed. Soon all the rich folk began to get sick. Before long, they realized what was happening and began establishing hospitals. The poor now had clean, comfortable surroundings, and the *Shechinah* had a proper place to visit. But now that the hospital will be closed, only the rich will be sick again!

Rabbi Yaakov Maza, the last official *Rav* of Moscow (also known as the *Kazyonnee Rabbin* or the *Rav-Mita'am* — that is, the government-appointed rabbi under the regime of the czars), tells how the Kelmer *Maggid* helped establish a Free Loan Society in his hometown of Mogilev (*Zichronos* [Memories], Book 3, p. 126). He describes the far-reaching influence the Kelmer had on the craftsmen of the town. At his urging, simple tailors, carpenters and the like were soon studying Rabbeinu Bachya Ibn Pakuda's *Chovos HaLevavos* (Duties of the Heart) and Rabbi Moshe Chaim

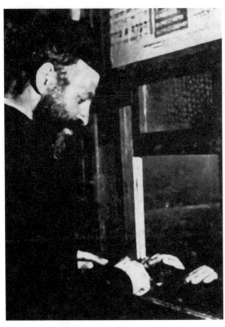

A communal Gemilas Chasadim

Luzatto's *Mesilas Yesharim* (Path of the Just), two ethical classics. They were all knowledgeable in *Chayei Adam*, a halachic compendium, and strove to polish their characters and piety. Whenever the Kelmer *Maggid* came to town, they dropped their work to welcome their *heiliger* (holy) *Rebbe*.

It was a craftsman, in turn, who influenced the *Maggid* to establish the Free Loan Society. The man complained that, though the prosperous sector of Mogilev gave a good deal of charity, craftsman like him didn't need charity — during most of the year they gave charity themselves. But they often needed to borrow money until the next harvest, when the peasants would pay off debts incurred for the purchase of crafts on credit. By law, a lending bank of this sort required a minimum of 5,000 rubles on hand. There were only 2,000 rubles in the fund.

"Who can put up the balance?" inquired the *Maggid*. (In those days, 3,000 rubles was roughly equivalent to $50,000 in today's currency.)

He was told of one elderly man by the name of Reb Yeshaya Shur, a wealthy businessman. His only son was also rich, but refused to donate the money. The Kelmer investigated the circumstances and learned that Reb Yeshaya himself had donated the largest part of the 2,000 rubles already in the fund, and would not respond to pressure to give more. He rightly expected others to join him in this *mitzvah*. Besides, in his will he had directed a fortune to be left to various charities, including the Loan Society.

Reb Yeshaya was a *talmid chacham* who owned his own *bais midrash*, a place where *maggidim*, as a rule, were not invited to speak. A shoemaker, commissioned to make a pair of shoes for the elder Shur, induced him to invite the *Maggid* to speak in his *shul* — and made certain that Reb Yeshaya would be there to hear him.

The *Maggid* began with a quote from *Yeshayahu* (46:12):

'*Hearken unto me, stout of heart, those distant from charity.*' Didn't the *Navi* know that those stout of heart do not listen, and those who are far away from charity do not understand what charity means? On the contrary — the *Navi* is addressing the generous men who dispense large amounts of *tzedakah*, but in their haste to do so, run the risk of losing sight of the very meaning of *tzedakah*!

It is the *Navi's* way to refer to people in terms of their ultimate status should they persist in their ways. For example, the *Navi* first says, '*We are almost similar to Sodom,*' and in the next passage actually addresses *Klal Yisrael* as '*officers of Sodom.*' And so, the *Navi* called the large contributors 'distant from charity' because charity is valued by the amount of *chesed* it involves. The more *chesed*, the greater the *tzedakah*. Performing acts of lovingkindness is more beloved before G-d than dispensing charity, offering sacrifices, or the merits of the Fathers."

The *Maggid* then described a dispute taking place in Heaven, as if he, and everyone in his audience, were witnessing it:

The archangel Michael, defender of Jewry, stands before the Heavenly Throne and summons the various craftsmen who were the Torah giants recorded in the Talmud. Here comes the elderly *Tanna* Shammai, with his trowel and level in hand; then his opponent, the great *Nassi*, Hillel the woodcutter with his axe; then Yochanan the shoemaker, and Reb Yosef Chalafta the tanner. As they wait, Yehoshua the tar-maker and Rabbi Yitzchak the blacksmith enter. Abba Zimra the tailor, threaded needle in hand, follows. They all pray for their fellow craftsmen below, in Mogilev, who follow in their path of labor, Torah, *mussar* and *middos*.

Then G-d responds by issuing an order: On the morrow, at 12 noon, the 3,000 rubles must be delivered! But wait — here comes the *Malach HaMaves*, the Angel of Death! He pleads, 'Let me bring the soul of that wealthy man tonight, and the money will be there. In his will, he designated half his fortune to charity. Actually, I'll be doing him a favor, for then his money will not only go to *tzedakah*, but for a *tzedakah* that entails *gemilas chasadim*!"

Tears were standing in everyone's eyes, and most of all in the eyes of Reb Yeshaya Shur. The *Maggid* then turned directly to him and said, "Reb Yeshaya, I know you are a very charitable man. Don't let the *Malach HaMaves* grant you the *mitzvah* as a favor. Do it on your own! As the verse says, "Bless your soul while you are alive, and you will be blessed, for it will do you good!" (*Tehillim* 49:19).

With tears rolling down his cheeks, Reb Yeshaya Shur stood up and promised to deliver the 3,000 rubles the following morning.

The Conscience of the People

It would be a mistake to assume that the listeners were naive or simpleminded. On the contrary, these were clever, learned and shrewd businessmen. Shur was a Torah scholar as well as a successful merchant. But the *Maggid* served as the conscience of the people. Knowing that he was right in his criticisms and demands, the people were receptive to them. For what, after all, was he demanding? *Chesed*, character improvement, and increased Torah study. He was the embodiment of *"Lo saguru*, Do not fear any man," and his honest and courageous words found their way into the listeners' hearts. Without trepidation he would face up to individuals and to entire communities.

My home town of Lomza had a large, beautiful central *shul*. The community had run out of money before the building was completed, and so the worshipers davened in a *shul* without a floor. Every Friday, the *shammas* would sprinkle yellow sand on the ground in honor of Shabbos.

One day a *maggid* visited the *shul*, and he chastised the people:

> "I feel sorry for the Jews of Lomza. *Chazal* say that when *Mashiach* comes, all the *shuls* will be transferred to *Eretz Yisrael* (*Megillah* 29a). So the four walls and the roof of this *shul* will be lifted from Lomza and taken to Yerushalayim — while you will remain here, since there is no floor to carry you!"

By the next Rosh Hashanah, a new floor was installed.

The Jews of Lomza surely knew that a *shul* needs a floor. However, it was a question of priorities; with other charities also demanding the money, the construction of the floor was postponed. Then the *maggid* came along and reminded the community of the dignity that was due to a communal structure used for prayer. Once again, it was his prodding which — by evoking smiles or tears — woke the people to the need for extra effort.

The Niggun

No *maggid* ever spoke without a *niggun* — the special sing-song melody of the trade. While they employed all the standard orators' techniques — motions and gestures, facial expressions and phrasing — when it came to the punch line, words were simply insufficient. The *niggun*, sweet, nagging, and heart tugging, emphasized a point and softened the *maggid's* harsh words. Some used it frequently, but only for short intervals; others sang their way through longer stretches, including the punch line. Words were the body of the sermon and the *niggun* was its soul.[1]

When the Kelmer *Maggid* published his *sefer, Tochachos Chaim,* he was asked, "Why doesn't the *sefer* have the same impact as your *drashos* (speeches?)"

He replied, "It is the printer's fault. He didn't put the *niggun* into the *sefer.*"

Rabbanim-Maggidim

In contrast to America, where Jews (in imitation of the gentile custom) routinely have a rabbi eulogize at funerals, the Eastern European rabbi would leave eulogies to others — except in the case of either an outstanding *talmid chacham* or an extraordinary tragedy. Also unlike America, where the eulogy can often be interchangeable with the introduction to a guest of honor at a banquet, in the *shtetl* a *hesped* (eulogy) aimed at bringing forth tears from its listeners. The audience always responded. The magic that drew the tears was not so much the words, as the *niggun*. Apparently, the rabbis had listened to the *maggidim* in their youth, then borrowed the *niggun* for the occasion: the key to the eternal wellspring of tears!

I remember the *hesped* delivered by the Rav of Tiktin, R' Avraham Kalmanowitz, for his young *rebbetzin*, who had died on the way to the hospital to deliver a baby, leaving him with very small children. It was during the Three Weeks (the period of mourning for the destruction of Jerusalem and the Holy Temple), and his voice, choked with tears, rang out at the funeral with his particular plaintive melody:

"Death crept into our palace, through our windows! (*Yirmiyahu* 20:9). Don't we have doors in Tiktin? Why windows? Because death

---

1. Some listeners, tired from a day's work, would be lulled to sleep by the *niggun*. Once a *maggid* heard someone snoring during his talk. He called out to the *shammas*: "Wake him up!"

Replied the *shammas*: "You put him to sleep — you wake him up!"

could never enter by the door; it would be stopped by 'children weaned on milk, who have not sinned, little children of *yeshivos.*' "

R' Avraham Kalmanowitz

The assemblage responded with weeping and wailing. The Kalmanowitz *niggun* had imbued his already moving words with a powerfully gripping emotion.

I also recall the *hesped* that our *Rav,* R' Moshe Shatzkes, delivered for the Chofetz Chaim. All of Lomza was there. The *Rav* suddenly broke off his speech, opened the *Aron HaKodesh,* the Holy Ark, and ordered everyone to sit on the ground. He, too, sat on the floor before the Ark. His famous oratory, borne aloft by the inimitable Shatzkes *niggun,* soared above the crowd:

All of *Klal Yisrael* is sitting *shivah* for its great *rebbe,* the Chofetz Chaim! There is only one left to perform the *mitzvah* of *nichum aveilim,* comforting the bereaved. Only You, *Kavayachol,* Master of the Universe. So send us — now! — *Mashiach Tzidkeinu!*

The crowd remained seated long after he finished speaking. The people were crying bitterly, for the melody of the Rav's words and the impact of the *hesped* had mesmerized them. No *maggid* could have done better!

Mashal and Nimshal (Parable and Moral)

Just as a *niggun* is essential to a *maggid's* delivery, so is the *mashal* an indispensable part of his portfolio. Whether it was a brief simile or a longer parable, the *mashal* served to enlighten every subject. Every *maggid* had a repertoire of *meshalim* for any topic and every occasion.

The Dubner *Maggid* once challenged his audience to quote any verse in the Torah; he would then ask a question on the verse, employing a *mashal,* and then answer it with another. The listeners opened a *Chumash* at random and selected a verse: "An Ammonite or a Moabite shall not enter into the assembly of the L-rd . . . Because they did not meet you with bread and water when you left Egypt . . . and they hired Bilaam to curse you."

The Dubner's parable-question was as follows:

> A bride and groom lived at a great distance from each other, so the families decided to hold the wedding in a town halfway between the two. After the wagon had been loaded up with all the food and drinks for the reception, and the bride's family had climbed aboard, her father galloped off on a horse to meet his *"mechutan"* in order to complete the arrangements.
>
> As the two were sitting and talking, his teen-aged son ran in breathlessly, telling his father that an accident had occurred and the wagon had turned over. "Food has rolled all over the road, the whiskey and wine have spilled into the fields — and guess what else, Father!
>
> "Mother got killed!"

The *Maggid* continued:

"To this child, the food and drink were the more important loss; the fact that his mother was killed was secondary to him. Now listen to the *pasuk* (verse): 'They refused the Jews bread and water' — that comes first. The fact that they hired Bilaam to annihilate the Jewish people is listed second — but is it logical to consider this as something of secondary importance?"

He then answered his own question with yet another *mashal,* as he had promised.

A Jewish farmer was envious of his neighbor and decided that he, too, would get a *talmid chacham* as a son-in-law. He went to the *rosh yeshivah*, who recommended one of his students to him . . . The farmer sat his new son-in-law at his table and shared his rough diet of black bread and onions with him. But the *yeshivah* fellow, accustomed to more refined, processed foods, could not handle the rough fare, and so shriveled away from hunger.

The farmer, upset, hired two peasants to force the delicate son-in-law to eat his food. The young man could not bear this treatment, and finally sneaked away to the *yeshivah*. The farmer came after him, but the *rosh yeshivah* stopped him: "A *yeshivah* student is not a farmer. He can't exist on rough food."

"But I can't afford any other food," the farmer protested.

"You can afford to hire two peasants to force your indigestible food on him," exclaimed the *rosh yeshivah*, "but to feed him proper food — for that you have no money?"

"The *nimshal* (message)," continued the Dubner, "is as follows. The Moabites might have argued that they could not afford to offer bread and water to the wandering Jewish tribes. Yet when it came to hiring Bilaam to curse the Jews, there was no shortage of money at all."

Maggidim versus Maskilim

One of the main battles waged by *maggidim* was against the threat of assimilation posed by the *maskilim* — the proponents of "enlightenment" in Eastern Europe (not to be confused with the "enlightenment" of the Reform movement in Germany).

These men naively believed that the source of anti-Semitism lay in the differentness of the Jews. Let "Mosheke the Jew" only be more like "Vanka," they reasoned, and the Russians, Poles, Ukrainians and Lithuanians would love him. Amazingly, these individuals — many of whom had studied Torah — developed inferiority complexes when faced with any insignificant Russian who carried the title "poet," "professor," or "doctor."

Their attempt to bring the "light" of *Haskalah* to the Jewish masses was met by three obstacles: *Chassidus*, which was an antidote in advance of the epidemic; the *rabbanim;* and the *maggidim*, who fought it head on. In their publications, the *maskilim* made a mockery of the Talmud, bitterly attacking their opponents as ignorant fanatics who were preventing the light of "enlightenment" from reaching the oppressed Jewish masses. "Permit the Jews to receive a Russian education," they declaimed, "and they will gain all the benefits of equal citizenship!"

The *maggidim* in turn discredited the *maskilim* from the pulpit: "Mendelssohn's children joined the Church during his lifetime; the children of the *maskilim* will follow suit. Do you want this to happen to your own children? Because the heretics have smothered the spark of *kedushah*, holiness, in their own souls, they lick the boots of any little learned heathen. Can't they appreciate the Torah way of life? Do the "Vankes" have a Shabbos? What a *chutzpah* to suggest that we lower ourselves to their level!"

It was the extremists among the *maskilim* who instigated the czarist education ministry against the famed Yeshivah of Volozhin, mandating the teaching of secular studies there, which led to closing of the yeshivah's doors in 1892.

The Last Word

Upon the death of Mordechai Aaron Ginzburg, one of the leading *maskilim* of Vilna, the local *maskilim* insisted that Reb Velvele, the *shtot-maggid* (official community *maggid*), deliver the eulogy in his honor. The *maggid*, being in the employ of the *kehillah*, could not refuse. He who had fought the *maskilim* all his life apparently had no choice.

But who has the last word, if not the *maggid*? At the memorial gathering, he delivered a warm *hesped* for two *rabbanim* from the vicinity who had recently passed away. Then, at the tail end of his oration, he tagged on mention of Ginzburg.

The *maskilim* were furious. One of them, the well-known poet Adam HaKohen, told the *Maggid*, "Your eulogy typifies the messenger who came to bring King David news of a Jewish defeat. The messenger is described as *"hana'ar hamaggid"* (literally, "the youth who told." In Yiddish, however, the word *na'ar* refers to a fool). Why is the *maggid* a *na'ar*? Because the most important tidings — the fact that King Shaul and his son Yehonasan were killed — he saved for last, as if it were least important... Which only proves that the *Maggid* is a *na'ar*!"

Reb Velvele was not at a loss for an answer. As usual, he replied with a parable:

A Vilna merchant who had extensive business dealings in Germany married off one of his children. He invited some Jewish businessmen from Germany to the wedding. The German guests were extremely impressed with the *badchan* (an entertainer who sang original couplets about the bride and groom), the famous Yitzchak Smargoner, who delighted everyone with his witty *grammen* (humorous verse), jokes and stories.

Some time later, one of these guests invited the Smargoner *Badchan* to entertain at his daughter's wedding. In Germany, however, the show was a flop!

The *badchan* apologized, explaining that he was accustomed to making up rhymes with names such as Yankel and Sarah. He had never composed *grammen* for a Hans or a Gertrude! "But," added the entertainer, "you just invite me to more German weddings, and I'm sure I'll improve."

"I am in the same position," continued Reb Velvele. "I'm used to saying a *hesped* for a *rav* or a *tzaddik*, but never for a *maskil*. However, let's have more funerals for *maskilim*, and I'm sure I'll improve!"

"Reshus": Permission to Speak

In order to establish his credentials, one had to request permission to deliver a speech in *shul*[1] from the *mara d'asra* —the "master of the place"; namely, the *rav*. This primarily affected unknown speakers. As opposed to secular society, where a book or speech is judged on its own merits, regardless of the author's or orator's personal life, the Jewish people demand that the speaker or writer be *tocho kebaro* — the same inside as he presented on the outside. No *maggid* could preach what he did not also practice.

By contrast, famous *maggidim* hardly needed permission, for they were generally recognized as empowered with the necessary *reshus* in the Torah's command: "You shall surely rebuke your friend" (*Vayikra* 19:12).

R' Chaim Soloveitchik once refused to grant permission to a particular *maggid* to speak in Brisk, when he found out that the *maggid* was lacking in *yiras Shamayim* (fear of Heaven). The *maggid* appealed to Reb Chaim: "I quote the Sages and strengthen *Yiddishkeit!*"

To which R' Chaim replied, "Kosher meat, when cooked in a *treif* pot, becomes *treif!*"

When the *Rav* of Slonim, Rav Eizele Charif, refused a *maggid* permission to speak, a delegation of townspeople came to plead his case. "*Rebbe*, being a *maggid* proves he is G-d-fearing!"

---

1. A *rav* seldom went to listen to a *maggid* speak. However, a certain *maggid*, while asking for permission to address the *shul*, once invited the *rav* to attend. Afterwards, the *maggid* asked the *rav* his opinion.

"The word *maggid* is mentioned three times," the *rav* replied. '*Maggid d'varav le'Yaakov*' — 'He tells His Word to Jacob, His laws and statutes to Israel' (*Tehillim* 147). This is the best type of *maggid* — the teacher.

"The second one says '*Maggid mereishis acharis*' — 'He relates the end from the beginning.' This is the *maggid* who draws on history and relates it to our lives.

"The third time, it says, '...*v'aini maggid*' — He challenged [Pharaoh's] magicians, but they could not speak' (*Shemos*). This *maggid* says nothing, but just wastes people's time!"

The *Rav* replied, "That proves nothing. When the Torah tells us, 'He said to Yosef, your father is ill,' *Rashi* explains that 'he' is *'echad min hamaggidim'* — one of the *maggidim,* or reporters. Question: Is it possible that one of the Jewish *maggidim* came to ancient Egypt? Of course not! This teaches us that one can be both a heathen and a *maggid* at the same time!"

There were also *maggidim* who would seem to have been unqualified for the task, but undertook it nevertheless as a source of livelihood. One such individual was known as the *Shtumer Maggid* (the "Mute *Maggid*"). He was a well-known millionaire who had lost his entire fortune. He did not have to speak; his mere appearance in a *shul* would awaken feelings of introspection and despair of material security, by demonstrating what can happen to even the most prosperous person. He delivered his best *mussar,* his most effective rebuke, without ever opening his mouth.

R' Yisrael Salanter is known to have taught several *drashos* (speeches) to men who lacked skills on their own. To help them earn a living, he would coach them on what to say, and how.

Visiting Maggidim

Lomza was visited by many *maggidim.* I personally remember the "Stuchiner *Maggid,*" the "Grayever," the "Ostrolenker," and others. This last one was a Novarodoker (though how a Novarodoker settled in a chassidic town like Ostrolenke is beyond me!). He would speak in installments; that is, he would end his speech in the middle of an interesting story, "to be continued tomorrow" —thus keeping his listeners in suspense. During his two-week stay in town he would visit many *shuls.* He also dedicated one evening to addressing the women of the town. This meant that both the ladies' section in the balcony and the men's section below would be filled with women. The only man in *shul,* he would stand in front of the *Aron HaKodesh* with a *tallis* pulled over his head so that it covered his face as well, and address them on subjects of particular interest to women.

One of his classic speeches dwelt on the expression, "Our sins are many, beyond count," from the *Selichos* prayers. "Are we really that sinful?" he would ask. Then he'd quote R' Avraham from Tiktin: "When one shaves his face with a razor blade, he transgresses five prohibitions for every two hairs. How often does that fellow shave — once a week? Twice? Daily? How many prohibitions in a week? In a month — in a year — over a lifetime? The numbers are astronomical! 'Our sins are beyond count,' indeed!"

With the annihilation of much of European Jewry, the *maggid* as an institution has all but vanished from *Klal Yisrael*. Apart from a few notable exceptions, there are no *maggidim* left today. I end my tribute to them with the traditional close that every *maggid* used: "May the Redeemer come to Zion, swiftly in our days!"

The Shadchan (Matchmaker): Sources for the Profession

"Since Creation, G-d has engaged in making matches — a task as difficult as the splitting of the Red Sea" (*Bereishis Rabbah* 68:4).

Shadchan, the Hebrew word for matchmaker, is related to the word *shidduch*, match, which literally means (believe it or not!) peace or rest. According to *Ran* (*Rabbeinu Nissim*): "It stems from the work *sheket* (quiet) and *menuchah* (peace), which a woman finds in her husband's house, as the *Targum* translates the passage (*Shoftim* 5:31) 'And the land was tranquil for forty years' ('*Vatishtok ha'aretz arbaim shanah*'): *veshiduchas ara*" (*Shabbos* 12a).

When the late Gerrer *Rebbe*, R' Avraham Mordechai Alter, was approached by his brother regarding a match between their children, the *Rebbe* said, "Go get a *shadchan*!"

The brother was shocked. "Can't I talk to my own brother about a *shidduch* for our children? I, of all people, need a *shadchan?*"

Replied the *Rebbe*: "Hashem offered His Torah to all the nations of the world, yet they refused to accept His offer. When He turned to the Jews, however, they did accept. Why? Because He offered the Torah through a *shadchan* — Moshe *Rabbeinu*. And a *shidduch* was made!"

Indeed, we find the source of this observation in the *Midrash*: "In what merit did Moshe's face glow? In the merit of his being the *shadchan* between Yisrael and *HaKadosh Baruch Hu*" (*Yalkut Shimoni, Yisro* 1, 279).

Every town in Eastern Europe had its matchmaker, while in bigger cities two or more plied the trade. Though generally poor, they were held in great esteem for the important position they occupied in the community. These were not merely brokers who brought the two parties together, as in a business deal. The *shadchan* was an agent of Heaven, fulfilling the Divine mission described in the Talmudic literature: "A person's mate is designated by the Holy One" (*Bereishis Rabbah* 68:3); "Heaven mates a man and his wife in accordance with his merits"; and "Matching up a couple is a difficult as splitting the Red Sea" (*Sotah* 2).

The *shadchan* was regarded as G-d's messenger, bringing mates together on His behalf. As such, he was respected and honored; after all, the fates of the town's children rested in his hands. And, ultimately, he was loved — or hated — depending on the outcome of the *shidduch.*

Prerequisites of an Effective Shadchan

A *shadchan* could never lie, lest he lose his credibility. Trust was the foundation of his business. This, however, did not hinder him from being a thorough expert in the fine art of *guzma'os* (exaggerations). He was adept at stretching the positive about a prospective mate, and minimizing the negative. Above all, he was skilled in the art of persuasion.

His fellow *shtetl* folk knew how to distinguish between hard fact and *guzmah*. They could tell where the core of hard truth ended and the embroidery began. If they chose to accept everything that was said at face value, it was only because they wanted to hear and believe the exaggerations. The *shadchan*, then, was clearly blameless for any later disappointments.

The matchmakers stored mental "computer files" of information on some 100 families in various towns. By sifting through his memory, the *shadchan* had to come up with a match that would work!

Matching the boy and girl — their looks, personalities, levels of intelligence and commitment to *Yiddishkeit* — was only half the mission; matching the families was just as important. This involved a consideration of the families' stature in the community, their level of Torah scholarship, their charitable activities, economic status, and — above all — their *yichus*, or genealogy.

In order to correctly evaluate the families' Torah level or *yichus*, the *shadchan* had to be something of a *ben Torah*. In fact, some highly regarded rabbinical figures were known to engage, on a strictly nonprofessional basis, in making *shidduchim*. (See "Torah Pioneers," *The Jewish Observer*, June '74, for some of the Alter of Slobodka's more eminent *shidduchim*.)

This Thing Called Yichus

The term *yichus*, with all its connotations, can never be fully translated into another language. Pedigree? Genealogy? Breeding? These terms are suitable when buying a dog or a horse! It is no wonder that the rabbis have stated, "*Ein yichus l'akum*": The concept has no counterpart in non-Jewish tongues. Indeed, the Jews pride themselves on tracing their lineage through Avraham, Yitzchak and Yaakov, and all the way back to Adam *HaRishon,* and directly to the Creator Himself (as opposed to the atheists, who trace their ancestry to apes!). Converts to Judaism become a new link in this same aristocratic chain.

There are actually two kinds of *yichus*: the legal or *halachic* meaning of the term, and the popular expression of deep reverence for family lineage. According to *halachah*, Jewish *yichus* is traced through the father: "...by their families, by their father's houses" (*Bamidbar* 1:2). Hence, if the father is a *Kohen* or a *Levi*, so are his sons. For the purposes of our discussion, however, *yichus* is the term used to express admiration for families that are part of the aristocracy of Torah. With the birth of the chassidic movement, the term was widened to include *Chassidus* and *tzidkus* (piety) as well. This type of *yichus* applies as much to the mother's family as to the father's.

Traditionally, *yichus* has figured in marriage, as is recorded in the *Mishnah*: "Twice yearly the daughters of Israel would go out in borrowed white garments and dance in the vineyards. Unmarried men would also go there. The beautiful maidens would say, 'Lift up your eyes to beauty, for a wife is primarily for beauty.' The daughters of distinguished families would counter with, 'Fix your eyes on family, for a woman is primarily for child-bearing' " (*Taanis* 31a).

And so, every matchmaker made it his business to know the *yichus* and stature of the families involved in every *shidduch* he arranged.

The Shadchan of Tiktin

In Poland, almost every city had a nickname, which was used to describe the nature of its inhabitants. For instance, one large Polish city was famous as the home of *ganavim*, or thieves. Of course, not all its citizens were dishonest; but the city had gained notoriety for the numerous pickpockets, flim-flam operators and common thieves that preyed on its visitors.

Tiktin was known for its "Tiktiner *Yachsanim*," a title that speaks for itself. Each householder considered himself a *yachsan*, a man of impeccable lineage, always measuring his own family against others to his own advantage. One can imagine the difficulties this posed for Reb Choneh (brother of my *Bobbe Faigl*), the local *shadchan.*

The residents of Tiktin were also known as the *"Farbeigene Fingers"* (bent fingers) because of their habit when talking about their *yichus.* Thus, "My father was the son of the *Rav* of Boiberik" — one finger bent. "My mother was the granddaughter of the *Rosh Yeshivah* of Shnipishok" — another finger bent. "My uncle was the *rebbi* of *Targum Onkeles"* — three fingers down.

Reb Chone worked very diligently at his trade. He carried the names of hundreds of clients in his memory bank. He knew people in the neighboring towns, all the way to Bialystok. Sometimes he even wandered as far away as Warsaw for a *shidduch*!

As a rule, he never matched up two families from the same street or village: They knew too much about one another. He preferred out-of-towners for Tiktiners. Reb Chone would quote a piece of native Tiktiner wisdom: "Why did the Jews make the golden calf? True, they thought that Moshe *Rabbeinu* had died and they needed a new leader. But why didn't they pick Aaron, Elazar, or Chur? Why a calf?" To which the good people of Tiktin would reply: "Let it be a calf — as long as it's a stranger!"

Another Tiktiner *"vort"* (teaching) went as follows: It says that Yehudah married the daughter of a Cana'ani by the name of Shua (*Bereishis* 38:2). Rashi explains that "Cana'ani" does not refer to the man's nationality, but rather to the fact that he was a businessman. Tiktiners would ask, "What was the girl's name? What kind of upbringing did she have?" There is not a word about these things. All we are told is that she was a businessman's daughter — and from such a match came such problematic children as Er and Onan! Hence the Talmudic statement, "If one marries for money, he will not have worthy children" (*Kiddshin* 70a).

Reb Chone would occasionally drop into the home of my *zeide* — Reb Shmuel Leib Shapiro — to consult with him on some contemplated *shidduch.* Tall, thin, and gray, Reb Chone would sway as though he were praying as he listened to the other's opinions. Once, as he left, I heard him whisper an actual prayer:

"Ribbono Shel Olam, I know I can't split the sea, but I'm doing Your work. *Zie mir matzliach* — grant me success!"

Unlike other professionals, who were finished with a *shidduch* once they received payment for their efforts, Reb Chone often became emotionally involved in his clients' lives. He would worry about a couple for years to come. When the family saw him silently pace the kitchen, a pensive look on his face, they knew he was worrying about a *shidduch* that wasn't working out, or about one that was doing well at the moment but might not fare as well in the future. Once, at a wedding, when congratulated by all about the "perfect match" he had arranged, Reb Chone repeated the old *shadchan's* saying: *"Kinderlach* (children), whatever you are wishing me today, let it happen to me. Whatever you will be wishing me five years from today, may it happen to you!"

As a rule, *shadchanim* preferred to work with young prospects rather than widowed or divorced people. Yet they kept lists of once-married too, and never let a good idea slip past. The personal gratification of helping an older person find a match surpassed even the joy of helping a younger couple.

When a match was successful, the couple showered a lifetime of gratitude on the *shadchan.* However, should the outcome be tragic, both sides spelled out the letters of his title, SH-D-CH-N, in a highly derogatory message: *Sheker Dover, Chessef Notel* ("Speaks falsely, takes money"; i.e, his matchmaker's fee).

A Do-It-Yourself Guide to Yichus

What of those individuals not born into distinguished, Torah-*chassidus-tzidkus*-steeped families? Simple: They are free to start a *yichus* of their own! As the old saying goes: *"Yichus* is admirable where it begins, not where it ends." In many families, *yichus* ended when the children went astray; the next generation did not appreciate the treasure it had inherited. These children might boast about their lineage, but its value dropped dramatically with their own behavior. As someone once retorted to a person he'd heard belittling a great *talmid chacham* who happened not to stem from a family of distinguished lineage: "*He* is the pride of his parents, while *you* are the shame of yours!"

Rambam actually prescribes a course for fashioning one's own *yichus*, based on a passage in *Avos*: "The Jews were crowned with three crowns. The crown of priesthood went to Aaron and his descendants. The crown of royalty went to David. And the crown of Torah is ready and waiting for everyone to come and claim it . . . Perhaps you think those two crowns are greater than the crown of Torah . . . [but] the Torah crown is greater than those two" (*Hilchos Talmud Torah* 3:1).

Pursuing this line of thinking, our Sages advise us: "A person should sell his possessions in order to marry the daughter of a *talmid chacham*, and he should marry his own daughter to a *talmid chacham*. This can be compared to clusters from a grapevine, a thing both pleasant and well received" (*Pesachim* 49a). *Maharsha* explains, "He, too, will be well received, for she will bear him fine children. Just as the grapevine does not accept a graft from any other tree, so, too, will your children be without flaw."

Even if a man finds it impossible to become a master of Torah, he can still build a house based on *Yiddishkeit* and charity, for "the crown of a good name is above them all." If one raises children with Torah-true values that they will remember and cherish all their lives, this provides them with *yichus* for generations to come. Such *yichus* is the greatest inheritance one can leave his children.[1]

In the absence of telephones, matchmakers would meet while traveling by train to various cities to investigate new "merchandise." Each *shadchan* would lavishly praise his "article," the

---

1. What of the *ger*, the convert? In his letter to Ovadiah the Proselyte, *Rambam* (Maimonides) writes: "Proselytes, do not underestimate your lineage! If we trace ours to Abraham, Isaac, and Jacob, you trace yours to the Creator." These individuals, too, can build a family of great nobility, as we find written about Pinchas, one of whose grandfathers was Aaron, the *Kohen Gadol* (High Priest), while the other had once fattened his calves to be sacrificed to idols (*Bamidbar* 25:1; see *Rashi*).

better to impress his "competitor." Often, they created partnerships and split the income.

The story is told of two matchmakers who became so immersed in presenting their fabulous "wares" to each other that they forgot to mention a very important item: the "green billet." (In czarist Russia, a youth would be drafted into the army for a period of five, seven, or ten years, depending on the particular army branch involved. Consequently, many Jewish boys, to avoid the draft, would cross the border to Austria and make their way from there to America.[1] Others went to the lengths of cutting off an index finger [one cannot pull a trigger without an index finger] or big toe [a soldier cannot march without a big toe], so that they'd be rejected by the draft commission. The proof of such rejection was the "green billet" [ticket].) A boy who possessed a green billet was preferable, for matchmaking purposes, to one who stood in danger of being drafted.

The two *shadchanim* agreed that it was a perfect match and shook hands on the deal. To clinch matters, one of them suddenly remarked triumphantly, "And mine has a green billet!"

"Mine, too!" replied the other.

---

1. The fear of serving a minimum of five years' army service, without Shabbos or kosher food, was so great that it provoked parents and children to extreme measures. My own grandfather did not want his son to go to America. He also rejected the expedient of having his son cut off a finger or toe, since, as a *Kohen*, he would be unable to do the service in the *Bais HaMikdash* when *Mashiach* arrived. My *zeide* went to another extreme. He hired a *"malach"* ("angel"), to present himself to the draft board in his son's place. This man had only one leg. As there were few photographs in those days, nobody would know about the switch. The "angel" was paid for such impersonations in various cities, and through his services many Jewish youths obtained the coveted "green billet."

In my father's case, however, something unforeseen occurred. The chairman of the draft commission fell ill, and was replaced by a *poretz* who had often done business with my grandfather.

"I know Sir Shmulki Shapiro," the new chairman exclaimed. "I have visited his home many times, and never have I seen a son with one leg!"

The *"malach"* turned white, giving himself away. He was immediately arrested. Another warrant went out for my father, then studying in Mir. It cost my *zeide* a fortune — but at the next meeting of the commission the chairman declared that he'd made a mistake. Shapiro did, indeed, have a son with one leg!

To their amazement, they realized that they had fixed up two boys!

A Shadchan in Lomza

Being blessed with two home towns, Lomza and Tiktin, I am able to share what I know about the king of the *shadchanim* for the entire vicinity of Lomza — R' Ever Frankel. R' Frankel even wrote a book on the subject, entitled *Nistorei Nechbados*, a veritable handbook of the trade. He claimed that matchmaking is a profession, and, as in any other profession, one must study its rules to become a master.

In that pretelephone era, the most impressive tool at the *shadchan's* disposal was the telegram. Its impact was much greater than that of a letter or oral communication. A flurry of telegrams often preceded a successful match.

Since telegrams charged by the word, the trick was to say the most with the least number of words. Matchmakers became adept at condensing descriptions, propositions, and plans into just a few words. The recipients — the parents of prospective brides and grooms — would study every word for what it said and did not say, discussing and interpreting every possible meaning to be derived from them. In the absence of commas, periods, and exclamation marks (telegrams had no punctuation), the word "stop" was strategically inserted. Apart from its use as a replacement for punctuation, the word also gave the reader a chance to catch his breath and digest what he'd read thus far. Such was the telegram's impact, however, that people tended to read it quickly to its conclusion, without bothering to pause for breath.

R' Ever Frankel, in his handbook, makes reference to this popular mode of communication. He writes: "Do not tell me of the first *shadchan* in history, Eliezer, who concluded the *shidduch* of Yitzchak and Rivka without a hitch — no difficulties, no arguments, no telegrams from Charan to Chevron. There the *shidduch* went smoothly because the *mechutan,* Avraham *Avinu,* did not ask for a *nadan* (dowry) from the *kallah*'s side. In our day, however, they sing a different tune. Every *mechutan* is from the *Asarah Yuchsin* and the wealth of Korach is not enough for these *Bnei Heichala Dichsifin!"*[1]

He goes on to describe one of his greatest achievements, a match that he brought to a happy conclusion where all the other *shadchanim* had tried and failed. It meant dealing with "... the famous, highly educated lady, Sarah Nimtzevitz from Bialystok, granddaughter of R' Yehoshua Leib Diskin, Rav of Lomza (later of Brisk and Yerushalayim). She spoke many languages; she was a *bas Kohen* and carried her *yichus* with pride, and she wrote a literate Hebrew which flowed like a swift river. She offered her only son along with a dowry of 10,000 rubles, but demanded in return 25,000 rubles from the *kallah*'s side. All the *shadchanim* in the country were out looking for a suitable *kallah,* but could find none."

Frankel found a prospective bride in Riga, in the province of Latvia (in those days, the three Baltic states were part of the czarist Russian Empire). He sent a telegram: *MATZASI* (I FOUND) STOP *MISHOMAYIM HITZLICHAH* (HEAVEN HELPED ME) STOP *KALLAH NA'AH VACHASUDAH* (A GRACIOUS PIOUS BRIDE) STOP A PERFECT MATCH STOP TWENTY THOUSAND STOP MAZEL TOV STOP

What was Sarah Nimtzevitz's reply?

HAVE SPOKEN STOP I GIVE MY SON STOP AS MUCH AS *BEN HAMDOSO* (HAMAN) STOP GAVE FOR ALL THE JEWS STOP IN THE KINGDOM OF ACHASHVEROSH STOP WE THE CHILDREN OF AARON HAKOHEN STOP WILL BLESS THE SHIDDUCH STOP ONLY WITH TWENTY-FIVE STOP

It took the wisdom, experience, and powers of persuasion of the king of *shadchanim,* R' Ever Frankel — along with a further exchange of telegrams — to conclude the negotiations. One must bear in mind that the telegrams and the haggling about

---

1. Talmudic and Midrashic references that defy simple translation.

money took place behind the scenes, without the children's knowledge. Then, if the chemistry was positive when they met, the parents would do nothing to derail the match. And if the principals were not interested, the parents were helpless to bring them together. The premeeting haggling was merely a matter of planning ahead to secure the financial future of the young couple.

P'gam: A Blemish in the Family

A *shadchan* had to be familiar not only with each family's *yichus*, but also with any *p'gam*, or blemish, in the family: a significant factor in the matching process. The following (in order of severity) were considered blemishes:

1. A *meshumad* in the family — someone who converted to a different faith (a rarity).
2. A *moser* — an informer against his fellow Jews.
3. A Communist.
4. A Bundist-Socialist.

It was the *shadchan's* duty to uncover the entire story and, in such cases, report the relevant facts to the interested parties.

Remarkable are the words of the *Maharsha*, who served as *Rav* of Tiktin (1620). (I can visualize him in the old *Bais Din Shtub* — still extant before the war — writing these words in his famous commentary on *Shas*.) "In our generation, most questions regarding *yichus* are not based on documented fact. Thus, if one casts aspersions on someone else's *yichus* to his friends, he is nothing less than a slanderer, seeking glory by shaming others. Whoever points out a *p'gam* in someone else is merely covering up his own shortcomings. They should be chastised and warned to correct their ways. The *shadchanim*, especially, are guilty in this matter, and should be punished" (*Maharsha, Kiddushin* 71a).

Shadchanus

A matchmaker's commission ("*shadchanus*") is protected by *halachah*, which raises many questions: Who is required to pay the *shadchan* — the bride and groom, or their parents? (It is the obligation of the young couple, as the main beneficiaries; however, it is customary for the parents to pay.) When is payment due — at the engagement or after the wedding? If one does not pay on time, does he violate the Torah prohibition against holding back a worker's wages? What if one *shadchan* introduces the couple and another steers the *shidduch* to its conclusion? What if the couple breaks off, and a different matchmaker then renews the match and brings it to completion? Responsa are full of such questions, geared mainly toward protecting the *shadchan*.

Community discipline was strict on the subject. Woe to those who failed to pay the matchmaker! In fact, some people are meticulous in giving a gift of some sort to everyone who was involved in bringing a couple together — to free the match from any misgiving on anyone's part. Some take unfair advantage of this tendency, as the following story illustrates.

A *shadchan* approached one of the fathers of the young couple after the wedding and demanded payment.

"I'm astonished at your nerve!" exclaimed the father. "It was Reb Dovid the *shadchan* who made the *shidduch*, not you. You never even spoke one word about us!"

"Indeed," replied the *shadchan*. "Had I said but one word about you, there never would have been a wedding."

The father got the message — and paid the *shadchan*!

In conclusion, *shadchanim* are a blessing for a community, For the past 30 years I have been involved in the *gittin* (divorce) process in Baltimore, and can testify that, in the hundreds or perhaps thousands of divorces I've witnessed, there were hardly two dozen from the *yeshivah* community. To what can we attribute this excellent record?

The Torah life, of course, with its built-in patterns of renewal, offers the best antidote to the plague of boredom and discontent. But in my opinion, *shadchanim* are also a contributing factor to the establishment of healthy marriages. The matchmaker brings an objective third party into the selection process and serves also as a buffer between the parties, who may be too eager, too reluctant, or too inexperienced for a smooth courtship. By contrast, when boy meets girl casually, Jewish patterns of modesty are violated at the outset. The couple may be unduly impetuous, without the guiding and sometimes restraining hand of detached people with mature judgement. This syndrome is obviated when a good *shadchan* is introduced into the process. He sees the whole picture from the start and has the experience and knowledge of human nature to carry the match to its proper conclusion, in the proper way.

As the Gerrer *Rebbe* put it: "Go get a *shadchan*! *Mazel tov*!"

Chapter 5: Charity in the Shtetl

*B*oth of my home towns, Lomza and Tiktin (Tykocin), were located in the district of Bialystok in northeastern Poland. Lomza was considered a sizable Polish city, with a population of 25,000, of whom some 12,000 were Jews. The Jewish community boasted a huge *yeshivah*, a 10-grade Talmud Torah, a Bais Yaakov, a hospital, 12 charitable institutions, 21 synagogues, two banks, two weekly newspapers (one in Yiddish and one in Polish), two orphanages (one each for boys and girls), a free loan society (no-interest, collateral required), *Hachnasas Orchim* (offering hospitality for travelers), *Hachnasas Kallah* (financial assistance for indigent brides), *Bikur Cholim* (visiting the sick), *Linas HaTzedek* (providing ice for fever-stricken patients), and a *Moshav Zekeinim* (old-age home).

And all this at a time when the words "tax deductible" had never even been heard of!

A Nation Like No Other

R' Assi said: "Charity equals all the other commandments" (*Bava Basra* 9a). Added R' Eliezer, "*Matan b'seiser* (where the recipient does not know the giver) is greater than Moshe *Rabbeinu*" (*Baba Basra* 9b).

No nation on earth can compare to the Jewish people when it comes to giving charity. In the *shtetl*, householders competed in inviting paupers to their Shabbos tables. Like every other aspect of Jewish life, charity is regulated by laws: how to give, how much to give, how to collect it (with two trustees), how to distribute it (with three trustees), and more.

Our poor do not beg; they "demand," as though they are collecting a debt! — as, indeed, they are. Life can be compared to a stormy sea. First you find yourself on the crest of a wave, on top of the world. Next thing you know, you're at the bottom of the trough, barely holding your head above water. The wheel of fortune turns; today's philanthropist is tomorrow's needy person, and vice versa.

The Moshav Zekeinim in Lomza

Lomza's Jewish hospital

There are two Hebrew words to denote a poor person. Each serves as a character description of the two different types of charity recipients. Each, in turn, demands a specific attitude on the part of the donors.

One individual was, only yesterday, a respectable, well-to-do homeowner. He was dispensing charity to others. Suddenly, he finds himself in the position of needing charity. In public, he *knepps the bakken* (pinches his cheeks) to keep them pink and healthy looking, trying to pass as the same prosperous *balebas* as before. While secretly hoping for charity, his pride will not permit him to extend his hand. He will not beg. This man is called an *ani,* and one who gives him a *matan b'seiser,* keeping his own identity hidden, is considered greater than Moshe *Rabbeinu.*

A typical case of an *ani* involved a man who came to the *Rav* of Brisk, the famous R' Yoshe Ber Brisker (Soloveichik). The man asked the *Rav* if it is permissible to use milk instead of wine for the *arba kossos* (the four cups of wine one is obligated to drink at the Pesach *seder*). The *Rav* looked the man over and replied that if a person was sick and the doctor forbade him to drink wine, he might get by with milk. Then he took out 25 rubles and offered them to the man.

The other man was embarrassed, insisting that he did not need charity. The *Rav* explained that the money was his own personal loan. "You'll be doing me a favor," he urged. "When does a *Rav* get a chance to acquire the *mitzvah* of lending money?"

After the man left with the rubles, the *rebbetzin*, who'd heard the interchange from the next room, complained, "If everyone who comes with a *sha'alah* (halachic question) leaves with 25 rubles, we will not have money for Pesach ourselves!"

The *Rav* replied, "You'll forgive me, but it is my responsibility as *rav* to read between the lines of the question. The man did not look ill. If he uses milk for the *arba kossos,* that means he won't have even a piece of chicken or a little chicken soup at the *seder* — for how could he have *milchigs* (dairy) and *fleishigs* (meat) at the same table? That man was not 'asking' — he was telling me something." The wisdom of a *rav*!

Sara Schenirer, mother of the Bais Yaakov movement, knew of a young man in desperate need; it was two weeks before Pesach. She approached Reb Binyomin Zusman, who *davened* beside that man in the same *shtibl,* and asked, "Please sneak these 50 *zlotys* into his coat pocket." R. Binyomin did just that, and watched the young man put his coat on after *davening.* When he placed his hand in his pocket and found the money, the eyes of that *ani* lit up and looked heavenward in thanks. That was a *matan b'seiser*!

Throughout the year, the community was divided into three categories: those who gave charity, those who received it, and the neutrals — individuals who could not afford to give but at the same time would be embarrassed to be offered charity. After Purim, however, when the *maos chittim* campaign began, the community was divided in two, omitting the neutrals. The rule that prevailed then was that one either gave or received. If one did not participate in the fund, he would discover a basket of *matzah,* wine and chicken delivered to his door one day, just like any other person in need.

In some communities, *maos chittim* was a straightforward drive for funds. In others, a voluntary tax was levied on every kilogram of *matzah* bought in the bakery, and every kilo of meat. This surcharge was then channeled into the *maos chittim* fund.[1]

The Evyon

In contrast to the *ani*, the *evyon* was the classic "*shnorrer*" who was not ashamed to beg openly for his sustenance.[2] Pride had no part to play for him; he stretched out his hand to ask for — indeed, demand — a contribution. The *evyonim* were easily recognized by the trademark *torbe* (sack) they always carried on their backs. Most of them were delicate souls, both men and women, who had lost their shame through sheer poverty. They had no trade, no education, no job. Unemployment insurance did not exist. Government jobs were denied to Jews unless they converted to Roman Catholicism — and, to the credit of these unfortunates, conversion was unthinkable even in the face of awesome poverty. They were reduced to begging to stave off starvation.

Every Monday and Thursday, they would go from door to door, to shops and private homes, collecting handouts. If there was no money, they would accept anything: half a *challah*, a piece of gefilte fish, a portion of chicken, a shirt, a pair of pants or shoes. That's what the *torbe* was for.

Upon entering a store, they would generally wait at the door or in a corner of the shop, with one hand extended and eyes downcast. Some, however, usually the men, could be arrogant. If someone remarked, "With your strong hands, can't you find a job?" a barrage of *klallos* (curses) would be his answer. "I was

---

1. By law, every Jew must have wine and *matzah* for Pesach. The term *maos chittim* literally means money for wheat (i.e., flour with which to bake *matzos*).

2. An *evyon* is even more indigent than an *ani*, and he has virtually nothing (see *Rashi, Devarim* 15:4).

once a respectable businessman, and my *mazel* overturned, may it happen to you. Next year, may I see you with a *torbe*. May you turn into a lamp, hanging by day and burning by night!" The townsfolk were terrified of a *shnorrer's* curse. With that kind of "blessing" in store, a person would give double just to shoo him off in peace.

In Lomza, the king of the *shnorrers* was Zavl. His *torbe* was immaculate. He used to explain: "I have to keep it clean, because it's my daughter's *nadan* (dowry). What else can I give the *chassan*? I'll teach him my trade!"

And some trade it was. The secret of Zavl's success was his native wisdom. My father would bemoan Zavl who, for all he lacked an education and a trade, was clearly so intelligent. What a shame, my father would say, to use such a mind for "*shnorrer shtick.*" Zavl could read a person's mood by his face, and would adjust his approach accordingly. He could cry at will, tell jokes and make faces like a polished actor. He could bless and curse for an hour, without repeating a curse twice.

He once entered our store while my father was closing a big deal with a *poretz*. Zavl bowed and, with a sycophantic smile, said to the *goy*, "*Pozmac pana po cholawe*" ("One can tell a gentleman by his boots.") (Rich Poles wore knee-high boots, and the glow of the leather was their pride.) The *poretz* handed him a large donation, which forced my father in turn to double his own regular donation. Zavl left with a smile and a blessing for both. "May the deal be a success for both, as the rain showers your farm with blessing."

Once Zavl went to Bialystok. He walked all night and reached the town in the afternoon, tired and hungry. He found a restaurant and, managing to hide his *torbe* beneath the table, ordered a full meal. Needless to say, he didn't have the money to pay the bill. The owner became angry, and opened the door to summon the policeman on the corner.

"Wait," said Zavl, in a businesslike manner. "*Reb Yid*, if I go to jail for a week or two, you still will not get paid. But I have a plan to pay you. In fact, I have three plans."

The owner took a chair. "Okay, I'm listening. How are you going to pay me?"

Zavl briskly presented his plan. "Number one: You extend me credit. Trust me — it will take me about 10 days to work over this town. After I collect my money, I'll come and pay you."

A silent negative was the owner's reply to this proposal.

"I understand," Zavl said promptly. "You don't want to extend me credit. Why should you? You don't know me. This is the first time you've ever laid eyes on me. So here's plan number two: You come with me from door to door, and whatever money comes in, you take it on account, until the bill is paid." A pause. "Again, I'll understand if you reject that plan. After all, you are a respectable citizen in the community, a restaurant owner with some real estate. It's below your dignity to walk down the street with a *shnorrer* like me." He smiled affably. "So here's plan number three: Since you don't trust me, and you are ashamed to walk with me — here's my *torbe*. Go yourself from door to door and collect for me!"

The restaurateur burst out laughing. Still laughing, he grabbed a broom and ordered Zavl out, together with his *torbe*.

Shnorrers also roamed the countryside, trudging on foot from town to town. If they were lucky, farmers driving to town would give them a lift. The larger cities suffered most from the addition of these out-of-town beggars to their own native ones. The Jewish *kehillah* of Vilna, it is recorded, once contemplated banning out-of-towners from doing their *shnorring* in Vilna. The situation, they felt, had gotten out of hand — and the *kehillah* had the law on their side. It clearly states: "*Ani'ei irchah kodem* — Your own poor come first."

As was usual at every important meeting, the city fathers invited the Vilna *Gaon* to attend. The *Gaon* chided, "I've asked you a number of times not to call me to a meeting unless you have to establish new *takanos* (laws)."

"But, *Rebbi*," insisted the *Rosh HaKahal*, "this is a new *takanah*. We want to enact the new rule that no out-of-town beggars be allowed in Vilna."

"No," interrupted the *Gaon*, "that is not a new *takanah*. It was already practiced in Sodom!"

The proposal died an instant death.

The more sensitive among the poor, who could not bring themselves to beg, became "street singers" or "street musicians," depending on their talent. In a preradio world starved for entertainment, in which the only music was provided by the gramophone (or Patephone) and records that only the rich could afford, these modest singers and players filled the void. One or two, or sometimes a combination team of a singer and a violinist, would turn up in a back yard. All at once windows would fly open. At every window, three or four heads would appear, listening and enjoying the show. Then a shower of coins wrapped in paper would rain down on the performers. Neighborhood kids used to follow these entertainers, hoping for some *"shikchah"* — that is, some small coin that the performer might forget to pick up.

These singers were true artists, poets and songwriters. Should a national or international tragedy occur, these men immediately came up with a song to tug at the heartstrings. I remember when a bus, en route from Lomza to Warsaw, plunged into the Narew River, drowning 18 passengers. That was a memorable funeral; even the rav attended and delivered a rare eulogy. Within a week, the *"hoif"* (backyard) singers had composed a song. The melody and lyrics opened all the windows, all the tear ducts, and all the pockets. I remember, too, when Italy attacked Ethiopia, and the *neggus* (their king) appealed to the League of Nations for help. At once the backyard singers composed *Neggus neggestye ratuj Abbesynia* (the Polish name for Ethiopia). They sang of Italian atrocities, and ended with *"U'mi yishveh lach, u'mi ya'aroch lach?"* ("Who can equal or compare with You?")

Then there were those who could neither sing nor play an instrument. They entertained the public with a *katerinke* (barrel organ). All they had to do was turn the handle and music would emerge. Some even had a talking bird sitting on the *katerinke* which, for a coin, would pull out a card telling the "future."

Charitable Societies

To assist the poor, a variety of charitable societies sprang up in the *shtetl*, some permanent and others organized for a specific task. For example, *Hachnasas Kallah* was a permanent group whose self-ordained task was to marry off poor girls. They formed temporary committees, such as women who volunteered to make a dress and other necessities for indigent *kallos*.

When I was studying in the *yeshivah* of Baranowitz, I once went to the shoemaker to get my shoes fixed. He refused to take money from me, because he was a member of *Malbish Arumim*, a society of shoemakers and tailors who fixed shoes and clothing for *bnei Torah* free of charge. When I insisted on paying, he agreed to accept money this time, adding that he had five other boys in the *yeshivah* whose shoes were beyond repair, and that he would speak to the *gabbaim* (Society officers) about paying for new ones.

In America, charity has been transformed into a "social science" in which caseworkers are armed with degrees and *gabbaim* have sometimes turned into directors with huge salaries and early retirement. How different it was in the *shtetl*, where the *gabbaim* were all volunteers. They used to donate their money and their time, strictly for the sake of the *mitzvah*. Their symbol was the *reite tichel* (red handkerchief). When a team of two set out to collect with a red handkerchief, the people knew they were trustworthy, and that 100 percent of their donation would go to the cause.

Hachnasas Orchim

In a world without hotels and motels, where was a traveler to stay for a few days or even just overnight? There was hardly any room to spare in private homes. In emergencies, people would line up three chairs against the wall and top them with a straw sack — that was a royal bed. Hence, almost every town

The Hachnasas Orchim building in Lomza

and village had its *Hachnasas Orchim* Society. A traveler could thus be assured of a clean bed and a cup of tea with sugar in the morning, free of charge. In some cities they were even served breakfast.

The *mitzvah* of *hachnasas orchim,* of providing hospitality to guests, was greatly cherished by the people. Once, in Tiktin, the charitable guest house burned down. Reb Yeruchom, the wine maker, soon bought another house for that purpose. He was a poor man, and the townspeople wondered where he had found the funds to make the purchase. It was years before the secret was finally revealed. The two sons of my uncle, Reb Mordechai Pines, had been asked to report to the draft board for induction into the Russian army. Reb Mordechai made a vow that, if his sons were rejected for military service, he would donate a house for the *mitzvah* of *hachnasas orchim.* He managed to conceal his identity for years by using the wine maker as a front for his charitable activity.

The *hachnasas orchim* house was always inhabited. There were travelers, guests, fundraisers for various *yeshivos,* and merchants passing through on business. On Shabbos, when one is required to eat three meals, these individuals would come to the *shul* on Friday night. The *gabbai,* noticing a new face, knew that the man was a guest in town. He'd look the man over from head to toe, as though assessing his personality, and then decide where to send him for his Shabbos meals.

Actually, who ended up hosting whom was more a matter of luck than of the *gabbai*'s psychological expertise. If a householder was fortunate, he got an *ore'ach* who was a bit of a scholar, or an intelligent person with whom it was a pleasure to have a discussion. Sometimes, on the other hand, he got a *fresser*, intent on his only square meals of the whole week. The same *mazel* applied to the guest. Sometimes he was placed with a well-to-do family, and other times in a home where, instead of gefilte fish, all he got was a piece of shmaltz herring.

R' Yosef Kahaneman, *Rav* of Ponevez and founder of the Ponevez *Yeshivah* in Bnei Brak, was born in a Lithuanian village called Kool, where his father served as *gabbai* of the *shul*. Whenever the town was hosting two guests, it was his custom to take them both into his own home on Shabbos. If there were three, he would take two and assign the third to his mother-in-law. Only if there were more than three strangers in *shul* did any other *baal habayis* have a chance to host one. The people didn't like it, but there was nothing they could do. Mr. Kahaneman had been elected *gabbai* on *Shabbos Bereishis*, and his term lasted a full year.

One Shabbos, some worshipers — apparently too lazy to go out to the *poloosh* (antechamber) — began to talk during the service. Mr. Kahaneman ascended the *bimah* and, in anger, announced: "I cannot be *gabbai* in a place where people talk during *davening*. Therefore, I am resigning the position!"

Silence reigned for a moment; the congregation was in shock. Then the town *meshuganer* leaped up to the *bimah* and, cackling with glee, asked, "So who will get the guests now?"

Mr. Kahaneman turned white. He jumped back onto the *bimah* and declared, "I rescind my resignation. I take it back!" Such was his love — the Jewish love — for the *mitzvah* of *hachnasas orchim*.

The story is told of a stranger who was a drunkard. The moment he walked into a house, he would surreptitiously study the table to find the bottle of schnapps there, along with the *challah*, wine, and gefilte fish. When they finally sat down to the table, the guest helped himself to one half-glass of whiskey, and then another. The host immediately recognized the "customer" he had landed.

The guest, realizing that it was not nice to finish the bottle all by himself, resorted to the old trick of pouring whiskey into his glass and then soaking his *challah* in it. Now no one could accuse him of drinking. He was merely eating *challah* — and wasn't a guest entitled to eat all the *challah* he wanted?

The *ba'al habayis* (householder) noticed that the bottle was empty. He said to the guest, "*Reb Yid*, did you ever attend *cheder*?"

"Of course I went to *cheder*," responded the guest. "What Jewish boy does not go to *cheder*?"

Asked the host, "Well, then, do you remember the story of *yetzias Mitzrayim* (the exodus from Egypt)?"

"Most certainly I remember. What do you take me for? The Jews were slaves in Egypt. Hashem released them from slavery, and then He split the sea so they could cross."

"Precisely my question!" exclaimed the *ba'al habayis*. "Why did Hashem have to split the sea? There were 600,000 Jews — more, if you count the women and children, too. Let each one dip a piece of *challah* into the sea, and it would be dry in no time."

The guest was no dummy, either. "With all due respect, my dear sir," said he, "you are making a bad mistake — indeed, a terrible mistake. It was Pesach! How could they eat *challah*?"

"Well," his host shot back, "it's true they couldn't dip *challah*, but they could surely dip *matzah*."

"Again with all due respect, *matzah* does not absorb as well as *challah*. Ask me — I'm an expert on such matters. Besides," the drunkard ended triumphantly, "there were a lot of *chassidim* there, and they would not eat *gebrochts*!"[1]

---

1. It is the custom of *chassidim* to refrain from eating *matzah* that has come in contact with liquid on Pesach.

Chevrah Korban Eitzim

Among the town's various charitable *chevros* (societies) was one called *Korban Eitzim* (literally, Sacrifice of Trees). The name goes back to the days of the *Bais HaMikdash*, the Holy Temple. There was a need for firewood to burn on the *Mizbe'ach* (Altar), and people would donate wood for that purpose. The wood had to be checked for worms which, if present, would disqualify it for the *Mizbe'ach*. In fact, during certain seasons of the year wood was not accepted by the *Kohanim* (priests of the Temple) because it was impossible to remove all the worms.

The main source of heat in the freezing *shtetl* winters, in the absence of electricity or gas, was firewood. Coal and peat were also available, but more expensive than wood. Peat — a type of dried mud cut into blocks — was cheaper than coal because it produced a good deal of ash and didn't burn as long. The Society, which supplied fuel for poor families, could not afford anything but wood.

The officers of the Society would personally drop off the firewood at the homes of the poor. At the same time, they would "smuggle in" a few sacks of potatoes or other vegetables, thereby acquiring an additional *mitzvah* on the side, as it were. Since there was no refrigeration, perishable vegetables were unobtainable during the winter. Every household that was capable of it would stock up on vegetables beforehand, which were stored in the basement during the winter months.

On one Shabbos each year, all the donations — pledged during the Torah readings in the *shuls* — were designated for the *Chevrah Korban Eitzim*. A story is told of the *gaon* and *tzaddik* R' Elya Chaim Meisel, *Rav* of Lomza (and later of Lodz). The officers of the Society complained to him about a certain prosperous man in the town who failed to support the Society properly. One Sunday morning, very early, the Rav went out in subzero temperature to pay a visit to Reb Mendel. The *Rav*, wearing his heavy winter *peltz* (fur coat) and high Siberian fur hat, knocked on the miser's door. The man, wondering who could be forcing him out of bed so early in the morning, grabbed his robe and bedroom slippers and went to open the door.

"*Rebbi!*" he exclaimed in astonishment. "Good morning! It's so early; come in, please."

The *Rav* refused to enter. "I'm on my way to the early *minyan*. I just wanted to know how you are."

"Oh, I'm fine, thanks."

"And how is your family?" continued the *Rav*, very much at his leisure.

"*Baruch Hashem*, fine, fine. We're all fine. But please, come in, *Rebbi* — it's freezing outside!" Reb Mendel was shivering from the cold.

But the *Rav* said, "No, I have no time to come in. I'm already late for *shul*. I happened to be passing by, so I wanted to see how everything is with you. How is business? How are the boys doing in *cheder*?"

"*Rebbi*, can't we discuss everything inside, where it's warm? It's below zero out here!"

"No, no, don't bother. I'm just leaving," the Rav answered. He fixed the other man with a penetrating look. "But you know, Reb Mendel, there are homes here in town that are just as cold on the inside as on the outside. That's why we have *Chevrah Korban Eitzim*. Have a good day!"

Reb Mendel got the message.

Buying cut firewood was too expensive. Instead, the *Chevrah* hired a lumberjack to go to the forest, cut down a tree, and chop it into logs that would fit the potbelly stoves of the *shtetl*. It was the custom of lumberjacks (as well as blacksmiths) to spit in their palms in order to give them a good grip on the handle of the axe, and to say, "Ha, ha," as they let the axe fall. The reason for this custom is unclear; perhaps the release of air from the lungs affected the force of the axe's blow.

One day, as the lumberjack was doing his job, Reb Zelig, the town *meshuganer,* was standing by observing every move. Each time the axe landed on the wood, Reb Zelig shouted, "Ha, ha!" Since he was a peaceful man who didn't bother anyone, he was amiably ignored. When the job was finished and the logs loaded onto a wagon ready for the Society members to deliver, the *gabbai* of the Society approached the lumberjack to pay him. At once, Reb Zelig jumped up and demanded that he, too, be paid.

"Why do you want to get paid?" asked the *gabbai*. "What did you do?"

"What did I do? Didn't you see? I said, 'ha, ha,' which made the axe dig deeper, and that made the lumberjack finish the job faster. So I'm entitled to get paid — not as much as him, true, but you can't get away with giving me nothing."

Had it been any other *meshuganer*, the *gabbai* would have chased him away, but this was Reb Zelig, who had been a respectable businessman and a member in good standing of the Society for a quarter-century. Ten years before, he had even served as president of the *Chevrah*. Then tragedy entered his life: His daughter died in childbirth, and Reb Zelig's mind snapped.

The *gabbai* had an idea. "Reb Zelig, let's go to the *Rav* for a *din Torah*." He winked at the other members, as if to say: "Let the *Rav* take care of this." Reb Zelig began rubbing his hands in glee. "I like a *din Torah*. *Oy*, did I have *dinei Torah* when I was in business!"

Reb Zelig was accordingly brought before the *Rav*, who asked him, "What did you do that justifies your demand for pay?"

"Oh, *Rebbi*, you see, when a lumberjack says, 'Ha,' the axe goes in deeper. Now remember, *Rebbi*, if you say, 'Ha,' one second before the blade hits the wood, you've wasted a 'ha.' If you say, 'Ha,' a split second after the blade touches the wood, that 'ha' is worthless, too. But I watched him very carefully. I said, 'Ha,' at the exact moment that blade hit the wood — and that's why he finished the job so fast. I'm entitled to some pay!"

The Society officers and the others present in the rabbi's *bais din shtub* were amazed at the strange logic of the *meshuganer's* case. They waited breathlessly for the *Rav's* verdict.

The *Rav* inquired how much the job had cost. Five rubles, stated the *gabbai*. In those days, most of the money was in silver or gold coins. Only the large denominations, like 50 or a 100 rubles, were on paper. The Rav took a five-ruble silver coin and knocked it against the table. The sound rang out: *dinggg.* Three times the Rav repeated this: *dinggg, dinggg, dinggg.* Then, to Reb Zelig and the puzzled onlookers, he declared, "This is my *psak* (verdict). You, the lumberjack who did the job, take the money. Reb Zelig, who made the *sound* of the job, take the sound of the money!"

The *meshuganer* was all smiles. "*Rebbi,* I thank you. I love the *psak.*" He stretched out both hands and grabbed the sound, while all those present marveled at the wisdom of their *Rav.*

The fact is that every society has "doers" and "Ha people." The doers make things happen. The "Ha people" just make noise and criticize — and then ask for payment!

Bikur Cholim and Linas HaTzedek

With medical knowledge so limited in the world of the *shtetl,* the only medicine for high fever (aspirin was virtually not obtainable) was ice. Cold compresses, wrapped in ice, were constantly changed on the sick person's head and body, especially at night, when fever was on the rise. It was the job of the *Linas HaTzedek* to ensure a steady supply of ice to the homes of the ill, especially in summer. During the winter, the members of this Society would cut blocks of ice from the frozen river and store them in a cold cellar against the coming summer.

Breaking a fever could take two or three days, by which time the family was exhausted. That was when the other *Chevrah,* the *Bikur Cholim,* took over. Volunteer members came in to watch over the sick person day and night, changing his ice, washing and feeding him, and attending to his every need.

Linas HaTzedek also carried a stock of all the primitive medical instruments used at the time — things like *bankes* and vaporizers

— which they loaned to the sick free of charge. *Bankes* were small wine glasses. Candles were lit inside them to draw out the air. They were then placed on the patient's back. The vacuum in the empty glasses sucked the flesh up to a level of one-half of the glass. After 15 minutes, the *bankes* were removed and the back rubbed with alcohol. This treatment was widely supposed to help cure a variety of ailments.

After massaging the back, some would also open the skin at the site of the *bankes* to let it bleed, while others used leeches to draw out the blood. The significance of blood pressure was unknown even to doctors, and no instruments existed as yet with which to measure it, but apparently, the thinning of the blood through incision or leeches often did make the patient feel better. In any case, this primitive treatment was the only one available, and the only acceptable method for effecting a cure for centuries.

The second most popular "medicine" was *ritzenoil*, a liquid that cleaned out the stomach. The saying went, "A pain from the waist down — *ritzenoil*; from the waist up — *bankes*." It tasted indescribably hideous. Forcing children to take it cast a household into a state of virtual warfare. The early pharmacies never thought of mixing the stuff with chocolate or some other sweetener.

The first thing a doctor would do, when summoned to the patient's bedside, was ask him to stick out his tongue. From the color, he was often able to make his diagnosis. Apart from the doctors, *feldchers* were also available to tell you the meaning of your symptoms. Just as the old-time farmers were "experts" in the treatment of sick animals, merely by virtue of their experience, so, too, were the *feldchers* "expert" in diagnosing human illness. Lacking formal training, they charged half the fee of regular doctors. In a time when there were no miracle antibiotics or sophisticated medical equipment, their lifetime of experience with illness — though in no sense constituting a formal medical education — was seen by many *shtetl* dwellers as something useful and valuable in its own right.

The Chevrah Kadishah (Burial Society)

The Jewish cemetery in the *shtetl* was always under the auspices of the *Chevrah Kadishah,* the Burial Society. Only pious and respected individuals were deemed worthy of joining the Society and, as members, to acquire the *mitzvah* of *chesed shel emes.* When we do a favor for a living person, at the back of our mind lies the thought that someday, perhaps, he will return the favor. However, when the recipient of our good is no longer living, such ulterior motives can be discounted. This type of kindness is *true chesed* — and one of the greatest *mitzvos* there can be.

The Society was never paid for its work, which it did only for the sake of this tremendous *mitzvah.* In the absence of doctors, it was the *Chevrah* members who declared a person dead; in the absence of funeral parlors, these same members prepared the body for burial. There were no eulogies. One had to be a great *tzaddik,* a great Torah scholar, or an exceptional *ba'al tzedakah* (philanthropist) to warrant a eulogy by the *rav,* who attended a funeral and delivered a eulogy only very occasionally.[1]

The 15th day of Kislev was set aside as a special day every year, when members of the *Chevrah Kadishah* throughout the country fasted and recited *Tehillim* and special *Selichos* to ask forgiveness from all the dead they had buried during the previous year, afraid that perhaps they hadn't fulfilled their obligation toward some individual or accorded his body the proper respect. In the evening, when the fast was over, they would celebrate by throwing a party in which the drink flowed freely. They enjoyed quoting an ancient source for this practice: "I do know that a *nazir* (ascetic) is forbidden to drink wine. But I thought that the *chachamim* (Sages) would permit it to me,

---

1. Standard funerals with benefit of clergy and a eulogy are a relatively recent innovation begun in America; the "unveiling" is also an American invention.

because I can't live without wine, or *because I bury the dead"* (*Nazir* 2:4).

During the rest of the year they found another, more involved rationale for indulging in drink. The Talmud (*Berachos* 35a) states that it is forbidden to eat or drink anything without reciting a *berachah*, the special blessing thanking G-d for that which is about to be eaten. The source of this law is found in a *pasuk* in *Tehillim*, which states: "To Hashem belongs the earth and everything in it" (24:1). However, another verse *(Psalms* 115:6) seems to contradict this: "And the earth He gave to mankind." The standard explanation is that the first verse, dealing with G-d's ownership of everything in the world, is applicable before reciting the blessing, while the second statement holds true afterwards, when He gives us to enjoy that which we have just blessed Him for.

The *Chevrah Kadishah* applied this piece of exegesis in another context. While they were obligated to bury the poor free of charge, the well-to-do had to pay for a grave. (In fact, if a rich man had been stingy in the giving of charity, the Society would make sure to "collect" from him when he got old, to make up for years of parsimony!) The question then arose: How could the Society charge for a grave if the earth belongs to Hashem? The members solved the problem by drinking a glass of schnapps — before which, of course, they made a *berachah*. The effect of this blessing, they claimed, was to place not only the whiskey, but also the earth itself, in the hands of the Society!

One year, two new officers were elected by the members of the *Chevrah Kadishah*: Reb Mendl, the furrier, and Yankl, the blacksmith. The two became close friends by chance, through an incident which occurred to Reb Mendl's wife.

Reb Mendl was a pious man and something of a Torah scholar who had inherited a tannery and furrier shop from his father. Like his father before him, he would buy sheepskins and horsehides from the surrounding farmers and landowners. He tanned them and made them into heavy winter coats which were in much demand by both city and farmer folk for miles around. The relative merits of sheepskin and horse hide were well known: While a sheepskin coat kept you warmer, it wore out much faster than one made of horse hide. The horse hide was very heavy but lasted much longer, and the Russians — particularly those in the military — preferred them to sheepskin coats.

Reb Mendl ran for the position of *Rosh HaKahal*, community leader, and lost. His defeat was attributed largely to his wife, who was not popular in the town. He had married a big-city girl who spoke Russian and French, but hardly any Yiddish. Because his wife couldn't bear the tannery smell, Reb Mendl was forced to hand the tannery over to a manager while he himself specialized in the furrier's trade. He made his wife a tricolor fur coat. It had yellowish sheepskin on top, black in the middle, and brown on the bottom. The coat won her the nickname "Frenchie," for the three colors of the French flag. The local women disliked her because of her supercilious airs. Dressed in her tricolor fur coat and leather hat made of red horse hide, "Frenchie" would sweep down the street looking down on the locals.

As a furrier, Reb Mendl suffered from the big needle used in his trade. The tip of the needle tended to prick the left hand, while the back of the needle pricked the right hand. To avoid infections, his sophisticated wife would dab alcohol on the left hand (for minor bleeding) and iodine on the right hand (for major bleeding). Then she would bandage his fingers with little rags (band-aids did not exist in those days). Every Friday he would remove the bandages, claiming that Shabbos itself cured him.

Yankl the blacksmith was not much of a scholar, but he was a pious Jews and a *gabbai* in the *Chevrah Chumash*. He was scrupulous in observing the *mitzvah* of *tza'ar ba'alei chayim*, the injunction against causing suffering to a living creature, and very careful not to hurt the horses whose hooves he was commissioned to shod. When his son, who lived in America, sent him money, he would donate it to charity. The son also sent packages of clothing, and Reb Yankl would distribute most of their contents to poor people.

He organized the *Malbish Arumim* Society, in which tailors remade used clothing for the poverty stricken, free of charge.

One such package once contained a "cylinder hat," also known as a "stovepipe hat." It stood up very high, but by pressing it down could become flat as a *matzah*. Reb Yankl wore this hat on Purim. One Purim, as Frenchie walked down the street in her tricolor coat, she noticed the blacksmith in his stovepipe hat. She turned around to stare and burst out laughing. In turning, her shoe sank into the wooden sidewalk, the heel stuck between two boards. She fell into the snow, and her laughter turned to cursing. She cursed the village, its sidewalks, and its people.

Yankl the smith walked over and asked, "You want me to help you?"

"Of course!" she sputtered.

"Then you must apologize to the entire village — in Yiddish — for your cursing."

A crowd had gathered around them, laughing at the chimney hat and at Frenchie. She did apologize, and in Yiddish. The smith then gave her his hat to hold while he extracted the shoe from the two snow-covered boards. While he was thus occupied, she tried on the stovepipe hat. The crowd roared with laughter. This was the turning point in her relations with the village people — a turn for the better. It also cemented the friendship between Reb Mendl the furrier and Reb Yankl the blacksmith. Though they never made it to the office of *Rosh Hakahal*, they did become the top *gabbaim* in the *Chevrah Kadishah*.

It was during their tenure that the Burial Society of Zembrove realized that the cemetery was nearly full. It was time to begin planning for the future. They finally reached the point of approaching my grandfather, the *Poretz* of Kollaki: "Reb Chaim Velvl, you probably notice that our cemetery is just about filled to capacity. In our days, people die more than they did in previous generations. We are not as pious as we used to be, and have no *tzaddikim* to protect us, as we once did. We must plan ahead. We would like to buy a piece of land for a new cemetery."

Reb Chaim Velvl knew what they wanted. They had no money to buy; what they wanted was a donation. It would be a dishonor to beg for the future generations of the dead, so they proposed to buy. The Society was following an old tradition established at the first Jewish grave. When Abraham, the first Jew, went to purchase a burial-place for his wife, Sarah, Efron offered him the grave free of charge — but Abraham insisted on paying the full price.

The Kollaker *Poretz* replied, "I will sell you several acres of land, at 10,000 rubles per acre. The deed will reflect this price. You pay me a deposit of three rubles; the rest you'll pay when *Mashiach* comes. Is it a deal?"

The bargain was struck. The newly "purchased" acres were right next to the old cemetery. The Burial Society members drank a *lechayim* with the *poretz* — a toast to life, to celebrate the new cemetery.

Then the *Chevrah Kadishah* went into action. Grass was cut and a fence dedicated with all the requisite prayers. A corner was set aside for *sheimos,* and a special section for "mothers in childbirth." In the *shtetl* it was announced that the new cemetery would be named for Reb Chaim Velvl: the Kollaker *Poretz's Beis HaChayim.*

Then an unanticipated problem arose. No one wanted to be buried in the new cemetery!

Old men, close to death, would state categorically that they wished to be buried in the old cemetery, close by the graves of generations of their family members. "Why, I'd be scared to death all by myself on the long winter nights!" In Jewish tradition, the wishes of a dying person must be fulfilled. What to do?

Finally, the Burial Society hit upon a plan. They decided that the only way to "trap a customer" for the new cemetery would be by offering a prize as inducement. An announcement was circulated throughout the *shtetl* to the effect that the first five burials there would be free of charge. However, since all the poor people received a free burial in any case, they tacked on an additional incentive: The family of the first person buried in the new cemetery would receive the amazing sum of 200 rubles. At a time when life insurance was unheard of and Social Security nonexistent, such a prize was tempting indeed. But still there were no takers.

Until Hirschl came along.

Hirschl was a poor man: no job, no income. It was already after Purim, with Pesach fast approaching. Hirschl's wife was after him to provide money for the holidays, and for shoes and clothing for the children. The daily nagging finally brought about the germ of an idea.

"Late tonight," Hirschl told his wife, "run out of the house and start banging on the neighbor's doors and windows. Cry, scream, pull out your hair, and tell them that I died. Tell the *Chevrah Kadishah* that I agreed to be buried in the new cemetery, and you'll receive the prize. Two hundred rubles — what a fortune!"

The wife laughed incredulously. "Hirschl, you've lost your mind! How can you convince the *Chevrah Kadishah* that you're dead?" (In the absence of a doctor in the village to sign a death certificate, the members of the Burial Society were the ones who determined death, by the simple expedient of placing a feather to the corpse's nose and checking whether it moved.)

Hirschl insisted, "I can hold my breath for a long time. I've been practicing. Besides, they will be so anxious to get their first customer that they won't bother to check me over."

Still the wife would not agree. "It's a crazy idea! Why, they'll bury you alive!"

"Don't worry about that," Hirschl replied. "Just don't let them take me out of the house until you get the 200 rubles. Now be a good wife and do as I tell you."

Just as Hirschl had predicted, in their enthusiasm the Burial Society forgot to check the body. In freezing weather a small group of friends and neighbors followed the funeral procession to the edge of town. Then they dispersed to their own homes. Hirschl's wife went home, too, to tend the children and her fortune. Only two men remained, the driver and the cemetery keeper. As the wagon passed the local *kretchme* (bar), the two decided to go inside and warm up with a drink of schnapps. The moment Hirschl heard them leave, he opened the box and ran into the forest. (In Europe, the body was placed in the grave on wooden boards; the box was only used for transporting the corpse to the cemetery.)

Later, when the two men arrived at the gravesite and lifted the box, they noticed its strange lack of weight. Imagine their shock upon opening it and discovering that there was nothing inside. Someone had made off with the body!

The cemetery keeper suggested that they report the theft to the police and the Burial Society, but the driver rejected that idea. "What are we going to tell them — that we stopped for a drink? During a funeral?" They finally decided to fill the grave and keep silent about the entire episode.

As soon as the sun had gone down, Hirschl slipped into his home, to the delight of his wife and children. He hid in the house throughout the *shivah*. When the *shivah* ended, the "widow" went on a shopping spree. To the amazement of the other villagers, she was the picture of glee. "Look at her," they grumbled. "The snow hasn't even melted on his grave and already she is having a ball — a real merry widow." The more she heard them talking, the more she laughed.

How long can a man remain locked up in the house? Passover arrived, and Hirschl decided to go to *shul*. Services began at 9 a.m. sharp. Five minutes before 9, Hirschl walked in. For a moment, the entire crowd froze. It was the first time in the history of the *shtetl* that a dead man had returned from the cemetery. Then Hirsch ventured to speak: "*Gut Yom Tov!*" Spontaneous laughter erupted as the congregation realized what had happened. Hirsch had tricked the officers of the Burial Society!

The Society was terribly embarrassed. The President approached Hirschl and loudly accused him of being a thief, a cheat, a *ganev*! Hirschl, he claimed, had stolen charity money, the holy funds of the *Chevrah Kadishah*. "Heaven will never forgive you," he concluded forcefully.

Hirschl was embarrassed. "Mr. President," he said, "I promise you here, before the entire congregation, that when my time comes you may bury me in the new cemetery. In the meantime, what do you care if Heaven has given me a few more years to live? Wait a little. Sooner or later, I'll be yours."

Soon after that, another poor old man died in the village. He, too, had agreed to be buried in the new cemetery. This time, the Society did not take any chances on being the laughingstock of the town. As they placed the body on the floor, feet facing the door as custom dictates, they ordered everyone to leave the room. Then they performed a number of tests on the dead man. First, the President pulled on the man's beard. Not a sound emerged from the body. Then the first *gabbai*, Reb Yankl the blacksmith, raised the man's foot and tickled the sole. There was no glimmer of a smile. Finally, the second *gabbai*, Reb Mendl the furrier, took his needle — which was much larger and thicker than an ordinary tailor's needle — and jabbed the dead man in a place that would surely have made a living man jump and cry out. There was no movement, no sound. The Society at last declared the man well and truly dead, and paid out the 200 rubles to his family.

Once again, the small procession made its way to the the edge of the *shtetl*. When everyone had gone home, including the widow, the driver and keeper were left alone. Nearing the *kretchme*, they began to consult in whispers.

"What do you think? Should we stop in?"

"Certainly!" whispered the other.

"But what about him?" asked the keeper, pointing at the box.

"Don't worry," replied the driver. "I prepared some rope. We'll tie him up. He won't go anywhere."

The *poretz* happened to be passing on his sled just as the two were busily wrapping rope around the box. He burst out laughing.

"You're tying him up? He won't go anywhere. He is dead. The other one — Hirschl — *him* you should have tied up!"

Hashgachas Yesomim —
The Orphanage in Lomza

The case of widows and orphans occupies a special place in the Torah, and likewise, in the heart of the *shtetl*. The great *mitzvah* to provide for them found a willing echo in the naturally merciful hearts of the village Jews, and developed into the community's foremost obligation. While non-Jewish orphans roamed the streets unsupervised, often turning to thievery and other mischief, the Jewish orphan was sometimes even better off than the child who had parents. Indeed, some of the children from impoverished homes were jealous of the orphans.

In normal times, the Lomza *kehillah* placed orphans in private homes. However, with the great increase in the number of orphaned children after the First World War, the situation became critical. In cases where a father died in battle, the mother was sometimes unable to support her children. Orphans from neighboring villages were also brought in, to augment those in Lomza. Though the community recognized that, by Jewish law, it was obligated to care only for its own orphans, how could they look a crying widow in the eye and tell her that her child was not accepted? Some of the girls were taken in by relatives, but others — and a great many boys — remained homeless.

When the number of children reached 80 boys and 20 girls, the *Chevrah Hashgachas Yesomim* realized that the need for a building had become urgent. A call went out to their American brothers. Their fellow Jews from across the ocean were quick to respond. The orphanage was built, funded partially by local donations but mostly by the American Joint Distribution Committee, the blessed overseas charity arm of American Jewry. Their generosity provided the orphans with dormitories, dining facilities, a *bais midrash,* and clothing. The institution housed boys and girls, in separate facilities, until the age of 18, when they graduated school and learned a trade. Some went on to *yeshivah.*

The Hashgachas Yesomim building in Lomza

When the new building was completed, the Lomza *kehillah* invited a delegation from the J.D.C. to the dedication ceremonies. The delegation duly arrived, bringing with them an American Embassy secretary. In the presence of Polish government representatives and city hall officials, the American diplomat delivered a speech — in Polish — critical of the Jewish community for constantly extending its hand to America. In diplomatic fine talk, he demanded that the community try harder to muster its own resources instead of begging from their more prosperous brethren overseas.

My uncle, R' Yechiel Kamchi, was one of the trustees of the *Chevrah*. He described how shocked everyone was at the tenor of this speech. But who could speak up against an American diplomat? And how to respond to it without insulting the Joint delegation, who were charitable Jews and certainly not responsible for the tactless speech of their embassy official? All eyes turned to the *Rav* of Lomza, R' Archik Baksht.

Now, R' Archik was not averse to criticizing his community. He constantly made demands on his Jews, urging them to rise to ever higher levels. But for an outsider to censure them — and a non-Jew, at that[1] — was something he could not abide. Like a faithful shepherd, he rose up in defense of his flock.

The *Rav* began calmly, telling of the various charitable activities that existed in the Jewish community.

"When it comes to charity," he said, "the Jews are second to none." He went on to explain that if the community had finally turned to America for help, it was because of the war and the poverty it had brought to the people.

Then he quoted a *midrash* which tells of a woman who came before King Solomon with a complaint against G-d Himself. A poor widow, she had been collecting grain in the field — to which she was entitled by law — when a fierce wind sprang up and blew away all the grain she'd gathered. She and her little children were forced to go hungry that night.

The king summoned the wealthiest merchant in Jerusalem and asked him how his business was faring.

"Business is excellent," replied the merchant. His ships had been out to sea, and a strong wind had brought them into port a full three days ahead of schedule, enabling him to bring his goods into a high market and make a killing.

"Pay this poor widow," ordered the king. "The same wind that made you rich, made her hungry!"

"Gentlemen," concluded the *Rav*, eyes piercing the diplomat, "the very same war that orphaned these children has made America rich. It is only right that you foot the bill!"

---

1. The diplomat, it turned out, was a Pole by birth.

Chapter 6:
Rest and Recreation

Shabbos

*J*n the *shtetl*, no Jewish store was ever open on Shabbos. An atmosphere of utter peace and tranquility reigned in the quiet streets on that day. Then, in 1916, in the throes of the First World War, the German military commandant of Lomza ordered all shops to remain open on Shabbos.

The Germans had just pushed the Russians out of Poland. The Russians soldiers were largely uneducated and hostile to those they conquered, while the Germans — especially the German officers — presented themselves as cultured, gentlemanly, and friendly. Yet the Russians, like the Poles, knew what Shabbos meant to the Jews. They knew that they could offer a Jew big business opportunities and the chance to make huge profits, but he would never accept on Shabbos. The German

A shtetl street on Shabbos afternoon

commandant, apparently, did not know how the Jews felt about Shabbos — or, if he did, he allowed his animosity to prevail. When the edict was passed mandating that stores remain open on Shabbos, a delegation from the Jewish community visited him to explain the matter — to no avail. It was war time. Civilians, they were told, must obey military orders.

Bobbe Shoshe forbade her husband and children to attend to the shop. "You'd better go to *shul*," she said. "I'll take care of the store." Taking her *Tz'enah Ur'enah* with her (the town, like almost all others, had an *eiruv*), heartbroken and tearful, for the first time in her life she opened the store doors on Shabbos.

None of the local Poles entered the store; they knew that nothing would be sold to them on that day. When German soldiers came, *Bobbe* Shoshe told them that the store was open only because of the commandant's orders. "I'm not selling anything. Take whatever you want, free of charge; we do not accept money today." Many of them took her up on this tempting offer, seizing what they wanted and leaving without paying.

Then a German captain came in. He wanted two kilograms of nails. *Bobbe* Shoshe invited him to help himself. She offered him a paper to wrap the nails, for she would not touch them on Shabbos. The officer became angry. He filled the paper with nails and took it to the counter, where *Bobbe* Shoshe was reading her

Tz'enah Ur'enah. "Wrap it up properly!" he barked. She wrapped the package in more paper, then with string — but she would not cut or tear or tie the string.

"How much for the nails?" he shouted. She repeated again that everything was free. He dropped a few marks on the counter and thrust the package under his arm, never noticing that the string had not been cut. He had walked two blocks when someone accidentally stepped on the trailing string, yanking the package from under his arm. It hit the ground. The paper burst open and nails rolled all over the street.

The other man apologized profusely and bent to pick up every nail, while the captain fumed and cursed the Jews.

Back in her store, *Bobbe* Shoshe read on in peace. After all, it was Shabbos.

Lag B'Omer

In every *cheder*, every child and every *rebbi* eagerly anticipated *Lag B'Omer* (the 33rd day of the *Omer* that is counted between Pesach and Shavuos). Preparations began immediately after Pesach. The children began producing "weapons": wooden swords, wooden bayonets, even wooden rifles. On *Lag B'Omer* day, the *shtetl* changed entirely. Its normal tranquility vanished, to be replaced by a beehive of happy activity. Every street corner was filled with children showing off their "arms" and waiting for the order to march to "war"!

The teachers would assemble their classes in rows like soldiers and march them off to the forest. On the way, the children tramped singing through the fields, filling their lungs with fresh air and their noses with the scent of freshly cut hay. During this march the "armies" were organized. The tallest and strongest of the boys became the "generals"; like Bar Kochba battling the Romans, they issued orders for conquest of the enemy.

Then the question of the salute arose. The Polish army — alone among the armies of the world — salutes with two fingers only, even to this day.[1] The Jewish children did not realize that other armies salute with the right hand fully open, differing only in the position of the palm, facing up or down. They knew only the Polish way, which did not appeal to them.

Then someone came up with the notion of a three-finger salute. The idea caught fire among the various Zionist youth organizations participating in the *Lag B'Omer* march. To the *Shomer HaDati*, the youth movement of the *Mizrachi* (religious Zionists), the three fingers stood for *Am Yisrael, B'Eretz Yisrael, al pi Toras Yisrael* — the people of Israel, in the land of Israel, according to the Torah of Israel. To the *Shomer HaLeumi*, the youth organization of the General Zionists (the Weizmann group), it meant *Am Yisrael b'Eretz Yisrael b'sfas Yisrael* — replacing Torah with the Hebrew language. For the leftist youth organization, the *Shomer HaTzair*, it stood simply for *Am Yisrael b'Eretz Yisrael*, according to the doctrines of socialism. And to the youngsters of Jabotinsky's army, known as Beitar,[2] it meant *Eretz Yisrael* for *Am Yisrael, al shnei gedot haYarden* — on both sides of the Jordan River.

On reaching the forest, each general assigned his troops to a section of the forest. Before issuing his orders, he greeted them with a mighty shout of *"Chazak!"* ("Be strong!") To which the troops replied, *"V'amatz!"* ("And be brave!") This became the unit's password in battle with the enemy. Only if one responded with the proper *"v'amatz"* in return to the offered *"chazak"* was he certain not to be mistaken for the enemy. Woe betide the unfortunate kid who forgot the right reply! He would be taken "prisoner" and tied to a tree, his part in the action at an end.

One tricky general devised a plan to confuse the enemy: He ordered his troops to say the password in reverse: first *"v'amatz"*

---

1. This practice originated in Italy, where General Dombrowski organized a Polish Legion to help Napoleon Bonaparte liberate Poland from the hated Russians. The salute meant, *"wiara i ojczyzna"* — "the faith and the fatherland." It was a rallying cry against the Russians, who tried to force the Poles from their Roman Catholicism and into the Russian Orthodox church.

2. "Beitar" is a shortened version of "Bris Trumpeldor," in memory of the Russian Jew who was killed by the Arabs while defending Tel Chai, and who declared before he died, "It's good to die for our land!"

and then *"chazak."* Another general changed the password to *"chazak, chazak,"* to which the correct reply was, *"v'nischazek!"* ("We will be strong!") These ploys wrought havoc on the battlefield, which became littered with many "dead" and "wounded."

David HaMelech's Giborim (King David's Heroes) was an elite unit of sharpshooters. These boys were experts at using a slingshot like the one David used to kill Goliath. The snipers swarmed up trees, rousing flocks of protesting birds who added their shrill noise to the general ruckus in the forest below.

Finally the teachers — the real generals — ordered a cease fire. The lunch baskets prepared by the children's mothers were opened. The troops recited their *berachos* and *bentching* (the blessings before and after meals) in unison. Then it was time to rest. The soldiers took a nap on the grass in the shade of the trees, while guards appointed by each general strode around, keeping an eye on the sleeping troops. In the afternoon, the children marched contentedly back to town, leaving their leafy battlefields in peace for another year.

A Shtetl Wedding

There were no big wedding halls in the *shtetl*. The custom arose in our town to erect the *chuppah* on Fridays, in front of the *shul*, with an indoor reception afterwards. Every house had one room called the *salle,* or living room. As the houses were small, so, too, was the *salle* — except in my uncle Shlomo Pines's house, which, having been built long, featured the longest and biggest *salle* in the *shtetl.* He donated the use of this room to every *chassan* and *kallah* as a gift.

This was a tremendous act of *chesed* and a real sacrifice on Reb Shlomo's part, for Friday was market day, the busiest day of the week. To accommodate the *shtetl's* wedding parties he neglected his business and inconvenienced his customers (his store was on the first floor, right under the *salle*). The gratitude and joy of the radiant young couple was ample reward for his efforts.

The Lomza Gemilas Chasadim (Free Loan Fund) committee

And so, from the *shul* grounds, the bride and groom and their families marched to Reb Shlomo's *salle* to the tune of the *klezmorim* (musicians), accompanied by half the town dancing and singing before and behind. The next morning, after the Shabbos *davening*, the *chassan* and *kallah* led the happy throng to the *kallah*'s parents' house, where all could wish them mazel tov and drink a hearty *"lechayim!"* in their honor.

There was a free loan society in the *shtetl* that lent money, interest-free, with the deposit of a collateral. Many women had the practice of leaving their Shabbos candlesticks on Sunday, doing some business with the loan money during the week, and paying off the loan on Friday in order to get the candlesticks back. The *Rav* of our town once learned that a certain widow, in order to have money to pay for her daughter's wedding *kiddush,* had deposited her pillows as collateral. Immediately, the Rav instituted a rule that no more than 10 people — the young couple's immediate family members — could take part in a wedding *kiddush.*

From that day on, the *kallah's* parents would stand outside their front door, inviting everyone inside: "You are one of the family — please, come in." But, as their *Rav* had intended, the *shtetl* population would politely decline the invitation and, with a warm *"mazel tov,"* pass on their way.

Storytelling in the Shtetl

Back in the times we're discussing, all medicines tasted terribly bitter. Children, naturally, refused to take the stuff their mothers referred to as *"retcept"* (literally, a "prescription"). Mother would induce them to open their little mouths for a lollipop, then slip in the medicine.

The same basic technique has been used by teachers for thousands of years. The Talmudic Sages, *rebbeim* in classrooms, *maggidim*, speakers and writers open people's minds and ears by using the story as a verbal lollipop — and then, while the minds are open and receptive for the "sweets," slip in the bitter "pill" that is the point of the exercise.

The Tale of Stories

Storytelling had its beginning on the long winter nights, in the era before electricity was invented, and grew with the passage of time. The peasants would work the land during the summer from sunrise to sundown; in winter, they would rest. By the flickering light of kerosene lamps or stubs of candles, stories were made up, told and retold.

A people may be judged by the stories it tells. Russians, for instance, have thousands of folk tales dealing with the trials and tribulations of princes and princesses, betrayal, infidelity and murder.[1] The Americans have their tales of the Wild West, with its Indian massacres and intrepid heroes whose guns held a

---

1. The Russians have published a number of volumes of *Ruskeye Narodnoe Skazkee* (Russian Folk Tales). All these stories, of course, had to be rewritten 60 years ago, to suit the taste of the Bolshevik revolutionaries. Religion, princes and princesses were replaced by Socialism, collective farms, collective farm directors and tractor girls. The Russians' folk tales come under periodic revision — just like their history, which also gets rewritten every few years.

notch for every man they killed.[1]

We, too, have our stories — Jewish stories. They deal with the lives of great men and their impact on the world around them: *tzaddikim*, chassidic *rebbeim*, miracles, *middos*, *mussar*, acts of charity and *chesed*. And then, of course, we have our sacred writings: *midrashim*, *Ein Yaakov*, and *Tz'enah Ur'enah*.

Traditionally, Jews had little time for storytelling, what spare time they had being occupied with saying *Tehillim* and learning *Chumash*, *Mishnah* and *Gemara*. The exception was on those long winter nights when the Shabbos Queen reigned. After the meal the candles guttered and went out, ending their lives in a last breath and a thin spiral of smoke — followed by total, sweet, scary darkness. The same darkness crept in on late Shabbos afternoons, after *Minchah*. We would huddle around the warm oven, where someone was always ready to tell a story.

The Birth of "Bobbe Ma'ases" — Stories Grandmother Told

On the long winter Friday nights, while the last of the Shabbos candles cast dancing shadows on the walls, *Bobbe* would tell stories to us spellbound children. The shadows on the wall would leap higher as the candles sank ever lower, and we would cling closer to *Bobbe*. When, one by one, the kerosene lamp and the candles went out, this was the signal for *Bobbe* Faigl to begin the story about King David, the narrative interwoven with proper verses from *Tehillim*, making us feel much safer. From the next

---

1. An exception to this rule was the American hero of the West, Davy Crockett, who boasted of killing bears instead of people. Apparently, in his Tennessee days, bears posed the greater menace. Hence, when Crockett ran for Congress, he boasted of killing 105 bears — to which his opponent immediately cried from the same platform: "That's a lie! Davy Crockett can't even count to 105!" Whether or not he could count that high, Crockett was elected to the U.S. Congress.

room we could hear *Zeide* learning *Gemara* by heart, and we were certain that the shadows on the wall were no less than *malachim* (angels). What else could fly around a house in which *Tehillim* resounds from one room and *Gemara* from the other?

The same scene was repeated the next evening, after *Shalosh Seudos* (the third Shabbos meal). As the lengthening shadows gave way to darkness, *Bobbe* was always ready with a story that stretched until it was full night, when she recited *"Gott fun Avraham,"* the famous prayer people say just before the departure of the Shabbos Queen. Thus were *bobbe ma'ases* transmitted.

Then came progress, and electricity was installed in private homes. As far as the stories were concerned, it was a regression. For a while the stories did continue to flourish, for electricity was expensive; but not for long. (In America, with universal cheap power and Shabbos clocks, there is no darkness even on the long winter nights — and the *bobbe ma'ases* have vanished from the scene. No one has time anymore to tell or listen to stories, for today, in the phrase coined by some progressive businessman, "Time is money.")

In a way, though, *bobbe ma'ases* and the telling of tales are still with us — transformed into literature. Despite cultural advances and philosophical pretensions, the basic purpose of all literature remains unchanged since the day of the *shtetl* and before: to tell stories.

Chapter 7:
East Meets West

They lived in two different worlds, separated only by a barrier and a border guard. The East European Jew and the German Jew were so close to each other — yet so very far away.

The following story, which made the rounds in Poland at one time, says it all.

A Polish *chassid* returned from a trip to Prussia (a German province) where he had happened to visit a Prussian town called Greiditz. The *Rav* of Greiditz was R' Eliyahu Gutmacher, a *tzaddik* and mystic who behaved like a full-fledged chassidic *rebbe*!

He would conduct a *chassidishe tish* (a ceremonial meal presided over by the *Rebbe*), where he handed out *shirayim* (i.e., the chassidic custom of partaking of the *Rebbe's* food), just like any *rebbe* in the East. The Polish *chassid*, newly returned from Greiditz, told his own *rebbe* about the visit.

"You say there is a *gutter Yid* (a good Jew) in Prussia?" asked the *rebbe*. (*Chassidim* refer to a *rebbe* as a "*gutter Yid*.")

"That's right, *Rebbe*. A *gutter Yid* — a *tzaddik* — a real *rebbe!*"

"With a beard and *payos?*"

"Yes, indeed, with a beard, *payos*, and a *shtreimel* (fur hat)!"

"A *shtreimel* in Prussia? Unbelievable!" The *rebbe* thought a moment, then asked, "And what about his *yiras Shamayim* (fear of Heaven)? He *davened* every day?"

"Why, of course, *Rebbe*. He *davened* with all sorts of preparations, including going to the *mikveh*. It takes him until midday to *daven*."

"And how does he *daven*, *nusach Ashkenaz* (the Ashkenazic liturgy)?"

"No, *Rebbe* — *nusach Sefard*, according to the *Ari HaKadosh*."

"And people travel to see him?"

"Certainly. On Shabbos there are five *minyanim* (quorums of 10) at his *tish*."

"You say five *minyanim*, and long hours of sitting at the *tish*, and *zemiros* (Shabbos songs)?"

"Yes, indeed, *Rebbe*. *Zemiros* — sweet *niggunim* (melodies), sung with enthusiasm and piety."

"And the *rebbe* says Torah?"

"Some Torah, and some *Kabbalah* (mystical secrets), too. The *Zohar* (the foremost Jewish mystical text)..."

"*Zohar* in Prussia? It's hard to believe! And you say he hands out *shirayim?*"

"Yes, indeed, *Rebbe*."

"And you also caught some of the *shirayim?*"

"Yes, *Rebbe* — but only fish."

"Why only fish?"

The *chassid* looked shocked. "Meat? Oh, no! My

conscience didn't let me eat meat. After all, this was Prussia!"

This, in a nutshell, was the typical attitude of an East European Jew toward the German Jew. Many things about his German brothers puzzled and irritated him. For one thing, the German Jew's well-known punctuality was irksome. Perhaps this was the self-conscience guilt of one who had rarely been on time to anything in his life, when confronted with a Jew who watches the minutes! He was mystified, too, by a person who had no beard or *payos*, who dressed like a gentile, and yet was full of Torah and genuine piety.

The Polish Jew also found amazing the fact that German Jews were doctors as well as Torah scholars, while in all of Poland not a single physician observed Shabbos! In Poland, the moment one registered for the *gymnasium* (high school) or university, he was at once cut off from *Yiddishkeit*. Yet in Germany, the Jews managed to remain fully observant, while also receiving a secular education. How did they do it?

Life in Old Germany

In his fascinating book, *Jewish Life in the Village Communities of Southern Germany,* Dr. H. Mandelbaum describes the Hebrew school — counterpart to the East European *cheder* — in these German villages:

> The Jewish traditional background and the observance of *mitzvos* were derived from the home and the short formal education imparted to the children in elementary school. Few Jewish communities in Southern Germany could boast of Jewish day schools. The children had to attend the non-Jewish public school. They would come to the so-called Religionsschule, maintained by the *kehillah,* for two hours. Attendance was as compulsory as the public school. In Geroda, the entire school was packed into a

single classroom. All the boys and girls, from first to seventh grade, were together from 4 p.m., when public school was over, till 6 p.m. During this period, all the grades had to receive attention and cover their respective subjects. This required no small amount of skill on the part of the teacher.

Page 23 of this book contains a picture of the community building of the Braunsbach *kehillah*. The ground floor housed the schoolroom for the community's children; the rabbi — charged with responsibility for about 25 rural communities in the district — had his living quarters on the upper floor.

Is it any wonder that, with the minuscule amount of religious education available to German Jews, "modernizers" and reformers should find them easy prey? Historians claim that the chassidic and *mussar* movements arose just in time to counter the anti-religious *maskilim* in the East. But neither *Chassidus* nor *mussar* found a true foothold in Germany.[1] Instead, Heaven sent a different Rock to stand firm against the avalanche of Reform. The Rock of German Jewry was R' Samson Raphael Hirsch.

Starting from nothing, this mighty man created a dam against the Reform movement. That he found the time to accomplish all that he did in his life — to dwell in the world of Torah, to study, lecture and write so richly and in such abundance, to impress people so deeply — is nothing short of amazing. R' Samson Raphael Hirsch was sent from Heaven just in time to perform an incredible task. And he succeeded!

Nor was his legacy lost during the Hitler years. Rabbi Dr. Breuer carried it to New York, where, beginning again from scratch, he re-created a perfect replica of Frankfurt.

---

1. There were exceptions to this rule. I was surprised when Mr. Yaakov (Kurt) Flamm of Baltimore told me that there had been a chassidic *shtibl* in his native Nuremberg, boasting some 50 families. And in the mountains of Wurzburg, some 30 families belonged to a *shtibl* called Achiezer.

Transplanted

I was once invited to Rabbi Dr. Breuer's *kehillah, Kahal Adas Yeshurun* in Washington Heights, to speak on a Shabbos. The minute I stepped into the *shul* I was amazed at the customs I saw. Whether in major ways or in the most minor detail, everything was exactly as it had been in Frankfurt. I stood astonished. A choir in an Orthodox *shul*, on an ordinary Shabbos? *Davening* in hats? There was no way to tell which men were married and which were not, as they were all wearing *talleisim* (prayer shawls)!

Picking up a *siddur*, I received a shock when I saw the German print — an old German type that I couldn't even read. I put that *siddur* down quickly and searched for a familiar one, but there were none that I could find.

I understood in a flash the rationale behind this transplantation. If Frankfurt was to be transferred to the shores of America, it must be in its totality. The evil that Hitler had let loose upon the world must not be allowed to interfere with or change even one iota of old, established custom.

R' Gelley, in his Shabbos *drashah* (sermon), did not speak about "Judaism," for all the congregants were already *mitzvah* observant. He gave a true *dvar Torah*, which demanded careful attention and real understanding. Watching the faces of the listeners, I saw that they followed and grasped the *Rav's* delivery to the very end. Most of them were clearly *talmidei chachamim*.

Even the perfect timing was exactly as it had been in Europe. Once, I was told, a small contingent from Lakewood had an appointment with R' Breuer scheduled for 3 p.m. When they arrived a few minutes early, they were not admitted. As R' Breuer told them, 2:56 is not 3. And when the *chazan* once began *davening* at 8:02, R' Schwab reprimanded the *gabbai* of many years' standing, Mr. Meir Loeb: "Two minutes after 8 is not 8 o'clock!"

R' Breuer, as a *Rosh Yeshivah*, would deliver his lectures standing up. Out of the corner of his eye he could spot students sneaking in late to the *shiur*. He knew where they were coming from: They had davened late with a chassidic *minyan*. The *Rav* gave a pointed, if oblique, commentary on their lack of punctuality: *"Tefillah lechud, Chassidus lechud,* Torah *lechud"* ("Each in its own good time"). The boys got the message!

Yekkes

If the Jews of Eastern Europe gazed with faint disapproval on what they considered the German Jews' lower level of religiosity, the German Jews looked down on the *"Ostjuden"* (Eastern Jews) because of their poverty and primitiveness. The Eastern European Jews liked to invent names: The Russians (excluding the Russian Jews) were called *"Funnyes,"* and the Germans were known as *"Yekkes"* — including the German Jews. Both titles were derogatory. In the case of the Russians, the nickname connoted ignorance and primitiveness. As for the Germans, a *"Yekke"* meant someone who was straightforward, not too smart, and did not understand the arts of subterfuge and sophistry which the Polish Jews knew so well. In Eastern Europe, to be straightforward, without subterfuge, was to starve. Poverty and government oppression had taught these Jews the fine art of survival by any means possible. In Germany, this art had been unnecessary, and so unlearned.

In the *yeshivah* world, the term *"Yekke"* took on a different, and much more positive, connotation. One was never called by his surname in *yeshivah,* as there were apt to be several students with the same name. Rather, a student was known by his place of origin. Hence, I was Chaim Lomzer (from the town of Lomza. Hardly anyone knew that my family name was Shapiro). In the case of foreigners, an exception was made; we couldn't even pronounce the places they'd stemmed from. These students were referred to as *"Yankel der Americaner"* (the American) or *"Moshe der Yekke"* (from Germany). Here, the title *Yekke* was not used in a derogatory sense. On the contrary — it was an adjective of distinction, even of reverence. A *Yekke* did not know how to twist and scheme. He was straightforward and direct — totally, truthfully *frum*!

On my arrival in Reb Elchonon Wasserman's Yeshivah Ohel Torah in Baranowitz, I met Moshe Schwab, the *Yekke*, brother of R' Shimon Schwab, *zt"l*. "Moshe the *Yekke*," followed the *mashgiach*, R' Yisrael Yaakov Lubchanski, like a shadow, and became a true *ba'al mussar* (student of self-improvement). Later, when I came to Kamenitz, I met his older brother, R' Mordechai Schwab. R' Mordechai was a genuine *"nichba el hakeilim"* (one who hides among the vessels, as the humble Saul did when the Prophet Shmuel came looking for him to anoint him king): a humble, quiet *tzaddik*; a *Yekke lamed-vovnick* (one of the legendary 36 hidden saints). He was always precisely on time, whether for *davening, shiurim,* or a *mussar* discussion. In other words, a typical *Yekke*!

In our day, the Reform *Yekkes* have either died out or assimilated; they do not exist any longer. The term *"Yekke"* has become a true title of distinction, respect and admiration. As a *Kohen*, I am often invited to officiate at a *pidyon haben* (redemption of the firstborn son on the 30th day of life). After reciting the blessing, I lean over and whisper in the child's ear, "Grow up to be a real good *Yekke!*"

Bais Yaakov

Not everybody is aware that the success of the Bais Yaakov movement is largely due to these very *"Yekkes."* Sarah Schenirer, mother of the Bais Yaakov schools, was a righteous and learned woman who foresaw what others failed to see. She accomplished great things in disseminating a Torah education to the girls of prewar Eastern Europe; but Bais Yaakov was in danger of expiring for lack of future teachers!

Without a seminary to train teachers the movement could have no future, yet Sarah Schenirer was not able to prepare a curriculum of this caliber, especially in the absence of books. Bais Yaakov was in desperate need. The Agudas Yisrael organization, Gerrer *Chassidus*, and R' Eliezer Gershon Friedenson (who volunteered as "propaganda minister") put Bais Yaakov on the map. But it was a *Yekke* who saved it.

Dr. Shmuel Deutchlander wrote a pedagogic program befitting an institute devoted to training teachers. Then he traveled over the length and breadth of Western Europe, hunting for talented young women who would become teachers, dedicated to the values of Torah and the ideals of Bais Yaakov. He did not believe in imparting Western culture to students of the East. He believed they could find all they needed to know in the holy books. His motto took up the words of Boaz to Ruth: "My daughter, do not collect in strange fields." To his students he used to declare, "Whatever you will find in other cultures exists with more beauty and truth in Torah!"

Dr. Deutchlander imported a faculty of academicians who sacrificed their own comfortable lives for an existence in primitive Poland. These included R' Dr. E. Ehrentrau of Munich, Rosaline Mannes and Betty Rothschild of Zurich, and Judith Rosenbaum of Frankfurt.

My aunt, Chana Shapiro of Tiktin — at the time, the first and only "*Litvachke*" in the Seminary (most of the girls stemmed from Chassidic homes in the Crakow area) — used to describe her shock upon arriving at the Seminary and seeing a "tall, modern-looking young woman, who looked like a non-Jewish *Yekkete*, davening with great *kavanah* (concentration) and *d'veikus* (sincerity). In Poland, we had never seen anyone like that!" She was talking about Judith Rosenbaum (presently Rebbetzin Dayan Grunfeld of London).

My cousin, Menucha Paley — also from Tiktin — was among the second generation of students. She subsequently taught in Bais Yaakov for 50 years in Poland and Jerusalem, and is the wife of R' Tzvi Paley, *mashgiach* of Hebron Yeshivah. She described the lectures of Dr. Shmuel Deutchlander: "In the summers we went to a Gypsy camp in the Tatra Mountains. There, the "Herr

Doctor" lecured on his favorite subject, *Tehillim*. This was a novelty for us. People in Poland used to say a lot of *Tehillim*, but who ever lectured on the subject? The treetops ceased whispering, the birds stopped singing; the whole world stood still while he spoke. We girls were mesmerized, transported to a different world. When he finished speaking, no one moved. We sat there waiting for more and more!"

The *Yekkes* saved the Bais Yaakov movement and put it on the firm footing that allowed it to flourish to this very day. More — they inserted their own special flavor into the brew and left it tasting even better than before!

Gedolim¹ in Germany

Although there seemed to be an iron curtain between the Jews of Germany and their brothers in the East, the sages of Eastern Europe knew the great men of Torah in Germany, and held them in high esteem. The Gerrer *Rebbe's* great admiration for and extraordinary opinion of R' Shamshon Raphael Hirsch is well known. In what constituted an expression of awe and a chassidic compliment of the highest order, the *Rebbi* once referred to "the *kedushah* (holiness) of that *Yid*." Indeed, at the founding of Agudas Yisrael, the *gedolim* of the East — the Chofetz Chaim, Reb Chaim Ozer, and the Gerrer *Rebbe* — joined with the great Torah figures of *Ashkenaz* (Germany), in becoming founding fathers of that organization.

The *tzaddikim* and Torah scholars of Germany are too numerous to list here; but one man deserves special mention. He was R' Pinchas Kohn of Ansbach.

R' Kohn's biography is most interesting. He was born in Kleinerdlingen in the northern corner of Swabia, one of the many little villages in the German countryside where clusters of 20 or 30 Jewish families clung together. Young Pinchas's dominant

---

1. Great Torah personalities

R' Pinchas Kohen

influences were his father and grandfather. His father, on the day after his wedding, returned the dowry he'd received, explaining that marrying the daughter of a *talmid chacham* was in and of itself good enough for him. Pinchas's grandfather, R' Dovid Weiskopf, took the boy into his home in Wallerstein when he was four years old, "to teach him the fundamentals of Jewish knowledge."

At the age of six a child was required by German law to attend public school, but Pinchas's father obtained permission for him to be taught by private tutors. Later, young Pinchas went to Noerdlingen three days a week for his secular studies. His sister was sent along to carry his books for him, in order to make the boy understand that it is beneath the dignity of a gifted student of Talmud to carry textbooks for mere secular learning!

Once, when Rabbi Ezriel Hildesheimer visited the village to raise funds for his Rabbinical Seminary in Berlin, a disagreement developed between him and Pinchas's uncle, Mr. Ettenheim, about the rabbi's program of *Torah im derech eretz* (Torah along with secular studies). In Pinchas's hearing, his uncle enumerated the dangers he perceived in such a policy, declaring, "Sooner or later, Torah will be relegated to second place!" These words made a deep impression on young Pinchas, and he was to repeat them often during the course of his life.

Eventually, he went to the *yeshivah* of Rabbi Selig Ansbach. Still later Pinchas Kohn became *Rav* of Ansbach in Bavaria.

The Steinharter brothers of Baltimore, Reb Jacob *z"l* and Reb Meir, remember Rav Kohn. As they tell it, "Whenever we traveled late at night for business, we would see the light in the *Rav's* window. He was learning, for what kind of *Rav* would he be if he didn't learn Torah? Busy all day long with communal affairs, when did he have time to learn? At night, of course.

"Our father, Reb Yissachar Steinharter, and many other *ba'alei batim* (congregants), would travel over 100 kilometers to the *Rav's* house every Thursday night to learn a *mishmar* (all-night study session). In the morning, after a nightlong *shiur* by the *Rav,* our father would catch a freight train back home, as there were no passenger trains at that hour. The German trainman once remarked, 'I wish I knew where this man comes from every Friday morning.' "

At the request of his counterparts in the East, R' Pinchas Kohn of Ansbach was most active in the Agudas Yisrael. He became the "matchmaker" between East and West. He was the one to resolve differences of opinion between *chassidim* and *misnagdim*, between *Litvaks* and Polish Jews. He was troubleshooter and peacemaker in one. Though hailing from the West, he was filled to the brim with Torah and Heavenly awe; he was versed in *Chassidus* and *Kabbalah*. As such, R' Pinchas Kohn became the darling of the Eastern *gedolim*.

Wurzburg

Thanks to the influence and labor of R' Samson Raphael Hirsch, Frankfurt-am-Main became the primary pillar of Orthodoxy in German-Jewish life. The activities and work of the "Wurzburger Rav," the *tzaddik* and *gaon* R' Seligman Baer Bamberger (1807-1878), also had broad influence.

Though engaged in community affairs as the leading Torah authority and *posek* (halachic authority) for German Jewry, Rav Bamberger still found time to publish six *sefarim*: *Meleches Shamayim* (first published in 1853), *Amirah l'Veis Yaakov, Shaarei Simchah, Moreh l'Zvachim, Nachlei Dvash, Korei b'Emes*, and many other writings. But his most important contribution to the life of German Jewry was founding the teachers' seminary in Wurzburg. With the standard of Hebrew and Torah knowledge among his countrymen at an all-time low, he was farsighted regarding the need to train good Jewish teachers.

On October 7, 1864, he opened the *Israelitische-Lehrer-Bildungs-Anstalt* (ILBA) in Wurzburg to produce Orthodox teachers of the highest caliber. These, in turn, spread Torah throughout Germany. They were the "foot soldiers" who stood up to the wave of Reform. They were the ones who influenced Jewish youngsters to observe Torah and *Yiddishkeit*.

The school existed for 64 years, from 1864 until 1938. A book published by the Alumni of the ILBA states (p. 104): "The day began, of course, with the *Shacharis* service, conducted by a member of the Bamberger family in a Western *Ashkenazi* and '*Yekkish*' fashion." (Note that they referred to themselves in this manner, which shows clearly that "Yekke" is not a derogatory term.) On page 145, R' Samson R. Weiss tells how he came to accept a position in that Seminary after four and a half years of studying in the Mirrer *Yeshivah* in Poland: "The institution itself somehow gave me the impression of a strange mixture, an exaggerated rigidity on one hand, lacking the warmth and soul without which no education can succeed — and, on the other hand, a pride in its traditions and principles which, if carried over to the student, could be an invaluable asset in forming the student's character and *weltanschauung* (worldview)." R' Weiss continues, "The typically German distance between teacher and student further exacerbated the difficulty of dialogue and communication. For me — who had been so deeply impressed, and literally transformed, by my *yeshivah* years [in Mir] — this was the very opposite of what I had learned to admire and revere in my great teachers, the Mirrer *Rosh Yeshivah* and the Mirrer *mashgiach*, teachers of what in the terminology of the Lithuanian *yeshivos* is called *mussar*.

"They had taught me that a *rebbi* must live for his students, share and shoulder their innermost problems and worries, and identify with them like a father with his son. I shall never forget the moment when I took leave for the first time from my *Rosh Yeshivah* to go home for a vacation, and he kissed me! It brought tears to my eyes, though I knew quite well that it was the custom in Lithuanian *yeshivos* that the *rebbi* kissed the *talmid* when he took leave and when he returned."

R' Weiss also describes in detail the "open house" for the students held on Friday nights in the home of Mrs. Bertha Neuberger, mother of R' Herman Naftoli Neuberger of Ner Israel in Baltimore. With pride, he relates that seven students went to study in the Mirrer *Yeshivah* in Poland; Naftoli — not a member of the Seminary, but through his family a part of its circle — was one of them. He then goes on to tell how Naftoli Neuberger traveled to Baltimore in 1938 to study in Yeshiva Ner Israel and how he subsequently saved the lives of Rabbi Weiss, his wife, and 23 students of the Wurzburg Seminary by sending them the necessary papers to emigrate to America.[1]

Smugglers

The Polish and German Jews were connected not only by Torah and holiness but also, on a more mundane level, by bonds of commerce — and not always of the most savory variety. Two small towns near the East Prussian border, Kolno and Myszeniec (not far from my home town of Lomza), were known as smuggler towns. When Poland declared its independence on November 11, 1918, the Polish government immediately began to monopolize certain items. As a result, prices went up, leading to wholesale smuggling.

Matches are a perfect illustration: The rural sections of Poland had no electricity or gas; wood and coal were used for cooking,

---

1. Another two of Rabbi Naftoli Neuberger's *zechuyos* (merits) are that the *Rosh Yeshivah* of Ner Israel, *HaGaon* Rabbi Yaakov Yitzchak Ruderman, bestowed on him the title, "the Bezalel (master architect) of Ner Israel," and that he brought a great number of Iranian boys to Ner Israel *Yeshivah,* thus rescuing them physically from the bloody hands of the Iranian ayatollahs and spiritually from the American melting pot. These were boys whose knowledge of Torah was minimal — practically nonexistent. Today they are great *talmidei chachamim* of whom any *kollel* or *yeshivah* would be proud!

baking, and for heating the house. This made matches a most essential item! The factories of the Shereshewskis, a Jewish family, supplied matches throughout the country. After independence, the government confiscated these factories and declared a monopoly on matches. The price of matches became prohibitive, leading consumers to look for alternatives.

Cigarette lighters were an option, but they relied on flint-stones, which were manufactured in Germany. The government slapped a tax on the import of flintstones and cigarette lighters. It became no unusual thing to see a man casually light a cigarette on some street corner — only to be approached by a policeman demanding to examine his lighter. If the tax stamp was missing, the smoker was charged with evading taxes!

In Myszeniec, a man would cross the border into Germany and return with his pants bound to his legs at the bottom so that he could hardly walk. Both legs were full of flintstones! This gave rise to the town's nickname, the *"farbundene hoisen"*: the tied-up pants. The border guards saw what was happening under their noses, but were amply rewarded for looking the other way.

Sugar became another government monopoly. The Polish government sold sugar abroad at a quarter of the price it charged its own citizens at home — sometimes even less. A less expensive option was saccharine, manufactured in Germany. Hence, in Kolno people carried packages of saccharine across the border, giving rise to that city's nickname: *"Kolner peklach"* (Kolner packages).

The Poles loved silk, and the cities of Lodz and Bialystok made plenty of it. The entire textile industry in these two great manufacturing centers was in Jewish hands, with Jewish owners and workers. But the Polish government derived a handsome income from exporting almost all this silk to countries abroad.[1]

Where could a Polish woman get her silk cheaply? From Germany, of course. A thin-as-a-toothpick woman would cross

---

1. Manchester, England was the world's biggest cloth and silk manufacturer. From there the English exported silk to all the British colonies in Africa and Asia, where it was protected by a heavy tax on non-British goods. But even with the tax, Lodz and Bialystok gave Manchester stiff competition in the British colonies.

the border in the morning at Kolno or Myszeniec, returning in the evening very chunky indeed, with a few hundred yards of silk wrapped around her waist!

The smugglers used an unusual currency to pay for all these German commodities: horses. The country's agricultural produce was inadequate to support it, forcing Germany to import food from its neighbors. The Germans loved horse meat, but they didn't have enough horses. Poland, on the other hand, had plenty of them. The smugglers would run a number of horses over the border, sell them to the Germans, and buy the goods they needed. To facilitate these transactions, they looked to their fellow Jews. The German Jews, realizing that the Polish government was essentially precluding Jews from participating in the legal economy, considered it a *mitzvah* to help their poorer brethren from across the border, though smugglers faced a stiff prison sentence if caught.

Wartime

Despite their different ways, the Eastern European and German Jews were brothers under the skin. This became evident — sometimes tragically so — during World War I.

By the standards of modern-day warfare, in which high technology has made it possible to destroy enemy strong points from hundreds of miles away, the First World War was primitive. Armies squared off in direct confrontations; men killed each other face to face. When the enemy was so close that shooting was counterproductive, the bullet was replaced by the bayonet. Perhaps the worst order of all was *"Na Shtickye!"* which meant to drive one's bayonet through the body of an enemy soldier.

The tale is told of one battlefield — though perhaps this happened on many of them — where a German Jewish soldier heard this dread order and saw the bayonet gleaming above him. Certain that he was about to die, he screamed, *"Shema Yisrael!"* whereupon the Russian soldier, who'd been on the point of

The Germans entering Lomza. The building in the foreground on the right was our home and store. I was born in that house.

stabbing him, continued, *"Baruch shem kevod malchuso...!"* Both dropped their rifles, and they embraced in tears.

"I almost killed you," exclaimed the Russian soldier, "and for what? Because you belong to the Kaiser?"

"And I almost killed you," replied the German soldier, "and why? Because you belong to the Tzar!"

It may actually have happened or it may be fiction, but it gives a true picture of a world gone by. The East European Jew and the German Jew lived in two different worlds, separated only by a barrier and a border guard. They were so far away, and yet at the same time so very close to each other.

Chapter 8:
A Yeshivah Is Born

The Lomzer Yeshivah

The Chofetz Chaim once remarked, "No *yeshivah* was ever born thanks to money, and no *yeshivah* was ever closed because of lack of money. Reb Chaim Volozhiner founded his *yeshivah* not with money, but with tears, with fasting, with *Tehillim* and *tefillah* (prayer) — hence he was successful!"

Until 1803, when Reb Chaim opened the doors of his *yeshivah*, every *bais midrash* was a *yeshivah* and every *rav* was also a *rosh yeshivah*. The local rav would give *shiurim* and tender *semichah* to those who qualified. Reb Chaim Volozhiner noticed that, under this system, brilliant minds were often lost. Without the proper elevation there was little opportunity for a budding scholar to develop his fullest potential. Reb Chaim's response was to open a *yeshivah* for the truly outstanding *talmid*. Many of the young men who attended were of near-genius caliber.

R' Eliezer Shulavitz

The idea caught on. Eventually, *yeshivos* were flourishing throughout Russia and Lithuania — but not in Poland. There, the custom remained true to pre-Volozhin times.

Poland's first *yeshivah*, in Lomza, was born because of a dream in the heart of R' Lazer Shulavitz. It was in 1883, with the passing of the founder of the *mussar* movement, R' Yisrael Salanter, that his student R' Lazer Shulavitz decided to turn his dream into a reality. He would establish a *yeshivah*, the first in all of 19th-century Poland, in the memory of his beloved teacher!

When one is about to embark on a new enterprise, he goes to an expert. Reb Lazer went to Stavisk, a small town near Lomza, to solicit the advice and support of its *Rav*, the Stavisker *Tzaddik*. A tremendous *gaon* and *posek,* the Stavisker was known as the only individual of his generation qualified to judge cases of "*dinei nefashos*" (capital crimes). He wrote the *Pnei Aryeh HaChai*, now out of print.[1] The Stavisker was the one who urged the Chofetz Chaim to write his classic compendium of *halachah*, the *Mishnah Berurah*. For consultation on an especially difficult ruling, the Chofetz Chaim would turn to the Stavisker *Tzaddik*, Reb Chaim Leib Mishkowski.

Divine Providence was evident in the timing of Reb Lazer's visit to Stavisk. He came knocking at the door of the *beis din* room, seeking guidance and advice — and found, when he entered, not only the Stavisker *Tzaddik*, but also his guest, the Chofetz Chaim! Reb Lazer immediately broached his concern: Would a "*Litvish*" type of *yeshivah*, with a *mussar* orientation, be

---

1. The Stavisker's son, R' Chizkiyahu Mishkowski (known as the Kriniker Rav), eventually founded the *yeshivah* in Kfar Chassidim.

The building of
the Lomzer
Yeshivah

successful in chassidic Poland? The two luminaries gave him their blessing and their promise of support — a promise they were to keep throughout their lives.

Reb Lazer had received a dowry of 3,000 rubles, plus an inheritance of another 3,000: a fortune in those days. After losing 1,500 in a business venture, he "invested" his remaining 4,500 rubles in the *"yeshivah* business" and purchased a lot for his *yeshivah.*

A local manufacturer of bricks immediately donated some 35,000 bricks for the new *yeshivah* building. When his wife found out about this, she summoned her husband to a *din Torah!*

"He donated those bricks without consulting me!" she declared. Then she anxiously inquired of the presiding rabbis: "In that case, will I have a share in the *mitzvah?*" The rabbis assured her that she would indeed have a share in her husband's good deed — but the woman was not satisfied until she herself had donated another 35,000 bricks!

The *yeshivah* was a tremendous success. At times its student body numbered 400, and could even climb as high as 500. Reb Lazer was an innovator. Unlike other *yeshivos,* where the entire student body was made up of a single class with only one *Rosh Yeshivah* lecturing them, the Lomzer Yeshivah had five classes; in addition, the third, or *"Gimmel"* class, was divided into two —

The Bais Midrash of the Lomzer Yeshivah

"Gimmel-Alef" and *"Gimmel-Bais,"* with separate *rebbeim* teaching them. Later, when the chassidic *rebbeim* opened their own *yeshivos,* they traveled to Lomza to see the miracle for themselves. Reb Yosef Yoizel Hurwitz, founder of Novarodok, spent time in Lomza and organized his *yeshivah* network along identical lines.

Reb Lazer liked to quote the Gemara's expression, *"Im ein gedayim, ein teyashim"* ("If there are no young kids, there will be no goats"). Accordingly, he opened 12 *yeshivos ketanos* (Torah institutions for teen-aged boys) in all the neighboring towns around Lomza. Reb Lazer personally nominated and subsidized the *rebbeim* of these *yeshivos.*

All too soon, however, the financial burden grew too heavy. Rumor had it that Reb Lazer was about to close down his entire enterprise — beginning with the 12 *yeshivos ketanos.*

When the rumors reached the Stavisker *Tzaddik,* he hurried to Lomza. That evening, the *Tzaddik* and Reb Lazer took a stroll through the town. Deep in discussion of a Torah topic, they passed one *bais midrash* after another. At that late hour, all the houses of study were closed and dark. Suddenly, the Stavisker stopped and said, "Reb Lazer, what do you hear?" In the stillness of the night, the only sound to be heard were the voices of the *yeshivah* students.

"I hear *kol haTorah* (the voice of Torah)," replied Reb Lazer.

"And where are the voices coming from? From the *shuls* we have just passed?"

"No," said Reb Lazer slowly. "They are all closed . . . dark . . . silent."

"And now you want to close the last *kol haTorah*, the *Yeshivah*, with its twelve *kruvim*?" demanded the Stavisker.[1]

With renewed vigor, Reb Lazer began to work even harder. The Chofetz Chaim, the Stavisker, and other *gedolim* (Torah leaders) issued appeals for the Lomzer Yeshivah. The Jewish community in neighboring Koenigsburg (East Prussia) responded mightily. In Germany proper, Rabbi Dr. Ezriel Hildesheimer, Rabbi Dr. Breuer of Frankfurt, and even Baron Rothschild, all answered the appeal. Then Reb Lazer dispatched *meshulachim* (fundraisers) to every corner of the globe.

A famous joke was born. Whenever the newspapers carried discussions on the question of whether life existed on Mars, the Jews of Lomza would laugh: "They should ask Reb Lazer. If he has no *meshulach* on Mars, you can be sure no one lives there!"

Reb Lazer's *rebbetzin* once told the Chofetz Chaim that their meager income was insufficient for the needs of their family, plus all the guests her husband brought home each day. She asked the Chofetz Chaim to intervene with her husband to raise his own salary by a few rubles. The Chofetz Chaim replied, "If Reb Lazer would accept a raise, he would have to raise the salaries of the entire faculty — and that he could not afford to do!"

No chronicle of the Lomzer *Yeshivah* would be complete without a description of three personalities. The first was the *Mashgiach*, Reb Moshe Rosenstain, a "graduate" of Kelm. R' Rosenstain virtually fasted for 30 years, eating only a little food

---

1. The 12 *yeshivos ketanos*, which he compared to the *cherubim* on the *Aron HaKodesh*, which had the face of a child.

Talmidim in the Lomzer Yeshivah. R' Moshe Rosenstain is in the front row, center.
The arrow indicates my brother Lazer.

after *Ma'ariv*, which a boy would bring to his room from the *yeshivah* kitchen. He lived in his room at the *yeshivah* all week long, going home only for Shabbos and *Yom Tov*. The *yeshivah* building was very long, allowing the *mashgiach* to pace the aisle of the *bais midrash* for hours at a stretch. He explained once that it takes five uninterrupted hours of concentrated thinking to produce five minutes of pure thought.

Then there was the *rebbi* of *"Gimmel-Alef,"* Reb Shabsi Viernikovski. R' Shabsi, a brother-in-law of Reb Yaakov Kamenetsky, stood nearly seven feet tall. He would invariably bend to the smallest *talmid* to answer his question, and not straighten up until the conversation was over and the boy completely satisfied.

Lomza, too, had an *"Alter."* Reb Yisrael Leib Ogulski was the *Mashgiach* before R' Moshe Rosenstain. In my day he was already elderly and retired. Reb Yisrael Leib was probably the only Torah scholar in the world who could not abide the sight of a boy who *"shockled zich"* — who swayed back and forth as he learned. A Litvak who could not pronounce the letter "shin," he would quote the line from the Torah about stoning an ox — a "shor" in

In the Lomzer Yeshivah.
L-R: R' Yehoshua Zelig Ruch, R' Lazer Ogulski, and R' Moshe Rosenstain.

Hebrew, though Reb Yisrael Leib pronounced it "sor." "*Sokel yisokel hasor*," he would complain (literally, "the ox shall be stoned"). "An ox should '*sokel zich*' — not a person!"

When his daughters grew to marriageable age, Reb Lazer asked his old friend, the *Alter* of Slobodka, to recommend two suitable sons-in-law. The *Alter* named the "Iluy of Trok," R' Yechiel Mordechai Gordon, later to be known as the "Prince of all *Roshei Yeshivos*," and R' Yehoshua Zelig Ruch, the "Rokishker," the most diligent student in Slobodka.

The wedding of R' Lazer's oldest daughter to R' Yechiel Mordechai Gordon took place in the *yeshivah* in 1905. The bride agreed to allow her new husband to return to Slobodka to continue his studies there. Sadly, within a year of their marriage the young wife died. Given the state of communications as they existed at that time, the tragic news did not reach R' Yechiel Mordechai until after the funeral.

Grief stricken as R' Lazer was, he did not want to allow such a gem to slip out of his hands. He traveled to Slobodka to plead with the young man to consider marrying his second daughter and taking over the *yeshivah*. R' Yechiel Mordechai refused. It had obviously not been decreed in Heaven, he said, that he be R' Lazer's son-in-law — and the reason for this was doubtless that he was not qualified to be a *Rosh Yeshivah*. Why put R' Lazer's second daughter at risk?

"Suppose the Chofetz Chaim himself promises you a long life together?" asked R' Lazer. R' Yechiel Mordechai agreed to travel to Radin to seek the Chofetz Chaim's blessing for the marriage. The blessing duly received, the wedding took place.[1] In the year 1907, R' Yechiel Mordechai became *Rosh Yeshivah* of Lomza at the age of 24.

Knowing he could safely entrust the *yeshivah* to the hands of his sons-in-law, R' Yechiel Mordechai Gordon and R' Yehoshua Zelig Ruch, R' Lazer realized another longstanding dream, and moved to Jerusalem.

The Job of Rosh Yeshivah

The job of the *Rosh Yeshivah* in Lomza was a demanding one, and especially so for the young man now holding the title. A young man himself, R' Yechiel Mordechai Gordon was called upon to deliver a regular *shiur* to the highest class in this place of outstanding Torah scholarship. (My father, a businessman, enjoyed a daily *shiur* with the *Rosh Yeshivah* every morning before *davening*; when the *Rosh Yeshivah* was called out of town, it was my father who substituted for him in delivering the *shiur* to the highest class.)

Crisis

The *yeshivah* — and the *Rosh Yeshivah* — faced its first major crisis during World War I, when Poland declared a general mo-

---

1. Some 25 years later, the *rebbetzin* became very ill. The *Rosh Yeshivah*, R' Yechiel Mordechai Gordon, went to collect on the Chofetz Chaim's long-ago blessing of long life for the couple. Once again, the Chofetz Chaim gave his *berachah*, and prayed for the ailing *rebbetzin*. She recovered. However, not long afterwards she passed away, leaving the *Rosh Yeshivah* with five children.

bilization. While Christian divinity students were granted army deferments, the blatantly anti-Semitic Polish government refused to defer the students of the Lomzer Yeshivah — the only such institution in all of Poland. R' Yechiel Mordechai set off for Warsaw to intervene.

He approached the leader of the group of Jewish members of the Sejm (Polish parliament), Dr. Noah Prilucki. Prilucki was an old-time *maskil* (proponent of the Enlightenment). While sympathetic to the *Rosh Yeshivah's* plight, the old spirit of *Haskalah* awoke in him.

"Lomzer *Rosh Yeshivah*," he said, "tomorrow I shall call on the Minister of War on your behalf. Can I tell him that you are training rabbis for all of Poland, and that your curriculum includes Polish history, grammar, and geography? Can you promise that the *yeshivah* will devote at least a few hours a day to secular studies?"

The *Rosh Yeshivah* replied, "Such a decision I cannot take upon myself. I must seek advice."

"Even though, in the meantime, your boys are being drafted and sent to the battlefield?" asked an incredulous Dr. Prilucki.

"Yes. Even at that price."

The *Rosh Yeshivah* could actually have decided on the spot, based on the Volozhin precedent of 1892. Acting at the instigation of the *maskilim*, the Czar's government had delivered an ultimatum to the *yeshivah* in Volozhin: They must either introduce secular studies into the curriculum, or close their doors. A special committee of Torah leaders convened in Vilna. It was the Brisker Rav, R' Yosef Dov Soloveichik, the "Bais HaLevi," who pronounced the final *psak*: "We are not Hashem's caretakers. We can only perform our duty. We created the *yeshivah* for *HaKadosh Baruch Hu*. If it is the Divine Will to close its doors, we have no choice but to conform. We can never agree to mix *kodesh* and *chol* — the sacred and the profane." The *yeshivah* was closed down.

Many at the time considered the closing of this major *yeshivah* a national tragedy and the action of the Torah leaders an error. However, the following years proved it a blessing. Instead of one single *yeshivah*, in Volozhin, a number of new *yeshivos* sprouted and flourished throughout Russia and Lithuania, all headed by former students of Volozhin.

Reb Yechiel Mordechai knew that the two situations were not exact parallels. There is a difference between a direct ultimatum, such as that issued to the Volozhiner Yeshivah, and the indirect offer Prilucki had made him. He was in a quandary.

Back in his hotel room, the *Rosh Yeshivah* fell asleep and began to dream. In the dream he heard the verse, "All leaven or honey you shall not burn as an offering to Hashem." The meaning of this verse is that no foreign elements — whether sour or sweet — can ever be mixed before Hashem. The message was obvious, but the *Rosh Yeshivah* would not rely on a dream when it came to closing the *yeshivah*. As the war had made communication with either the Chofetz Chaim or R' Chaim Ozer in Vilna impossible, R' Yechiel Mordechai returned home to seek the advice of his *Mashgiach*, R' Moshe Rosenstain.

After much deliberation, the *Mashgiach* said, "It is clear that Heaven requires *mesiras nefesh* (sacrifice) from us for Torah. We are not obligated to display *mesiras nefesh* for secular studies, however. We cannot mix the two, *kodesh* and *chol*. The sacred and the profane cannot dwell together."

The *Mashgiach* was a firm believer in the Vilna Gaon's "*gorel*" — a lottery by which one derives a decision through the selection of a verse from the Torah. The verse that came to his hand was a Divine command to Moshe Rabbeinu. It read, "From 20 years old and upward, all that are able to go forth to war in Israel: Thou and Aaron shall number them by their hosts" (*Bamidbar* 1:3).

The *Mashgiach*'s own name was Moshe. He picked a student whose name was Aharon Zlotowitz[1] and the two set out to solve the *yeshivah's* dilemma. They established contact with the chairman of the local draft board, who agreed — for a quantity of

---

1. Rabbi Zlotowitz was known in the *yeshivah* world as Arke Droschiner, after his home town of Droschin. He later became one of the leading rabbis in the United States, serving as a vice president of the Agudas HaRabbanim and spearheading the battle for *halachic* circumcision and organized *kashrus*. Rabbi Meir Zlotowitz of ArtScroll/Mesorah is his son.

money, in American dollars only — to free all the *bnei Torah* (*yeshivah* students) from army service!

Though possession of any foreign currency was against the law, those were the only terms the official would accept. The *Mashgiach* justified this "illegal" approach by reasoning that the *yeshivah* students should have been deferred from army service in the same way that Christian divinity students had been. Polish anti-Semitism had denied the Jewish boys their legal rights.

R' Aharon Zlotowitz

If general Polish society was alive with anti-Semitism, the army was 10 times worse. Keeping the laws of Shabbos and *kashrus* were impossible for soldiers. Hence, students of other *yeshivos* threatened with conscription hurried to Lomza to establish residency and find a place to learn. As long as they had the necessary funds in American dollars, they were safe. For the next 20 years, Lomza served as a haven for *bnei Torah*.

Branching Out

When return to the land of Israel became a reality, the *Rosh Yeshivah* began to speak of the concept of the Torah following the people. He decided to establish a *yeshivah* in *Eretz Yisrael*. While all *yeshivos* in those days were located in Jerusalem, Lomza broke ground for its newest offshoot in the city of Petach Tikvah. In the year 1926, R' Yechiel Mordechai took 40 students from Lomza to the newly established branch in Petach Tikvah. (All 40 were of draft age and lacked the necessary funds to buy their deferments.)

Now that the *Rosh Yeshivah* had two institutions to care for, the debts began piling up. He was forced to travel to America and Africa to raise funds; en route, he would stop off in Petach Tikvah to give *shiurim*. And so it came about that in September, 1939, just as he was about to return from the United States to Lomza, Germany invaded Poland. The *Rosh Yeshivah* was forced to remain in America.

The Va'ad Hatzalah

As one of the only European *Roshei Yeshivah* in America, R' Yechiel Mordechai Gordon was the prime force behind the creation of the Va'ad Hatzalah, dedicated to rescuing Jewish souls from the inferno that was sweeping Europe. Though he himself was in a state of personal poverty, somehow he found the money to send packages to *bnei Torah* in Russia. In addition to the parcels sent by the Va'ad Hatzalah, R' Yechiel Mordechai sent along some personal packages as well. I had firsthand knowledge of this fact.

As a tank officer in the Polish Army, stationed in the USSR, I faced death daily on the battlefield. I was desperate to let someone know that I was alive, so that after the war they could inform my parents. (Not a word was mentioned in the Soviet press about concentration camps and the wholesale slaughter of the Jews. At that point, I had no idea that my whole family had perished.) Accordingly, I mailed a postcard addressed to Rabbi Y. M. Gordon, Delancey Street, New York. I didn't recall the house number. And I dared not write my return address in the army, lest my correspondence with a foreign country arouse the ever-present Russian suspicion of espionage. I never knew whether my postcard reached its destination until after the war.

When the war was over, the Va'ad Hatzalah organized a *yeshivah* in Windsheim-bei-Nuremberg, attracting surviving *bnei Torah* from all over Europe. I later learned, from students who were there, that a stream of packages began to arrive with my name on them. At first they were standard Va'ad Hatzalah packages, but soon a private parcel began arriving for me every two weeks, from my "relative," Gordon, in New York! I had no

My tank crew.
I am on the left.

relatives in New York; clearly, the *Rosh Yeshivah* presumed that I'd remained with the Kamenitzer Yeshivah in Siberia and was now on hand to receive his personal packages. The other boys hadn't a clue as to my whereabouts, but they realized that, if the packages were not quickly claimed, they would be stolen by the hungry postal employees. The boys forged documents with my name and accepted the packages in my place. Those parcels saved many a *yeshivah bachur* from starvation.

The "Public Domain"

It seems that the *Rosh Yeshivah's* entire life was a long series of tribulations. It brings to mind the recorded life of R' Yochanan in the days of the Talmud. R' Yochanan lost 10 sons during his lifetime. The 10th fell into a fire and was entirely consumed, except

R' Yechiel Mordechai Gordon

for a small bone. R' Yochanan dedicated his life to comforting people in distress. He would point to the little bone of his youngest son, to show that life must go on. He was his own lesson's clearest example.

Married at 22, R' Yechiel Mordechai lost his wife in their first year of marriage, and could not even be present at her funeral. His second wife bore him five children and then died. His son, Shneur, standing guard at the yeshivah in Petach Tikvah during the Arab pogroms, was shot down at the age of 20.

When his daughter, Chaych'ke, married an outstanding Talmudic scholar in the Mirrer Yeshivah, R' Eizl Kostukowski (a nephew of R' Chaim Ozer), R' Yechiel Mordechai was not able to attend the wedding for lack of fare from America to Lomza! The young couple had two children, the *Rosh Yeshivah's* grandchildren, whom he had never seen. His youngest son, Yudele, became a *bar mitzvah* while he was away in America. And finally, they all perished at the hands of the Nazis, including his 18-year-old daughter Itkele. (One son died in New York.) For 60 years he was a *Rosh Yeshivah*. For 60 years he carried two great *yeshivos* on his shoulders. And in the end — except for his many students and admirers — he was alone.

In spite of all this, R' Yechiel Mordechai remained undaunted. Every letter I received from him in Germany was like a shot of penicillin, awakening me and recalling me to life! In the aftermath of the war, many who had survived were broken in spirit. After losing one's entire family, who has the will to go on living? But the *Rosh Yeshivah* radiated *emunah* and *bitachon* —an unshakable faith and trust in the Almighty. He was filled with life and vigor, despite all that had happened. Life must go on; he, personally, served as the best example of this!

What was his secret? What was the source of the strength that enabled him to overcome his personal tragedies? I learned the answer when I arrived in America. His closest friends told me that R' Yechiel Mordechai cried bitterly in the privacy of the night, weeping over his lost children and students, and the terrible destruction of the war. But not a sign of his grief was visible during the day, when he faced people.

His father-in-law, R' Lazer Shulavitz, would tell of an encounter between his *rebbi*, R' Yisrael Salanter, and another Jew, on the day before Yom Kippur. R' Yisrael greeted the man and inquired after his welfare. In reply, the man began to weep.

"I'm terribly worried about the Day of Judgment we are facing tomorrow," the man sobbed. His gloomy countenance was enough to frighten anyone who saw it. R' Yisrael admonished him, "Your heart is a *reshus hayachid* — a private domain. Within its borders, you can cry all you want. But your face is *reshus harabim*, the public domain. You have no right to burden others with your fears. The rule in *Pirkei Avos* (1:15), to 'receive all men with a cheerful countenance,' applies even on Yom Kippur!"

Such was the practice of the *Rosh Yeshivah*. I'll never forget his radiant face when he met me with my wife and baby for the first time. Wreathed in smiles, we kissed and embraced. When he saw our baby, he cried, "If I would have seen this baby among 10,000 babies, I would recognize him at once as Reb Alter's *einekl* (grandson)!"

Soon afterward, I shared a personal experience with him that revealed even more of his greatness and his *emunah*. Though seven long and terrible years had passed since I'd last seen the *Rosh Yeshivah's* children and grandchildren in Vilna (they'd escaped from Lomza to Vilna together with the *yeshivah*), he loved to hear whatever I could tell him of them. In a sense, I served as his final link to his loved ones. Time and again, I would relate everything I could remember, until there was nothing left to tell. Once, while we were riding the subway together to the *yeshivah* office, I mentioned the *kiddush Hashem* (sanctification of G-d's Name) that his daughter, Chaych'ke, had created in Lomza. There were several versions to the story and I was not sure which was authentic, but I did my best with what I knew.

Chaych'ke was preparing for her marriage to R' Eizl. All the arrangements fell on her own young shoulders, as her mother had already died and her father was far away, in America. Her uncle, the *Rosh Yeshivah's* brother, lived in Boston; he gave R' Yechiel Mordechai a personal check of $500 to send Chaych'ke as a wedding gift.

The check duly arrived — but Chaych'ke put it to a different use than her uncle had envisioned. She had three friends, girls from the neighborhood who were also engaged to be married but whose weddings had been postponed due to poverty. Chaych'ke divided the $500 — a veritable fortune in impoverished Poland — among the three girls!

As R' Yechiel Mordechai listened to the tale, the tears streamed down his cheeks into his gray beard. I began to feel sorry I'd brought up the story. Then, to my embarrassment, he embraced and kissed me, right there in the crowded subway car. Holding my hand, he repeatedly whispered to himself an expression that was unfamiliar to me: "*Nachas* in *Olam Haba.*" A short time later, as we parted, he said, "Look up the *Midrash Tanchuma* on the *pesukim* (verses) on *orlah.*"

I was puzzled, for the laws of *orlah* pertain to the planting of trees in Israel: During the first three years, the fruit of the tree is forbidden. How did this relate to the *Rosh Yeshivah's* personal tragedy, and to the strange expression he'd used?

I lost no time in dropping into one of the Hebrew bookstores that lined Delancey Street, and found the *Midrash Tanchuma* (*Vayikra* 19:23-24). "And you shall have planted all manner of trees for food, then you shall count as forbidden the fruit thereof; three years shall it be sealed unto you; it shall not be eaten. And in the fourth year all the fruit thereof shall be holy for giving praise unto the L-rd." To which the *Midrash Tanchuma* comments: " . . . This refers to a child. For three years he does not converse; the fourth year he is holy, for his father dedicates him to Torah, when he begins to praise Hashem; and in the fifth year you shall eat his fruit, referring to the child embarking on Torah study ... In this world, a man gives birth to a son, leads him to school, works hard with him to teach him Torah; then he dies, and has no *nachas* from him ... However, in the World to Come I shall remove the *yetzer hara* from your sons; you shall give birth and be happy, with *nachas*."

Such was the source of strength of a Torah giant, even in the face of personal and national tragedy!

Among the first of R' Yechiel Mordechai's students to emerge from the concentration camps alive was Reb Moshe Mordechai Krieger (presently of Ocean Parkway, Brooklyn). The *Rosh Yeshivah* immediately sent him funds to travel from camp to camp in search of other surviving *bnei Torah*. When I told the *Rosh Yeshivah* that Moshe Mordechai had endured five years in various concentration camps without ever tasting non-kosher food, he was astounded and deeply moved. "Only Torah and *mussar* can bring a person to such *mesiras nefesh*," he declared. He credited the *Mashgiach*, R' Moshe Rosenstain, with this achievement. In those dark days, this was the sole ray of light to reach the *Rosh Yeshivah*. R' Moshe

A group of talmidim in the Va'ad Hatzalah yeshivah in Windsheim-Nuremburg, Germany, after the war. L-R: Moshe Krieger, Yaakov Kiniel, Eli Shapiro, me, Moshe Kalmanowitz and Yosef Linczewski.

Krieger had the special *zechus* (merit) to survive Buchenwald; the *nachas* he brought the *Rosh Yeshivah* was an additional *zechus*!

The *Rosh Yeshivah* remained active on the Torah stage after the war, as well. For the sake of his students who survived the concentration camps and Siberia, he established a *kollel* in Brooklyn. Then, as soon as everyone was settled, he moved to Petach Tikvah to be with his *yeshivah* there.

The *Rosh Yeshivah* passed from this world at the age of 83. Before he died, he published the first volume of his *Nesivos Yam*. (His students published the second volume after his death.) The Lomzer Yeshivah still exists in Petach Tikvah, under the leadership of Reb Lazer Ozer, a grandson of its founder, R' Lazer Shulavitz.

R' Yechiel Mordechai Gordon had endured a bitter life that spanned tragedies of recent history, but he brought joy, courage, and purpose to the lives of so many — including myself. May he enjoy great *nachas* in *Olam Haba*!

Bais Yosef: The 70 Novarodok Yeshivos

I first became acquainted with the Novarodok Yeshivah in Bialystok by accident. One summer, before my *bar mitzvah*, I visited my father's family in Tiktin. I spent a great deal of time in the *bais hamidrash*, where my *zeide* was learning behind the *bimah*. He learned mostly from memory, for he was nearly blind. For years he led a daily *Gemara shiur* for 40 or 50 men, always from memory. (In fact, there had been one occasion when he'd left his seat for a few moments, and some pranksters turned his Gemara upside down. My grandfather returned to his seat and *continued* learning for two solid hours without turning the *Gemara* right side up!)

On this particular day, I told my *zeide* that I was hungry and was going home to get something to eat. Just as I was about to leave, a very poorly dressed young man entered the *shul*. Without a word to anyone, he washed his hands, took a seat, and began to learn *Gemara*. I asked the other kids who the fellow was, and they informed me that he wasn't from those parts. "He must be a Novarodoker," they decided.

A Novarodoker! When *Zeidie* heard that, he told me to run home and tell *Bobbe* that a Novarodoker was in *shul*. "She'll know what to do," he said. "Hurry!"

Curiously, I asked, "But who is he, *Zeidie*?"

"I'll explain later. Now go!"

I went.

It was Tuesday — market day. I found the store packed with customers, and my grandmother with her hands full.

"*Bobbe*, I'm hungry," I began.

"Don't you see how busy I am?" she threw back. "Go into the kitchen and find something to eat."

That reminded me. "Oh, *Zeidie* said to tell you that some Novarodoker just walked into the *bais midrash* — whatever that means."

My grandmother immediately dropped everything she was doing. Calling on my Uncle Kalman to take over the shop, she rushed to the kitchen, where she heated up some rice and milk. Next she wrapped up three sandwiches of bread and cheese. When all this was loaded into my arms, she added a large glass of milk, and ordered me to take the food to the stranger. "And don't forget to tell him you'll bring him supper, too."

"But what about me?" I asked pathetically. "I'm also hungry."

"You'll eat when you come back. The Novarodoker is hungrier than you!"

Afterwards, *Zeidie* explained to me all about Novarodok.

"In the *yeshivah* in Bialystok," he said, "there are men who are '*ba'alei madreigah.*' That is, they are high-level students of *mussar*. These men insist that *emunah* and *bitachon* cannot be acquired merely by reading words in a book. Rather, they are traits that must be developed and put to the test through practice. So they leave the *yeshivah* without a penny in their pockets. They walk to town on foot. If someone offers them a ride they'll accept, but they will never ask for one. Because they focus on *shmiras ha-lashon*, guarding the tongue, they don't talk much to anyone. When they arrive in a town, they go straight to the *bais midrash* and, without a word, begin to learn. Food? That's part of their test of faith — Heaven will supply their needs! They will never accept an invitation to a house, for that would mean compromising their *shmiras halashon*. Also, their custom is to look down at the ground when they walk in the streets, something they could not politely do in someone's home. With Tiktin so close to Bialystok [only some 50 kilometers separated the two towns], we get these exceptional young men very often. *Bobbe* and some of the other women already know their duty to feed these *ba'alei bitachon* — these masters of faith!"

Such was my introduction to Novarodok. From that time, whenever I traveled home from the *yeshivah* in Baranowitz for the holidays, I would seize the opportunity of changing trains in Bialystok, first to pay a call on my uncle (director of a bank), and then to visit the Novarodok Yeshivah for a few days.

Novarodok was shaped by its originator, R' Yosef Yoizel Hurwitz, better known as *"der Alter fun Novarodok"* (the Novarodok Elder). He founded his first *yeshivah* in the city of Novarodok, and the name clung to the *yeshivos* that followed. Two verses best encapsulate his credo: *"Na'eh doreish v'na'eh mekayem* (Preach beautifully and live accordingly)," and *"V'yafutzu ma'ayanosecha chutzah* (Your springs shall flow outward)."* His students followed his teachings and founded *yeshivos* all across Russia, Ukraine, and White Russia. In Poland alone, there were eventually 70 Novarodok *yeshivos*!

R' Yosef Yoizel was a businessman who, inspired by the *mussar* of R' Yisrael Salanter, broke with his past and decided to dedicate his own life to spreading Torah and *mussar*. He demanded from his students that they sever all ties with their own past lives without delay. "Why doesn't a person change his lifestyle for the better?" he would ask. "Because he is held back — by weakness of character, by family obligations, by earthly desires. All of these factors will be with him 10 minutes from now,

10 days from now, 10 months from now, 10 years from now — or a lifetime from now! If one doesn't break away from his past this very moment, he never will!"

The break, he claimed, must be a total one. The process of trying to change gradually was something he compared to the situation of a man who decides to keep kosher but cannot afford to buy a whole new set of dishes. He buys them instead one piece at a time, week by week. But at the end of the year, instead of having a full set of kosher dishes, he'll have a set of completely *treif* ones, through mixing the kosher with the non-kosher. In this way, claimed the *Alter*, a person's bad habits will eventually overcome the good ones, and end by making them all *treif.*

Rambam teaches that spiritual ailments are no different from physical ones. One can either treat the symptoms or cure the very source of the illness. *Mussar* aims at the root of the spiritual ailment, by eradicating evil within a person and replacing it with good.[1]

---

1. In the early days of the *mussar* movement, when its founder R' Yisrael Salanter had just brought forth his ideas, there was opposition from some Torah leaders. A page of *Gemara*, they claimed, constituted a lesson in *mussar* in itself. The *Alter* of Slobodka thought otherwise. In his great wisdom, he arranged *shidduchim* between his best students, all *ba'alei mussar*, and the daughters of various *Roshei Yeshivos* who opposed his *mussar* system — thus effectively "planting" the seeds of *mussar* in those *yeshivos*. The Mirrer Yeshivah was one place where he did not succeed. Though he "planted" his own son there, the *Rosh Yeshivah*, Reb Elya Boruch Kamai, was definitely against the idea.

In due time, however, the winds of change and revolutionary ideas began to penetrate the *yeshivah* from the world outside. Some of the Mirrer students were affected. R' Elya Boruch Kamai sent an urgent S.O.S. to his *mechutan*: Save our *yeshivah*! The *Alter* of Slobodka responded by sending ten "Cossacks" to the Mir — young men who were great in Torah as well as *mussar*. Among them were my own father (known as Alter Tiktiner), and Reuven Grozovsky (Reuven Minsker), later to become *Rosh Yeshivah* in Kamenitz. Their arrival at the Mir led to an amusing incident.

R' Kamai had earlier instructed the *shammas* to burn any "*treif*" (unkosher) books he might find while cleaning the boys' rooms. The *shammas*, a simple man, asked how he was to distinguish a *treif sefer* from a kosher one. He was told that the pages of a kosher volume were marked with the letters of the *alef-bais* (Hebrew alphabet), while *treif* books were numbered.

In due time, the "*Mussar* Cossacks" arrived, armed with the first *mussar*

My father with some of his fellow talmidim in Mir, c. 1910. Standing at the left is Beinush Friedlander, later a Rav in Baltimore. Seated on the left is my father.

The *Midrash* relates G-d's promise to His people: "My children, pierce your hearts with an opening [of repentance] as tiny as the tip of a needle, and I shall open for you a passage wide enough for wagons to pass through." Asks the *Alter* of Novarodok: "Is it possible that we never open such an opening? Of course we do! But there are all sorts of holes. If one drills a hole in steel, it remains open forever. When a person puts his hand into a bucket of water, he creates a hole, too — but the moment he removes his hand, the 'hole' closes up. *Mussar* makes the hole a permanent one!"

If one has *emunah* (belief in Hashem), then he must also have *bitachon* (trust) that Hashem will supply all his needs. One who works hard, as though everything depends only upon his own efforts, demonstrates a lack of trust in his Creator. Hence, *bitachon* is always pitted against human *hishtadlus* (exertion of effort). How is one to determine the correct balance between the two? How much effort should a person apportion to the fulfillment of

---

works to enter the Mir: copies of the newly published *Mesilas Yesharim* (Path of the Just). As luck would have it, the new *sefarim* were marked with numbers instead of the usual Hebrew letters. One day, to their horror, the new arrivals discovered that every copy of *Mesilas Yesharim* had disappeared!

Luckily, someone remembered the simple *shammas* in the nick of time — and the precious volumes were rescued from the fire.

his needs, and how much must he leave in the hands of Hashem? The Talmud records a debate on the subject (*Berachos* 35b), in which R' Yishmael prescribes a normal measure of involvement in one's work, while trusting in Hashem for success, while R' Shimon bar Yochai calls for an extreme approach: all *bitachon* and no *hishtadlus* at all.

While the topic is further debated by later authorities, the *Alter* of Novarodok — from the moment he first broke with his past — practiced total *bitachon* his entire life. Others would sometimes remind him that Abbaye, on the same page in *Berachos*, declared, "Many ('*rabim*') attempted to follow R' Yishmael's way and succeeded, while many attempted to follow R' Shimon bar Yochai's way and failed." The *Alter* would point out that the key to this statement is the word *rabim*. R' Shimon's way, he agreed, is certainly not for the masses — but individuals can and should work to reach the ultimate level of *bitachon*, of trust in Hashem. And this labor requires drastic measures. One cannot learn how to swim by tying one hand to a tree for safety's sake, nor lay claim to genuine *bitachon* while in possession of a well-filled bankbook.

The *Alter* had a unique method for establishing *yeshivos* over the length and breadth of Russia. He would send a young man with 10 students into a town. The newcomers would immediately "occupy" a *shul* and begin to learn Torah. The townsfolk had no choice. How could they stand by and let *bnei Torah* go hungry?

A committee was organized at once to take care of the boys' eating and sleeping arrangements. Then the fledgling *yeshivah* would go about its business of attracting new students, by the simple method of knocking on doors and picking boys up in the streets. Almost overnight, a *yeshivah* was born — without any funds. It was a *yeshivah* based totally on *bitachon*. As the Chofetz Chaim was heard to remark with admiration, "We are sitting and writing *sefarim* (learned works), while R' Yosef is creating *yeshivos*!"

The Bolsheviks posed a lethal threat to Novarodok. At first the *Alter* tried to fight their influence, but he soon realized that there could be no discussion with these criminals. Soon after his death, his *talmidim* consulted with the Chofetz Chaim who advised them to cross the border into Poland. Only some 600 made it across; some were killed, others arrested and shipped to Siberia. Those 600 settled in the city of Bialystok. From that headquarters the *Alter's* son-in-law, R' Avraham Yaffen, went on to establish 70 *yeshivos* throughout Poland.

For the serum of *mussar* to be effective, taught Novarodok, it must be injected with zest and emotional intensity. One cannot be cured or build up immunity against evil merely by reading a book on the subject. The Novarodok way was for each student to attack his personal weaknesses and insecurities in a vehement, almost violent manner. One summer, a passer-by was attracted by the raised voices exploding through the open windows during a typical *mussar* session. He entered the building and asked the *Alter*, "Is this a crazy house?"

"Indeed it is," the *Alter* replied. "People enter the *yeshivah* crazy, and when they leave, they are refined and normal!"

I was familiar with the Novarodok method, having spent some time in the Bialystok Yeshivah each time I traveled home. But I was to get a much more personal taste.

Ready-made suits were unheard of in Europe at that time, so before I returned home for Pesach one year my parents sent me money to buy material and have a good tailor make me a suit. The perfection of a suit's fit was a tailor's pride, and a good measure of that pride rubbed off on me. As was my custom, I decided to stop into the *yeshivah* before switching trains in Bialystok. Entering the *yeshivah*, dressed in my brand-new suit, I felt like a millionaire among paupers, for poverty and tattered clothing were the "fashion" in Novarodok. I wondered if any of those boys had ever owned a new suit. (The *yeshivah* had three decent suits, sized large, medium, and small, which were used exclusively by boys meeting a prospective *shidduch*. The story is told that a button once fell off a suit when it was worn on a Shabbos. The girl in question knew Novarodok; she kept the button, and when, some two weeks later, another boy came wearing the same suit, she sewed the button on!)

I walked into the middle of a"*birze*" — literally, a money-exchange center, but with a rather different twist here. Black markets flourished in every city, with people busily exchanging foreign currency and passing on the price of the American dollar or the British pound. The *Alter* instituted a *birze* of another kind. Instead of money, it was *middos, mussar,* and character traits that were exchanged.

The idea came to him during one of his solitary strolls through the forest, when he chanced upon a secret gathering of anti-czar revolutionaries. The men were walking around in pairs, discussing ways of deposing the czar. The sight inspired the *Alter:* "If they can refine their ideas in pairs, why can't *bnei Torah* do the same with their *middos*?" In short order, he established a *mussar* system whereby the students worked in pairs on the refinement of their characters.

As I walked through the doors of the *bais midrash, yeshivah* students were walking up and down the long study hall in pairs, immersed in heated discussions. One of them, a teenager like me, spotted me at once and came right over. He gave me a warm "*Shalom aleichem,*" took me by the arm, and immediately started talking.

"Did you ever wonder," he asked, "why we never use the *berachah* (blessing) that Avraham gave us, or Yitzchak, or Moshe *Rabbeinu?* In our day, when we want to bless our children, we use the words that Yaakov spoke to Yosef's sons, Efraim and Menashe. Why?

"Let me tell you how Novarodok answers this.

"All four of them — Yaakov, Yosef, Efraim and Menashe — knew the importance of a *berachah.* Remember, Eisav had wanted to kill Yaakov because of a *berachah!* Yet, Yaakov, in blessing his grandchildren, bestowed seniority upon Efraim, the younger son. Menashe should have screamed! He should have complained, 'Zeidie, you've deprived me of my rights as the *bechor,* the elder son!' But Menashe was silent. He had the trait of brotherly love, as well as a tremendous respect for his grandfather.

"Yosef, the boys' father, tried to intervene. He attempted to remove his father's right hand from Efraim's head, pointing out that

Menashe was actually the *bechor*. Now it should have been Efraim's turn to complain. 'Father, why are you interfering? If *Zeidie* wants to give me the *berachah*, why are you trying to stop him?' But Efraim, too, was silent. Again, we see the enormity of his love for his brother, and his respect for his father and grandfather.

"And that's why we use the words of their blessing to this day. Both brothers were silent. Neither one sought honor. Many a man has fallen from great heights because of his desire for glory. We should take an example from Efraim and Menashe, whose brotherly love, and whose silence, has proven the exact opposite of honor and arrogance."

I was deeply impressed by his words. The boy looked me in the eye and continued, "Tell me, why don't you go into the street, stretch out your hands, and call out to the passers-by, 'Look at my ten fingers! Marvel at the way they operate! And take a look at my head — my two eyes, my two ears. The wonder of me!' " He smiled, and finally came to the point of his harangue. "No. You'd never do that, because who doesn't have the same ten fingers, the same head and the rest? And yet, when you put on a silly suit, made to fit perfectly, you want the whole world to stop and admire it. What *ga'avah*! What pointless arrogance!"

The boy paused, and then added philosophically, "Of course, you may be right. *Rambam* established a rule: If the absence of something is considered a *chisaron* (shortcoming), then when it is present, it is not a *ma'alah* (asset). However, if an item's absence is not a shortcoming, then its presence is an asset. Without hands, a person is considered a cripple who suffers from a great lack — so possessing hands is not regarded as an asset. But owning a magnificent suit is something else again. Its absence is no *chisaron* at all; one can live a lifetime without a new suit —which makes its presence an asset." He pointed a finger at me. "*There's* the justification for your *ga'avah* — your silly arrogance!"

I was astounded. Here was this young fellow, a teenager just like me, who'd probably never owned a new suit of his own. And yet he understood, with uncanny exactitude, my innermost thoughts and feelings. That was the essence of Novarodok.

It was much later that I realized the real importance of the *birze* system. The method involved much more than simply criticizing one's partner and tearing him apart. It was also, in the deepest sense, a tool for self-improvement — in the spirit of the words, "He who comes to teach, and stays to learn." As a person launches into an enthusiastic analysis of his friend's shortcomings, how can he fail to start looking inward eventually, and to ask himself with painful honesty, "And what about me?"

Novarodok, with its rejection of luxury and emphasis on living the simple life, seems far removed from contemporary America, so overinvolved with sensual experience. The *Alter* insisted that teaching in the smallest *yeshivah* was of greater significance than being a *rav* in the largest community. His demand for constant introspection and self-improvement could not fail to leave its lasting mark on all who came into contact with him or his great *yeshivah*. The old saying goes, "Whoever touches the doorknob of a *bais hamussar* — a house of *mussar* — will never enjoy an *aveirah* (sin)." I might add, "Whoever touches the doorknob of Novarodok will never stop digging within his character and breaking apart his inner self!"

Chapter 9:
The Winds of Change

Revolt!

Rumors of revolt were circulating all over the Russian Empire. The people were muttering against the czar; the Poles were pitted against the Russians; the peasants despised the big landowners. Government officials were being assassinated with alarming frequency. Laborers went on spontaneous wildcat strikes. Peasants all over Russia demonstrated their animosity toward the landed class by setting fires that burned down luxurious palaces and stables. They would have loved to kill the *graf*, too, but the *graf* was never home; he and his family resided in Paris, Berlin or Moscow. The peasants expressed their anger by taking revenge against the Jewish *pritzim*, who lived on the land and were always at home. Outright murder took place.

My grandfather, Reb Chaim Velvl, had many close friends among the peasants. There was Yannek, in charge of the horses;

Vladik, who tended the cows; and Yoozef, who oversaw the planting and harvesting. They spoke to him in a broken Yiddish. Their fathers had been his friends; he even remembered their grandfathers. "Voolvki" felt safe among his peasants. He would ride his horse daily to *minyan* without fear — until, one day, he noticed that the two giant dogs, who were supposed to be guarding the house, were chasing him instead.

Wondering how they had got free of the chains that kept them tied to the gate, he turned his horse around and tried to chase the dogs back home. To his astonishment, for the first time in their lives they refused to obey him. Finally, he gave up and continued along the forest road, the dogs trotting alongside.

As they entered the forest, the dogs spurted ahead. Suddenly, he heard screams. "*Voolvki ratuj! Voolvki ratuj!*" ("Velvl, save me!") Galloping ahead, he found the two dogs mauling a figure on the ground. A rifle had been knocked out of the man's hands and lay on the ground nearby. He lay helpless and screaming as the dogs tore at his clothes and bit his flesh.

Velvl called off his dogs and helped the other man to his feet. It turned out to be Stefan Kowalski, a farmer he had dealt with in the past. Kowalksi owed the *poretz* money. The route that Velvl followed each day passed right by Kowalski's farm, and the farmer had lain in ambush in the forest, waiting to kill him. The very man who saved his life had been his intended victim! The dogs, messengers of Heaven, had ruined his evil plan and saved their master's life.

To the end of his days, my *zeide* would double his *tzedakah* donation on that day, and make a *seudas hoda'ah* — a special meal of thanksgiving — to which the poor of the town were invited. At this meal, he would re-tell the tale of the dogs who had saved his life, relating every detail of the miracle and calling the dogs "my angels."

After that incident, Reb Chaim Velvl always had an armed man ride escort with him. He still believed that, in general, he was fairly safe among the peasants he knew so well. But he'd miscalculated the extent of the violent turmoil that rocked the times, and especially the power of the Church and its clergy, that ancient source of hatred and evildoing toward the Jews.

He learned of his error in judgment, to his sorrow, soon enough. One morning, a heinous discovery was made: The entire Solomon family had been murdered.

The Russian police didn't even bother to come down to the village to investigate the crime. The chief of police told Voolvki openly: "We are not dealing here with murder for the sake of robbery, but with a nationwide uprising of the sharecroppers against the landowners. The police are powerless to stop it. Their real target was probably you, even though you have no sharecroppers."

Reb Chaim Velvl was shocked and shaken to the core by the crime and by the unwillingness of the police to help. After the funeral of the six murdered Jews, his three "best friends" among the peasants — Zajkowski, Kormornicki, and Novinski — came to visit. They assured "Panie Voolvki" that he had nothing to worry about: They personally guaranteed his safety! But the *poretz* didn't trust them anymore. Though he did not believe that these particular men would harm him, he harbored no such certainty about the local priest. In fact, he was convinced that the priest was behind the slaughter of the Solomons. The Church had been organizing such pogroms for centuries.

The czarist government tightened its grip on Poland, imposing the Russian language on its citizens, and trying to impose its religion as well. As a Jew, this was not R' Chaim Velvl's business, but his political sympathies definitely lay on the side of Poland. In his business dealings and his constant contact with the Russian officials he played the role of loyal-to-the-czar citizen; secretly, however, he supported the Polish revolutionaries. This led to his first contact with a young Pole who would come to play an important part on the stage of Polish history.

Jozef Pilsudski, of the Vilna district, organized the *Legjony* to fight the Russians for Poland's independence. The czar's secret police, the *ochrana*, placed a huge bounty for his capture, dead or alive — all to no avail. Pilsudski, who later became the George Washington of modern Poland, was a friend to the Jews, and the Jews reciprocated in kindness. Once, when the *ochrana* came in hot pursuit of Pilsudski to the city of Baranowitz, a Jewish black-smith by the name of Yankel Zakay dressed the Polish revolutionary as his apprentice and hid him in the smithy for weeks. The Russians finally instituted a house-to-house search. Realizing the danger Pilsudski posed to himself and his family, Zakay quickly wrapped the Pole in *tallis* and *tefillin*, handed him a *siddur*, stood him facing the wall and instructed him to *"shockel zich"* (sway) like a Jew at his prayers. Pilsudski did as he was told — except that he held the *siddur* upside down! The *ochrana* man went so far as to look into the *siddur*, but didn't bother glancing into the face hidden by the *tallis*!

Some time later, when Pilsudski and his group ran out of money, they robbed a money-train in the city of Lomza. The cash — totaling some millions of rubles — had been destined for the payroll of the Russian Army and government officials. When the governor ordered an intensive search for the robbers, Voolvki's three Polish friends brought Pilsudski to the village of Kollaki to hide. They asked the village's Polish blacksmith for cooperation in Pilsuski's concealment, but the frightened man refused. Then, as they continued to plead, he relented and said that he would hide Pilsudski in his shop only if *Panie* Voolvki gave his consent.

If he was hoping that the *poretz* would refuse, he was disap-pointed. *Poretz* Voolvki cooperated fully. He not only helped hide the "revolutionary criminal," but even personally assisted him in burying the millions of stolen rubles in the forest.

Velvl's Polish friends confided in him that Pilsudski had warned them not to trust the local priest. It was Pilsudski's belief that the Catholic clergy were cooperating with the Russian au-thorities on the Vatican's orders. He further suspected that a secret deal had been hatched between the Vatican and the czar: The Church, on its side, would not support any uprising against the czar's rule in Poland, and in return the czar would refrain from imposing the Russian Orthodox Church on the Poles.

Years later, when Lenin established the USSR and opened the secret archives in Moscow, the documents proved Pilsudski's allegations to be well founded. A secret deal had, indeed, existed between the Vatican and the czar. By that time, Poland had declared its independence and Pilsudski was the Prime Minister, First Marshal, and semidictator of Poland. When his suspicions about the Church were proved correct, he publicly proclaimed himself an atheist. (This, in a country immersed in medieval Catholicism, took a great deal of nerve!)

Escape

One Sunday, Kazymierz, Chaim Velvl's housekeeper, burst into the living room crying, *"Panie* Voolvki!" The man could hardly breathe from his desperate run. When he was at last able to speak, he spilled the bad news. He had heard people secretly whispering in church. "Tonight, or the next night, they are coming after you! Just like the Solomons!"

Reb Chaim Velvl didn't waste a minute. He loaded his family onto his wagon, along with the *sefer Torah,* the *sefarim,* the gold and silver jewelry, and two rifles. Kazymierz and the two dogs came last. Off they started for Zembrove, where *Bobbe* Shoshe's parents lived.

It wasn't easy leaving behind the house he had built, and all the furniture. *Bobbe* Shoshe, tough businesswoman that she was, held back her tears until she reached the *mezuzah.* Then she broke down in tears. The children had never seen their mother cry before. Now she was sobbing, and they cried along with her. Though they were fleeing to safety, the ride to Zembrove was a far from happy affair.

Zembrove proved too small for Velvl's plans. He moved his family to Lomza, a much larger city, where he purchased real estate right in the center of the city across the street from the *magistrat* (City Hall). There he opened a large business dealing in hardware and building materials. His boys went to *yeshivah*, his girls to school. He never did return to the village; Kollaki continued to be administered through managers.

Reb Chaim Velvl was very pleased with his sons' progress in *yeshivah*. Lazer, the oldest, was especially beloved by his *rebbeim*. They admired his quick grasp of a subject, and his prowess at debate. And no wonder: The Kollaker *Poretz* debated *Gemara* topics with his sons daily. Shoshe took great pride in the boy. She would remind her husband often, "Chaim Velvl, our Lazerke will not be a farmer. He will be a *rav*, our great *nachas!*" In those days, to a have a son become a *rav* was a Jewish mother's lifelong dream.

War

In the year 1914, a shot in Sarajevo began the First World War. For the *shtetl*, war spelled ruination. Territory changed hands with lightning rapidity — Russians, Germans, Poles, Bolsheviks, Whites, Lithuanians — and always with terrible consequences for the Jews. Besides the "normal" animosity toward them, generated by centuries of the Church's teachings, the Jews were always mistrusted and accused of siding with the enemy — no matter who the enemy was.

"*And where was Dinah? Yaakov hid her in a chest... lest Eisav cast his eyes upon her*" (*Rashi* on *Bereishis* 32:23).

The fact that Jewish girls and women — unlike their non-Jewish counterparts — hid in their homes rather than run out to greet the conquering soldiers was "proof" to every army that the Jews were hostile. Many Yiddish songs were composed about this subject:

> *Dearest mother, my loving mother*
> *Remove the pearls from my neck*
> *The soldiers are coming*
> *Heaven forbid, they might like me.*

Daughter of mine, my golden child
Tell your heart not to worry.
I don't want the soldiers to like you;
You'll not wear any jewelry.

Dearest mother, cover up my white complexion.
Dearest child, I shall cover your face with chimney ash.
Dearest mother, I am constantly crying
How can I hide my eyes?

Dear daughter, run like an arrow.
I'm afraid that if they see your eyes
They'll never let you go!

During World War I, my *zeide*, R' Shmuel Leib the *Pike'ach* (Wise One) — known among the gentiles as *Panie* (Sir) Shmulki — was the *Rosh Hakahal* (community leader) in Tiktin. When the czar's army mobilized civilians to dig trenches, R' Shmuel Leib pleaded with the commanding officer to exempt the Jews from digging on Shabbos, offering Sunday instead. The arrogant Russian general had him arrested at once for interfering with the war effort. My grandfather was scheduled for a military trial. Before it could take place, however, R' Shmuel Leib's many Polish and Russian friends organized a delegation to assure the general of his patriotism, honesty, and religious devotion — and "*Panie* Shmulki" was released.

In due course, the Russian army retreated and the Germans came in to occupy the town in their place. In those days, the Germans were better educated and were considered more humane than either the Russians or the Poles. However, they had two major problems — communication with the local populace, and provisions for their troops — which sometimes drove them to extreme measures. The further east they penetrated, the less the Germans were able to communicate with the local population. The exceptions were the Jews, who made do with Yiddish.

When the Germans occupied Tiktin, the first order they gave was for the rebuilding of the bridges over the Narew River, which had been destroyed by the retreating Russians. My grandfather, who spoke German fairly well, once again went to the commanding officer to plead for the Jews. He asked the German commandant to permit them to substitute Sunday for Shabbos, and even offered a number of Jews to serve as interpreters on Shabbos. The German, though more polite and less arrogant than the Russian general had been, refused the exchange and ordered R' Shmuel Leib arrested. No charges were specified. My *zeide* languished in prison for two days and two nights. Meanwhile, the Jews, having no one left to intervene for them, turned to their last line of defense: *Tehillim.* The heartrending sound of prayer poured through the *shul's* opened windows as the people pleaded with Heaven to come to their leader's aid. Two German-Jewish officers, passing by, heard the noise and inquired as to its cause. Then they went to the commandant, who was persuaded to release my grandfather.

A few days later, the German commander summoned Reb Shmuel Leib to his office with a fresh demand. He wanted the Jewish community to supply food for his soldiers. (Germany imported food even in peacetime; during the war, its troops were all the more dependent on local sources.) *Zeide* explained that the city folk did not grow food, and that the farmers would no longer extend them credit because the currency was worthless. As a result, supplies had diminished, and the people were going hungry themselves. The German listened, nodding his head, and *Zeide* thought the case was closed — only to discover otherwise on the following day, which happened to be a Friday.

Every *erev Shabbos,* an elderly Jew volunteered to check the town's *eiruv.* That week, he was arrested while making his rounds of the *eiruv* wire, and charged with supplying the enemy with information through the rusty old wires. The accusation against the innocent old man amounted to nothing less than espionage!

The commandant set the hour of the man's execution for 10 a.m. on Saturday. The town was in shock. The ridiculous charge had obviously been trumped up to pressure the community into delivering food supplies to the army. Again, R' Shmuel Leib appealed to the commandant: "You'll kill an innocent man, but food will still not be forthcoming. That deaf old man is as much a spy as I am."

The German, shrewdly realizing that the Jews would be more responsive to his threats if they were aimed at the life of their leader, turned on *Zeide* in anger: "You have just confessed to spying. You are under arrest!" He sent the old man home, with instructions to advise the family of "*Herren* Shapiro" that he would be shot the next morning at 10. The whole town was in turmoil. Again the people flocked to every *shul* to say *Tehillim*.

My grandmother, known variously as "Faigl the Businesswoman" or "Faigl the *Tzaddeikes*," had her own special methods of reaching Heaven in an emergency. She had to act swiftly now. Entering the big *beis midrash* where her husband always davened and learned — to the considerable shock of the men reciting *Tehillim* there — she took *Zeide's Gemara* and placed it inside the Holy Ark. Then, sobbing and burying her face in the *sefer Torah*, she prayed that in the merit of the *chesed* he'd done, of the Torah he'd learned, and of his children and grandchildren who were learning Torah, Heaven crown her plan with success.

Thereafter, without a word to anyone, she marched off to the commandant's office. As the wife of a prisoner under sentence of execution, she was admitted. Casually she explained that she had a houseful of hungry children and grandchildren, and that she had been on her way to her favorite farmer friend to get some supplies when word had reached her of her husband's plight.

The officer swallowed the bait. Smiling slyly, he said, "*Ach so, Frau* Shapiro. You have hungry children to care for. Go home at once. When you get there, your husband will be waiting for you."

Faigl walked out, pretending to be unaware that she was being followed. Praying and murmuring *Tehillim* under her breath, she walked all the way to the house of Jan Szymanski, on the outskirts of Tiktin. This Mr. Szymanski, the most vicious Jew-hater in town, prided himself on the fact that no Jew had ever crossed the threshold of his home. *Bobbe* Faigl walked up to his front gate, opened it halfway, and then turned around suddenly. "Discovering" the sergeant and two armed soldiers just behind her, she quickly closed the gate again and continued along the dusty farm road. A deep sigh went up to Heaven, and a plea that they, too would swallow her "bait" — and they did. They would not be fooled by the stupid old Jewess who was trying to conceal her supplier from them!

Running through fields and side streets, *Bobbe* Faigl made it home — where she found *Zeide* waiting for her.

No one ever learned the exact amount of food confiscated from Szymanski, but everyone did know that he spent the next two months recuperating from the terrible beating he suffered at the hands of the German soldiers. When he finally reappeared in the streets of Tiktin, supported by two crutches, the Jewish citizens could not repress their smiles. And my grandmother gained yet another title: "Faigl the *Chachameh*" — "Faigl the Wise Woman!"

The War of 1920

After World War I, all the mighty empires of Europe — Russian, German, and Austro-Hungarian — fell apart. President Wilson of the United States proclaimed self-determination for all the little countries that had comprised these empires and they, in turn, promptly declared their independence.

On November 11, 1918, Jozef Pilsudski declared independence for Poland. He himself became Prime Minister, Marshal, and semidictator. His old *Legjony* cronies became generals and colonels in his new army, though their military knowledge was practically nonexistent.

The nations of the West feared Communism above all, and wished to halt it in its tracks inside the borders of the new Soviet

Union. They were especially anxious lest it spread into Germany; the combination of Russian resources and German know-how would have posed a catastrophe for the rest of Europe. Poland, with its natural and longstanding animosity toward its Russian neighbor, was the logical place to hold the tide.

In order to fight a war, a country needs both arms and military brains. Poland lacked both. To help alleviate the first problem, England and France began shipping arms to Poland. Then a military mission arrived from France, headed by General Waygand and his assistant, Colonel Charles de Gaulle. These two actually managed the war of 1920.

Marshal Pilsudski, eager to demonstrate his military capability, ordered his troops to travel in a circle many miles in diameter for some 48 hours. This ploy was intended to deceive Trotzky and his Red Army spies. The Soviet spies indeed reported to Trotzky, their commander-in-chief, that a huge Polish army was marching on Kiev! However, the trick backfired: Trotzky mobilized two divisions and beat the Poles all the way back to their capital, Warsaw.

Then, on the banks of the Vistula River — practically at the gates of the city — the Red Army ran out of supplies and ammunition. An army on foot and horses cannot resupply quickly. The Poles proclaimed a miraculous victory for their country. Finally, tired and worn out, both sides sat down to the peace table in Brisk, where they signed the peace treaty of 1922. The Poles called their victory *"Cod nad wisla"* (the "Miracle on the Vistula River")!

Both sides were forced by the treaty to give up territory. As was natural in every debacle, most of the blame was laid at the door of the Jews. Pogroms took place, and the pulling or cutting off of elderly Jews' beards was in order. One general, Haller, and his soldiers — known as the Hallerchiks — were especially vicious and murdered many Jews. When General Haller visited the United States, a young lawyer from Baltimore named Joseph Paper organized a protest against the killer. Haller was forced to leave America.

Pilsudski's Regime

The first law the new government passed was agrarian reform. This meant that all the big estates were parceled out to the farmers who worked them. The farmers were supposed to pay the owners a certain price per acre. Then the government passed a second law, which instituted a 25-year moratorium on payments. As it turned out, the country didn't last that long.

For my grandfather, Reb Chaim Velvl, the agrarian reform bill meant that he lost Kollaki, and that his "good friends," the Polish peasants, got the land for nothing.

(On July 30, 1965, a press report from London noted that the city government of Zambrow [Zembrove] erected a monument in the village of Kollaki, in memory of the 1,000 Jews killed by the Germans. Did any of those Kollaki farmers remember Voolvki?)

The new government also declared the Communist Party illegal. Marshal Pilsudski, a former Socialist, declared, "I was riding a train called socialism, and I got off." Involvement in Communist activity or propaganda brought with it a 10-year prison term. Even the Socialist Party, the PPS (Polska Parta Socialisticzna) and the Bund were looked upon with suspicion.

Cemetery on the Border

In the aftermath of the First World War, the League of Nations had a hard time deciding whom the city of Vilna belonged to. The newborn Republic of Lithuania declared "Vilnius" their historical capital, while the Poles claimed it as a Polish city and part of the new Polish Republic. The Jewish members of the Lithuanian delegation backed their country's claim by presenting an ancient volume of the Talmud, whose first page stated, "Printed in Vilna, capital of Lithuania."

The League finally decided in favor of Lithuania, and the

happy Lithuanians celebrated in their newly renovated capital of Vilnius. Their triumph was short lived, however. Marshal Pilsudski of Poland would not accept the verdict. He categorically refused to yield Vilna, his own birthplace, to the Lithuanians!

In 1920, Polish General Lucjan Zeligowski mobilized a few divisions to occupy Vilna and its environs. Marshal Pilsudski innocently claimed that Zeligowski had acted on his own, without his knowledge. Lithuania was no match for the larger Polish army. Swallowing its pride, the government of that country declared in its constitution that "the capital of Lithuania has temporary been moved to Kaunas (Kovno)."

From that date, a state of war existed between the two countries. It lasted nearly 20 years. There was no mail between Poland and Lithuania, and no communication of any kind was allowed between its citizens, even between members of the same family. The border sliced many families in two. It was a bizarre situation.

My uncle, R' Eliyahu Kamchi, was *Rav* of Novo-Swiencany, a town which found itself during this interlude on the Polish side of the border. The town's Jewish cemetery, however, remained in the strip of no man's land between the two countries. This strip was zealously guarded by soldiers of both "enemy armies." No one was permitted to visit.

R' Kamchi met with his counterpart, the *Rav* on the Lithuanian side, in neutral Latvia. The two decided to launch a campaign in both their capitals, demanding access to the cemetery. Both countries nominally guaranteed freedom of religion, and the Jewish religion requires visiting the cemetery before the High Holy Days.

Both Poland and Lithuania eventually agreed to the rabbis' demand; in fact, that was the only time representatives of the two countries actually spoke to one another! From Rosh Chodesh Elul until after Succos, the guards were ordered to stand aside and permit Jews from both sides of the border to visit the cemetery.

The visits turned into family reunions. Seeing the hordes of Jews foregathering at the cemetery, the puzzled guards would wonder: "There are only 50 graves here. How many children did these people have?"

There were many non-Jewish families — Poles, Lithuanians, and White Russians — that had also been split apart by the "wartime" border. Jealous of the Jews' good fortune, many pretended to be Jewish themselves, simply in order to meet with relatives at the cemetery in no man's land. The border guards kept a sharp eye on the visitors. People who crossed themselves or opened a bottle of whiskey were arrested immediately!

Life After Pilsudski

Marshal Jozef Pilsudski was good to the Jews, who had proved themselves his friends when he needed them. The Jewish community was able to breathe easier for a time, despite the occasional pogrom. When the Marshal died, he left a will ordering his body to be buried on the Vavel (burial grounds of the Polish kings), his heart in Vilna (his birthplace), and his brain to be donated to medical research. (He considered himself a genius.) The clergy refused to attend his funeral, and the church bells did not toll at his death in the customary way. The majority of Poles had never liked him much, considering him a Jew-lover. The only people who mourned him were the Jews and Pilsudski's supporters in the military, who had fought with him for Poland's independence.

The new government, made up of generals and colonels, immediately appointed a new marshal, Ridz Smigly, who postponed the funeral for a few days. Meanwhile, the Vatican was pressed to order the Polish clergy to attend the former marshal's funeral and to ring the bells across the land. As usual, the Vatican yielded, following its old practice of "rendering unto Caesar that which is Caesar's."

With the demise of Marshal Pilsudski, both government and populace — nurtured by the clergy's centuries-old antagonism toward the Jews — pursued an openly anti-Semitic policy. In an attempt to undercut the Jewish merchants who were engaged in the country's commerce and industry, the government supplied capital for Polish stores to open. However, this newly arisen "merchant class" lacked both the brains and the inclination for business. Their enterprises consistently failed, forcing the government to come up with yet more funds to prop them up again.

The government declared an open boycott on the Jews. The Prime Minister, General Skladkowski, declared in Parliament: "Pogroms, no! But economic boycott against the Jews, *owszem* (certainly, please.)" Hoodlums, protected and encouraged by the police, appeared in front of every Jewish store to prevent Poles from entering. Their slogan was *"Swoj do swego za swojego."* ("One should buy from his own, products produced by his own.")

Thus began a dark era for Polish Jewry. Poverty increased, and desperation was widespread.[1] Emigration was impossible. The entire Christian world, including the United States, locked its doors to the Jews. The United States had a 10-year waiting list; Palestine was closed by the British and their "White Paper." Australia, Canada, and South Africa were closed.

Then came 1939, and the German attack on Poland.

World War Two

The Poles were a coarse people, immersed in medieval Catholicism. Invited by the early Polish kings to vitalize the country's economy, the Jews were promised certain rights despite the Church. Indeed, the Jews wrought miracles in the backward country. They built cities and industries; they were the major writers and poets. The "thanks" they received was the full cooperation of their Polish neighbors in the obliteration of three-and-a-half million Jews in Poland — one-tenth of the country's population.

---

1. A Jew could help himself and his family by converting to Roman Catholicism. The Church would help him get a government job. Yet, despite the poverty and oppression, there were few takers. I don't know if there were two dozen converts in the entire country.

The Poles benefited from the annihilation of their Jewish countrymen. They were able to take over Jewish homes and businesses with impunity. With the clergy fanning the flames of hate, the Germans were sure of full cooperation from the locals and the Church. For that reason, most of the concentration camps were established in Poland. After a great deal of enthusiastic labor, the Poles and their Church achieved their aim: a Jew-free Poland.

Churchill had a very low opinion of the Poles, calling Poland "a beast of prey... glorious in revolt and ruin, squalid and shameful in triumph" (*The Gathering Storm*, p. 323). It was a nation of sycophants who cherished their so-called honor above all. Every bum and beggar must be addressed as "Sir." As a Pole would say, *"Pieniaddze nie mam ale honor man"* ("I have no money, but I have my honor"). In this quest for self-aggrandizement, Polish history books have been routinely falsified: Every king was a hero and every soldier courageous. Yet in a thousand years they rarely won a war. Gorki, the great Russian writer, perfectly characterized the character of the people with the term *"gordee Lyakh"* — Polish hubris.

In 1939, Poland boasted an 18th-century army of horses and sabers. Not surprisingly, when Germany attacked in September of that year, the entire country fell apart in a matter of weeks! The Commander-in-Chief, Marshal Ridz Smigly, abandoned his post and vanished without a trace, while President Ignacy Moscicki pulled out his dusty old Swiss passport and fled to Switzerland. Government officials and army generals were ludicrously pathetic in their haste to reach the Romanian border in search of asylum.

The ignorant Polish government had called on 12 cavalry divisions — that is, soldiers riding on horses — to defend their country against Germany's 17 armored mechanized divisions! The cavalry actually lost the war to German motorcycles. The Germans used three-wheeled motorcycles which seated two: A basket adjoining the driver's seat held a soldier with a machine-gun. An armada of these motorcycles would burst into a town at full speed, backed by tanks. The horses panicked merely from the roar of the motorcycles! They would go wild, rearing up so high that the mounted soldiers could hardly stay in the saddle; indeed, more often than not they'd fall over together with their horses. With sword in one hand and horse's bridle in the other, the Poles stood ready to chop off their enemies' heads — while the enemy marched against them with spitting machine-guns. These motorcycles, sowing panic among the infantry, engineered the defeat of Poland.

The Eastern Army, charged with the job of holding the Soviet border, gave up without firing a shot. The country was mortified and humiliated. Poland's honor had been terribly mutilated.[1] But instead of blaming the calamity on the blindness and stupidity of its leaders, the nation found an excuse in "the Russian stab in the back" — and, of course, they blamed the Jews. In Vilna, the populace expressed its frustration at the country's defeat by instigating a pogrom against the Jews. However, with the appearance of only five Soviet tanks in the streets, the pogrom was over. The cowards took to their heels and disappeared.

The Polish Underground and the Jews

The well-armed Polish underground, known as the A.K. ("*Armja Krajowa*"), fully cooperated with the Germans in destroying the Jews. General Komorowski, commander of the A.K., refused to donate a single bullet to aid the Jewish uprisings in Warsaw, Bialystok and other towns. Acting on instructions from the Polish government-in-exile in London, the Polish Army in the USSR, under the command of General Anders, kicked out all the Jews (including me) before departing to Iran, Iraq, and Palestine. The clergy preached that it was a sin to save a Jewish life. Hence,

---

1. The humiliation grew worse when it became known that large army units and their officers crossed the border into Lithuania. That tiny country — under the impression that the "*Lankijos*" (Poles) had invaded them, and ignorant of the fact that the Polish army had already disintegrated — mobilized their own minuscule army . . . only to find the Poles laying down their arms and asking for asylum!

when the Poles captured Rudolf Hess, the commandant of the Auschwitz concentration camp and put him on trial, the local priest of the city of Auschwitz stepped forward to testify for the defense! He stated under oath that the commandant and his family — along with all the other camp officials and their families — attended church every Sunday. It was well known, too, that any Jew who managed to return alive from one of the death camps or from the forest was enthusiastically hounded down and butchered by the Poles.

The Prime Minister of the Polish government-in-exile, Stanislav Mikolajczyk, published a book entitled *Zgwalcenie Polski* (The Rape of Poland). In the entire book of 309 pages, he spared exactly 15 words on the subject of the annihilation of Poland's Jewish population. On page 123, he writes that "3,200,000 Jews were put to death in Poland, in history's greatest outrage against a nation."

Chaya Elbaum Dorembus and her husband managed to escape from the Warsaw ghetto. They lived in Warsaw with false papers, posing as Polish Catholics. In her book, *Oyf Der Arisher Seit* (On the Aryan Side), she recalls the fierce animosity of the Poles. After the Jewish ghetto uprising, the Germans burned the place down. Poles, witnessing Jewish women holding their children in their arms as they jumped from windows to their deaths, danced with glee. "*Zydki sie pala* (The Jews are burning)! *Zydki sie snaza* (The Jews are being fried)!" Their only regret was reserved for the furniture. "Such good furniture going up in flames. We could have used those things. They should have eradicated the Jews with poison, like rats. Then all the furniture and the apartments would have been left for us!"

The Role of the Ukraine

Historically, the most vicious pogroms of all took place in the Ukraine. In the Ukrainians' centuries-long bid for independence, they set awash a sea of Jewish blood.

The Cossack Bogdan Chmielnicki (1595-1657) organized a Ukrainian army and led a revolt against the Poles. Apart from his political agenda, he was bent on eradicating the Jews from the Ukraine. During the massacres of 1648-9, known in Jewish history as the *gezeiras tach vetat*, he wiped out some 300 Jewish communities, murdering 100,000 Jewish men, women, and children.

In the end he was forced to abandon his dream of Ukrainian independence and to hand over the Ukraine to the *Moscales*, the Russians of Moscow. Today the Ukrainian city, Chmielnicki, is named for him.

The next "freedom fighter" was Mazzepa (1645-1709). He, too, tried and failed to win independence for the Ukraine, spilling a great deal of Jewish blood in the process.

After the First World War, Semyon Petlura (1879-1926) proclaimed himself *Attaman* (commander-in-chief of the Ukrainian Army). In 1919 he declared the Ukraine an independent state and joined the Poles in fighting the Red Army. Petlura was responsible for butchering thousands of Jews.

When the Bolsheviks pushed the Ukrainian Army and their Polish allies out of the Ukraine, Petlura moved his headquarters to Kamenitz-Podolsk in southern Ukraine, which was then under the control of his friends, the Poles — only to be betrayed by Poland's signing of the Brest-Litovsk treaty with the Bolsheviks in 1922. Petlura escaped to Paris, where he announced the establishment of a Ukrainian government-in-exile.

On May 26, 1926, a Jew named Sholom Schwartzbard assassinated Petlura on a Paris street. He then went to the police and declared, "I just killed Petlura the Pogromchik, who murdered many Jews, including my family." The greatest lawyers of Paris volunteered to undertake his defense. After studying the tragic tale of the pogroms, the French court acquitted Schwartzbard.

～○～

In 1935, the Polish Minister for Internal Affairs, Colonel Pieracki, was assassinated on a Warsaw street. The police arrested one Stepan Bandera, a student at the Politechnicum and a leader in the Ukrainian youth organization. Bandera was convicted and sentenced to life imprisonment. However, when the Germans attacked and defeated Poland in 1939, all the prisons were opened and Bandera was released. He was free to become the leader of the Ukrainians.

Bandera went to Berlin, where he was presented to Hitler. The German Führer promised him an independent Ukrainian state; in return, Bandera promised to help with the eradication of the Jews and to organize a number of divisions to fight the Russians.

Of course, Hitler never had any intention of freeing the Ukraine. "Give me the Ukraine, and I will feed all of Europe," he wrote. But he did permit the raising of the Ukrainian flag on the Polish border.

Bandera, on the other hand, lived up to his promises. He organized two military divisions, which were armed by the Germans. And in every town he established a Ukrainian *Hilfs Polizei* (auxiliary police) whose primary job was to kill all the town's Jewry. In Babi-Yar alone, they massacred 130,000 Jews. Most of the ghetto and concentration-camp guards were Bandera men. (John Demjanjuk, who was recently put on trial in Israel, was a Bandera man.)

At the end of the war, with the Germans in retreat, Bandera's men — knowing the fate that awaited them at the hands of the Russians — fled to Germany. The Christian nations, including America, which had locked their doors to every single Jewish refugee, opened them wide for the Bandera murderers. With the Vatican's help, they all emigrated to Canada, Australia, and America.

Bandera himself established his headquarters in Munich, Germany, the more easily to maintain underground contact with his gangs inside the USSR. In 1959, a Ukrainian named Stashinski managed to worm his way onto Bandera's staff. One rainy day, as Bandera waited for a streetcar, the man pointed his umbrella at him and fired one shot. It was a poisoned bullet. Bandera dropped to the pavement, dying instantly. To the

Germans, the assassin presented himself as a Soviet agent. In those days the Germans were afraid of the Russians. They gave the agent a light sentence.

Revolutionary Winds

Every Shabbos, in the spacious home of the Kollaker *Poretz* in Lomza, the younger generation met to debate the Jews' political situation under the czar. Every home and every group of young people was a mirror of the times: a hodgepodge of Democrats, Social Democrats, constitutional monarchists, anarchists, Socialists and agrarian reformists.[1] Communists — that is, the Marxist left wing of the Socialist Party — were a rarity. Despite

---

1. It is interesting to study the ideas that are born out of desperation. Brooding on the cruel pogroms that periodically rocked the Jews of Eastern Europe, Dr. Eliezer Zamenhoff, resident of Bialystok (some 80 kilometers from Lomza), came up with an innovative notion. In a lengthy article published in 1882, entitled, "Finally, What Can We Do?" Dr. Zamenhoff wrote:

> "We should find a relatively unpopulated corner of the United States of America. We should announce that this spot is designated for Jews from all corners of the world, and we should direct all refugees there. In the beginning, they will be governed by the authorities of the U.S. When they become a majority and their numbers reach 60,000, they will be permitted, according to the constitutional laws of the U.S.A., to legally proclaim statehood and join the federation of the other states ... This is the best way to solve the refugee problem and the easiest way to solve the Jewish problem — a most easy way, because there is no need for great fortunes, for wars, or for bloodshed. For that purpose, we need only one thing: to ask for that piece of land and present it to the people." He ended the article with these words: "Go, my people, to our home on the banks of the Mississippi."

Desperation, it seems, is the mother of naïveté. This same Dr. Zamenhoff, in his great innocence, claimed that wars arise through the inability of different peoples to communicate with one another. Hence, he devised a new "international" language, called "Esperanto," to enable nations to communicate! Esperanto clubs sprang up in major cities all over Europe — but peace did not come.

(In his later years, Dr. Zamenhoff realized that Esperanto could not replace *chibas Tzion* [love of Zion], and he raised funds to support the *Bilu'im* [young Russians who pioneered land settlement in Palestine].)

vehement differences among the proponents of these points of view, all agreed on one thing: The czar must go. The labor class was nothing more than a slave class, as were the millions of peasants in the Russian Empire.

Within the Jewish community, the Socialist Party or Bund was the most prominent political party. In their naïveté, they claimed that removing the czar and educating the Russian *muzhik* (peasant) would make anti-Semitism vanish. The Zionists, however, laughed at them. "You want to give every Russian a doctorate? They'll hate the Jews even more! Anti-Semitism comes to them with their mother's milk, taught by their Church. Let's get out of here and build our own land — our own *Eretz Yisrael*."

The *Rav* and *Rosh Yeshivah* of Lida, R' Yaakov Reines, said, "Ninety percent of the Jews are *frum* (Torah observant). Let's take over the Zionist organization and build an *Eretz Yisrael* based on Torah." He founded *Mizrachi,* the religious Zionist organization. This group, like all of Zionism, was forbidden under the czar, and its operations as well as the raising of funds strictly illegal.

Reb Chaim Velvl loved to listen to the young people's discussions. From time to time he would take part in them, taking the role of "elder statesman."

"You youngsters are like the motor in a machine," he would say, "running away at full speed. It can maim, damage, and kill. You need us, the older generation, to put the brakes on you."

There was one girl, daughter of his chassidic neighbor Reb Mendel Olach, who would answer him with spirit, "Reb Chaim Velvl, you older people are not the brakes. You are the sand in the machine. You slow the machine down, and will end by ruining it altogether. You kill the enthusiasm of the young! Of course you are scared of the revolution — you're a former *poretz*, and still a wealthy man. But the revolution will come, like it or not!"

Rosa, an avid Bundist, was very bitter about the Zionists. She called their vision of rebuilding *Eretz Yisrael* "an empty dream, a false dream. Who wants to go to the desert and die of malaria?

Lenin is right: Zionism was invented by the Jewish capitalists to divert the attention of the Jewish labor class from the fight against capitalism and the czar. We Socialists (the word "Communism" had not yet been coined) are for building a better life for all people!"

But even outspoken Rosa Olach listened when Reb Chaim Velvl spoke. He told them, "In our Torah, one of the greatest of all sins is idol worship. An idol does not necessarily have to be a human being, an animal, or an inanimate object. It can also be an idea. In our day, Marxism is an idol *par excellence!*

"We Jews are concerned not only with a book's contents, but also with the character of its author. Now let's take your new idol, Karl Marx. He is a genius, no question about it. The fact that he's convinced so many people to accept his ideas proves his greatness. But who is the man who wrote this book? Did he practice what he preached?

"Marx's entire family converted to Christianity when he was only five years old. He grew up hating Jews — a result of normal Church teachings. Even later, when he proclaimed himself an atheist, his animosity toward the Jews remained, and his writings are full of anti-Semitic slogans.

"Karl Marx had a faithful follower whose name was Friedrich Engels. Neither Marx nor Engels was able to earn a living, but luckily Engels' father died and left him millions. With those millions he supported Marx. When Marx's two daughters reached marriageable age, he turned again to his patron: 'I need a dowry for my daughters. Friedrich, you don't expect my daughter to marry some common laborer!' Here is your idol, revealing his true face. Here is the man who would save the labor class — who would save the whole world — yet would not dream of permitting his own daughter to marry a common working man.

"Foolish children, the oppression of the czar makes you grab at anything, the way a drowning man will grasp even at a straw. You place your faith in a man who cannot and will not help you or your world. The Torah says that poverty and the poor will never vanish from the face of the earth. Along comes Marx and says that he will do just that — and you believe him! My children, remember one thing: Every socialist leader, every socialist writer, was anti-Semitic. From Karl Marx to Lenin, they all hated the Jews!"

⊸◦⊶

The end of the First World War found the Russians tired of fighting. Four years of destruction and millions of casualties were enough for them. The country's Social Democrats persuaded the czar to abdicate. A *Duma* (parliament) was elected for the first time in a thousand years. The Russian masses got their first taste of democracy.

It lasted just six months. Then the left wing of the Socialist Party, under the leadership of Lenin and Trotsky, proclaimed a Bolshevik majority and organized gangs to encircle the parliament building and arrest government officials. (The Prime Minister and Minister of Justice, Professor Kerenski, managed to leap from a window; eventually he made his way to America.) Lenin established a Soviet government based on Marxism, and Trotsky organized a Red Army of Workers and Peasants.

The generals and soldiers who remained loyal to the czar were known as the Whites, and for a while they fought the Reds bitterly. The Whites also found time to murder thousands of Jews, whom they accused of undermining the czar's regime, in vicious pogroms. At the same time, the Reds accused the Jews of being capitalists and opposing the Revolution!

In Poland, Marxist agitation was against the law. The Socialists held a May Day demonstration every year, at which young Rosa Olach was always present. With the years she became one of its most fervent orators. It wasn't long before she was arrested for possession of Communist literature. At her trial, her brokenhearted parents, old Reb Mendel Olach and his wife, pleaded with the judge to have mercy on their only child. The judge relented; instead of the mandatory 10-year sentence, he sentenced her to "only" eight.

By that time, my grandfather was bedridden and dying. The old couple, his neighbors, came to visit, and begged Reb Chaim Velvl to write to Marshal Pilsudski, asking for clemency. "After all, Kollaker *Poretz*, you once saved his life!"

It grieved my grandparents to think of the only child of their dear neighbors spending her best years in prison. *Zeide* dictated a letter and *Bobbe* wrote:

To the Savior of Poland, *Marszalek* Juzef Pilsudski

Dear Sir,

If you remember the blacksmith's shop in the village of Kollaki, *Powiat Lomze* (Lomza district), you will, sir, remember me. I am Chaim Velvl Szeniak, owner of Kollaki until the agrarian reform took away my land. I am writing to plead for a young, brilliant girl named Rosa Olach. She has been convicted to a term of eight years for Communist activities. She is the only child of two old parents, broken now in pain and humiliation.

I'm not writing to argue about the law. I fully approve of the law, for Communism is the enemy of Poland and also of the Jews. However, Sir *Marszalek*, we of the older generation, who suffered so much and so long from the tyranny of the czars, must look into the matter. What makes young people cling to this terrible idea of Communism? The girl in this case is young, has a brilliant mind, and is a gifted orator. How did she fall into the clutches of Communism? Why, in fact, does Communism appeal to intellectuals?

I do not speak only of Jewish youngsters. Look at the Ukrainians. The government changed their name to Ruthenians and doesn't permit them their own schools — all in order to cut them off from their Soviet Ukrainian brethren. Did it help? The fact is, that while the old Ukrainians hate the Russians as much as the Poles do, and oppose Communism like sensible people, the Ukrainian youth is poisoned with Communism. Many of them have crossed the border to the Ukrainian Soviet Republic. Why?

The answer is — discrimination. Give a young person hope, a decent living, and an opening in life, and he will reject Communism. As much as the Jews have hoped, prayed and fought for an independent Poland, we've been terribly disappointed. In this entire country of ours, except for the army and the *Sejm* there is not a single Jew on the government payroll. Government jobs are totally closed to qualified Jews, while the Soviets spend millions on propaganda about free education, jobs for all, and the lack of discrimination under their system. Is it any wonder that the younger generation falls for these Bolshevik lies?

The parents of this young girl are very religious people. They raised her in the old faith and taught her loyalty for our country. They did not fail in the upbringing of their only child. It is the government — our government — that has failed her!

So please, *Wielemorzny Pan Marszalek* (Most Honorable Sir Marshal), do something about this girl. I think she can be saved. Once she's had a taste of prison life, we can persuade her that a Communist life is actually no different. Please grant her a pardon for the sake of her old, suffering parents.

Marshal Pilsudsky did indeed remember Kollaki and the *hrabia* (*poretz*). He immediately sent his recommendation for a pardon to the president. The president subsequently informed Rosa's parents that he would be glad to sign a pardon, provided Rosa would openly declare that she rejected Communism and was resigning from the Communist Party. The parents happily took the letter to the prison warden and requested a meeting with their daughter.

The Olachs showed the letter to Rosa. They begged her to do what the president asked and go home with them, a free woman. Rosa replied, "Suppose they asked you to convert to Catholicism

— would you do it? Of course not. Well, I cannot do this either!"

The poor old mother fell to Rosa's feet, weeping, but still Rosa persisted in her refusal. Then her father cried out in rage, "You compare Communism to our holy faith? You say you want to change the whole world. You want to save all the proletariat — but you have no mercy on your own mother!" With great difficulty, he pulled his wife from the girl's feet and took her away.

Before he died, R' Chaim Velvl wrote once again to Pilsudski, telling him that the president's conditions could not be met. "Please, Sir Marshal. Before I die, I hope to see the girl free."

Pilsudski did as he asked — but my *zeide* died one day before Rosa was unconditionally released from prison.

Following the Communist Dream

Communist propaganda was very strong among the younger generation — and very successful. Millions poured into Poland from Moscow for the underground propaganda apparatus of the illegal Polish Communist Party. As a result of Polish oppression and joblessness, young Jews did not see a future for themselves. The world of emigration was tightly sealed; there was a long waiting list to enter America, a very limited British admissions policy in Palestine, and hardly a crack open in Australia, South Africa, or Latin America. The young people, in their frustration, turned to the USSR as their new Garden of Eden.

The Polish Ministry would not issue passports for travel to Communist Russia. Hence, hundreds — perhaps thousands — of naive boys and girls stole across the border into the USSR. Once there, they quickly discovered the true conditions of life in that country — but by then it was too late to return. They were not permitted to go back to Poland or even write a letter home which might tell the tale of their disillusion. As was later discovered, many of them were subsequently accused of spying for Poland, for the fascists, or for America. They wound up in prison for life, though no one in Poland ever knew about it. Frantic parents made inquiries at the Soviet Embassy, but to no avail. Their children had disappeared without a trace. Poland, with all its poverty and anti-Semitism, was a haven compared with the Soviet regime.

After her release from prison, Rosa lived quietly for a year — and then vanished. Everyone knew that she must have gone to Russia. Her mother died of a broken heart. The father sat *shivah* for his wife and mourned for his daughter. The mother had gone to Heaven, and Rosa — to the Soviet "heaven!"

What Happened to Rosa

Rosa Olach's story is historically interesting, in that it follows the fate of one Jewish girl in the difficult years between the two world wars — a path that in many ways mirrored the ideals of the youth of her time. Let us follow the story to its conclusion. To do so, we must take a slight detour into Soviet territory.

At that time, the Soviet Kommisar[1] for Foreign Affairs was Maxim Litvinov. His real name was Meyer Wallach. Like other hard-core Bolshevik revolutionaries, he'd stopped using his original name for fear of the czar's *ochrana*, or secret police. Hence, Ulyanov became Lenin; Bronstein became Trotsky; Dzugashvili became Stalin; Skriabin became Molotov; and Meyer Wallach became Maxim Litvinov. Litvinov served as foreign minister for over 20 years. In 1939, when Stalin decided to make his infamous pact with Hitler, he found the Jew Litvinov an encumbrance. He was replaced by Vyacheslav Molotov.

Litvinov had been born in Bialystok to a family of Orthodox Jews. The Polish government did not bother the family of the mighty Soviet Union's foreign minister; still, one of the Wallach brothers feared the authorities enough to change his name to Olach and sever his ties with his Soviet nephew. This was the

---

1. Lenin dreamed of creating a "Soviet" person, totally devoid of capitalistic tendencies! Thus the title *Minister* was changed to *Kommisar*.

very same Mendel Olach, my grandfather's chassidic neighbor and father of the missing Rosa. The fact that Reb Mendel was uncle to Maxim Litvinov was a closely guarded secret.

When Rosa disappeared into the Soviet Union to follow her socialist dream, her father feared for her life. He was certain that the Soviet authorities would accuse his daughter of spying for Poland; after all, the usual 10-year sentence the Polish courts meted out to every Communist had been shortened to eight, and Rosa had actually been released from prison after only one year. The Soviets, he believed, would reason that Rosa was a provocateur — a Polish agent within the Communist Party, sent into their country to spy on them.

After six months without word from Rosa, Reb Mendel Olach went to see his brother in Bialystok. "According to the newspapers, your son is coming to Geneva as head of the Soviet delegation to the session of the League of Nations. Please, Yankel, go and see him. He must find my daughter, my Rosa. She might be languishing in a prison there!"

Yankel Wallach hadn't seen his son in years or held any communication with him; but his brother's tears extracted a promise from him to go to Geneva. The Swiss police charged with guarding the Soviet delegation were shocked and astounded when the bearded Jew came up to them, claiming to be father to the Foreign Minister of the USSR. They reported the matter to their Soviet counterparts, who replied that the man must be crazy: Litvinov's father had died in Russia years ago. But Yankel Wallach declared a hunger strike and refused to leave until his son agreed to see him!

The Swiss guards finally permitted him to enter the building, where he convinced the Soviet guards to deliver a note to Litvinov, written in Yiddish. He was finally admitted. No one knows what father and son discussed in their meeting. But there was still no word about Rosa.

It is time now for another detour on the road to Rosa.

There were two cousins named Yaffe. R' Yisrael Yaffe lived in

Lomza. He was the great-grandson of R' Chaim Volozhiner, the founder of the first great *yeshivah* in Europe. Reb Yisrael, an illustrious *talmid chacham* in his own right, married the daughter of the Lomza Rav, R' Eliezer Simchah Rabinowitz, and settled there. He was a well-to-do man, earning his living by appraising lands and forests. When large landowners bought or sold forest or land, R' Yisrael was called in as an expert: He could calculate to the minutest degree the amount of timber and firewood the land contained, and cannily estimate their quality and value. He was a great philanthropist. Not only did a large share of his money go to charity, but he was personally involved in helping many people as well. If, for example, a family was evicted from their apartment for not paying the rent, Reb Yisrael would pay up for the next six months — and then help carry the furniture back into the apartment.

R' Yisrael Yaffe died childless. My father and a few friends published a small book in his memory; it was entitled *HaTzvi Yisrael* (The Beauty of Israel). My father wrote a moving eulogy to Reb Yisrael, in which he speculated that Heaven had held back from granting children to Reb Yisrael in order to eliminate the possibility that the illustrious heritage that went back to R' Chaim Volozhiner would remain untarnished through possibly unworthy offspring. "Rest in peace, Reb Yisrael. You have fulfilled your task completely. You have restored the crown of *yichus* to the way it was in previous generations."

One day, Mendel Olach received a visit from Reb Yisrael Yaffe, a fellow Lomzer. He came with good tidings. "Reb Mendel, we are now related. My cousin in Moscow wrote to me that he married your daughter!"

Reb Yisrael Yaffe's cousin was Vladimir Yaffe, a Bolshevik who worked his way up the political ladder in Moscow. Lenin appointed him his Vice Kommisar of Foreign Affairs, the equivalent of the American Assistant Secretary of State. An interesting story is told about the time Vladimir Yaffe was appointed as head of the Soviet delegation that was slated to meet with a delegation from tiny Lithuania to settle a border dispute. His counterpart in the talks was Dr. Shimshon Rosenbaum, Vice-Minister for Foreign Affairs of the newly independent Lithuania. When the two teams had sat down at the table, Kommissar Yaffe, tongue-in-cheek, asked Dr. Rosenbaum, "How far would you like the borders of your republic to go?"

Dr. Rosenbaum, also tongue-in-cheek, replied, "As far as the Jews *daven nussach Lita* (the Lithuanian variation of the Jewish prayer book)."

An old Russian member of the Soviet delegation

My father's tribute to R' Yisrael Yaffe

thought they were talking about a few villages. "Well, now," he said, "I think there are grounds for a settlement."

Both Jews burst into laughter. Said Yaffe, "Comrade, he wants not only Minsk, but Kiev and Moscow too!"[1]

It was this same Vladimir Yaffe who had married Rosa Olach. It was the first news of Rosa since her disappearance. Like the rest of her adopted countrymen, she did not dare write a letter to her father back in Poland. To everyone's surprise, however, the two Yaffe cousins corresponded openly, apparently unafraid of repercussions in either Poland or the Soviet Union. Rumor had it that Reb Yisrael did not fear the Polish authorities because of his connections with the aristocracy of that country; but more importantly, because the Foreign Ministry used him as their "back door" to his cousin in the Soviet foreign ministry, and vice versa.

---

1. It is interesting to note that Dr. Rosenbaum, Yaffe's counterpart, was Consul General of the Lithuanian Republic in Jerusalem until the day he died.

Then Lenin appointed Vladimir Yaffe the Soviet Ambassador to Berlin. Old Reb Mendel finally received his first letter from his daughter, posted from Berlin. But his happiness was short lived. The historical events soon to take place in Moscow had their effect on Mendel Olach and his daughter, Rosa.

In 1918, Lenin was shot by Dora Caplan, a Jewish student at Moscow University. A Social Democrat, she attacked Lenin because he had destroyed democracy in her country. Lenin's bodyguards shot and killed her on the spot, but Lenin himself lingered on in the hospital for several years before he died. During those years, Stalin wormed his way into power and took over the reins of government.

The first thing he did was order a *chistka* (clean-up job), which killed off all the old party Bolsheviks and revolutionaries. Vladimir Yaffe, Ambassador to Berlin, was recalled. Knowing what to expect, he committed suicide. Rosa, his wife, disappeared from the face of the earth, like so many of her unfortunate fellow citizens.

How she survived all those years of imprisonment no one knows. But in 1985 a report filtered back from Tel Aviv: "The 90-year-old Mrs. Yaffe, wife of the former Soviet Ambassador to Berlin who committed suicide in fear of Stalin, has arrived in Israel!"

Mother Zion opens her arms to all her children, even the renegade children who had once spat in her face and rejected her. She opened her arms and heart to welcome Rosa Olach Yaffe. After years of suffering, Rosa had come home.

Chapter 10:
Destruction and Renewal

The Holocaust

Questions. There are so many questions. We, the Jewish people, are used to pogroms, "little" ones and big ones; but the extraordinary scope of the Holocaust boggles the mind. Six million individuals, a million and a half children — this amazing enterprise of killing is something unheard of in the history of humankind. Entire nations — Christian nations — dedicated their energy to the eradication of our people. Poles, Lithuanians, and Ukrainians, our neighbors of yesterday, turned overnight into bloodthirsty beasts — not to mention, of course, the Germans themselves. And the rest of the Christian world locked their doors, so that no Jew might escape.

To those like myself, who lost an entire family in the inferno, the questions bombard the mind through sleepless nights: Why? How? For what purpose? And then there's the opposite question: Why me? Why was I chosen to remain alive? Guilt!

In my tank uniform

The questions are there, and they are pressing. But there is not a single human being who can answer even one of them. When Aaron *HaKohen*, the High Priest of Israel, saw his two sons die right before his eyes, he too must have had many questions. But the Torah says, *"Vayidom Aharon."* ("And Aharon kept silent.")When there are no answers, silence is the best — the only — answer.

In the absence of a humanly comprehensible rationale for the events we've witnessed, we are forced to conclude that there is an invisible, Divine logic behind it all. This is the meaning of *emunah*, faith. This faith in the transcendental should not be difficult for the modern-day mind to grasp. We have become accustomed to believing in the unseeable. For instance, we see no one playing an instrument, yet we can hear music. Up until a short time ago, no one knew of the invisible waves that carry sound through the air. The human ear is limited: It can pick up sounds for 100 feet, perhaps 200, but no more. A radio, however, can pick up sounds from across the globe!

Who would have thought, 100 years ago, that a person might stand in one room and see things that are taking place a 1,000 miles away? Yet now we know that invisible waves carry images through the air — images that can be discerned by wires and cables, but not by the human eye.

Now we come to the human brain, which, along with our power of speech, distinguishes us from animals. We can teach a dog all sorts of tricks, but never that two plus two equals four. Yet even our mighty minds are limited. When Albert Einstein died some 40 years ago in Princeton, New Jersey, his family discovered that his brain was missing. They finally tracked down the culprit: the local pathologist. He protested that a brain such as Einstein's comes along only once in 1,000 years, and should be preserved for scientific research. The family gave their consent. The pathologist, now retired, lives in Witchita, Kansas, where he keeps Einstein's brain in a glass jar. During the last 40 years he has handed out slices of the brain to scores of scientists who wished to study it. To date, not one of those scientists has found anything in Einstein's brain that is different from any normal human brain! The difference, obviously, is qualitative, not quantitative. The awesome mystery of human intelligence is not something that can be discerned by the tools at our disposal. Here, again, is something intangible, whose effects can be witnessed and measured — but not its Source.

When Moshe *Rabbeinu* asked to "see" G-d, he was refused with the words, "*Ki lo yiraini odom vachai.*" ("For no human being can see Me and live.") We cannot see Hashem with our eyes, nor grasp Him with our puny human brains. And just as we are unable to see Him, so also is our understanding simply too limited to encompass His reasoning.

We all know that a chair does not grow in the forest. A lumberjack cuts down the tree and slices it into lumber; a carpenter takes that lumber and builds a chair from it. But does the chair know who built it or how it was made? Certainly not! A chair is inanimate; it has no mind with which to understand. When it comes to G-d, we humans are like that chair. Our human intelligence is not capable of encompassing the Divine. As *Rambam* explains, we can know Him only through His handiwork. And just as we do not — *cannot* — know Him, we cannot know His ways or the reasons for His actions.

We of the Torah world know that the Vilna *Gaon* was greater than 10 Einsteins, and that the Talmudic sage Rabbi Akiva was greater than many Vilna *Gaons,* or hundreds of Einsteins. Yet when the 10 sages of the Talmud were killed, they too, apparently, had questions. The answer came from Above: "*Gezeirah hi milfonai vekabluha!* ("It is My decree — accept it!")

In other words, don't ask questions.

A true believer asks no questions, for he knows that the answers are inaccessible to him. An awareness of the inability of some people to cope with tragedy prompted a certain chassidic *rebbe* to comment that the reason so little is recorded about the pogroms and massacres in Jewish history is because it was feared that the details of suffering and death could drive an individual to apostasy. If that was true in the past, then how much more so in the case of our recent *Churban* (Holocaust), whose sheer scope and brutality in the avowed goal of trying to annihilate our entire nation could drive a person to insanity and apostasy!

Of Bombs and Plows

I remember when the United States dropped the atom bomb on Hiroshima. I was still in the Polish Army in the U.S.S.R. then, and information was hard to come by. The only news we used to get was the weekly lecture by the *politrook* (political officer), which was invariably full of lies and communist propaganda. Hungry for hard facts, I would lock myself in my tank and play with the radio. Though a tank radio has a limited radius of only 25 kilometers or so, sometimes I would pick up a German station, or occasionally a Russian or Polish one. That day, I heard a brief line about the "atomic bomb" that had been dropped on "Giroshima." (The Cyrillic alphabet does not contain the letter H. The Russians can't pronounce this sound, and replace it with a G. Hence, Eisenhower is Eisengower and Hiroshima is Giroshima.) I knew what a bomb was — I'd witnessed its effects in Lomza, Stalingrad, and Warsaw — but the word "atomic" was a puzzle to me, as was the name "Giroshima."

It was only on the following Sunday that the *politrook* told us all about the ultrapowerful bomb that had been dropped on Hiroshima. For days, I went about in a trance. "*Ribbono Shel Olam*! You have such a beautiful bomb, and you drop it on Japan? What a waste! On Germany, Poland, Lithunia, Ukraine — that's where the bomb belongs, not on Japan! You should have asked *me* where to drop it!"

I was reading the Book of *Job* at the time, from the small *Tanach* I always carried with me (I have it to this very day.) I didn't understand much of it, yet I came upon four words that stuck in my mind: *"Aifo hayisa beyosdi aretz?"* ("Where were you when I created the world?") At once, all my questions vanished. It was as though Hashem was speaking directly to me. "You little nobody, you little fly, here one minute and the next in the grave! Are you going to tell Me how to run My business?"

The Dubner *Maggid* has a beautiful *mashal.* The last lines of the *Navi Amos* tell us, "The plowing man will meet the harvester." Apparently, we are talking about two different people, for one man cannot meet himself. Plowing is done in the spring, while the harvest takes place in the fall, six months later. How, then, do the two meet?

The Dubner answers with a parable. A city man walked out into the countryside for the first time in his life. He was tremendously impressed by the scenery, the beautiful landscape and lovely green grass. Then he noticed, in a nearby field, a farmer beginning to plow up the soil.

"That's outrageous!" he thought indignantly. "He's ruining that field. Instead of beautiful grass, we now have dirt!" Then he saw the farmer scatter kernels of wheat into the turned-over soil. "That crazy man could have used the wheat to bake bread for the poor! Why is he being so wantonly destructive?" He went home to the city, full of anger, complaints, and unanswered questions.

Six months later, as he walked in that vicinity once more, he saw the beautiful field full of growing wheat, each stalk of which brought the farmer a profit 25 times greater than the original kernel he'd sown. Suddenly, all the man's complaints vanished, and all his questions were answered.

The *Navi* is telling us this: When Heaven plows under the Jewish people, we are full of complaints, full of questions. But the day will come when all will be understood, and all the questions answered at last.

Christianity and the Holocaust

Professor Harry James Cargas, Professor of Literature and Language at Webster College in St. Louis, author of more than 20 books, and a Catholic, published a book entitled *Shadows of Auschwitz*, or "A Christian Response to the Holocaust." Dr. Cargas was the first Christian to state openly that "Christianity died in Auschwitz." He had the courage to bring into the open the criminality of the Christian clergy — not only during the Holocaust, but over a 2,000-year span.

He quotes R' Michoel Ber Weissmandl from his book, *Min Hameitzar*, telling how Father Tiso, president of the puppet state of Slovakia, paid Eichmann 100 marks for every Jew he'd take out and kill, and how he helped load up 20,000 Jewish men, women, and children for deportation to Auschwitz. Rabbi Weissmandl managed to escape from the train and made it to the residency of the Papal Nuncio, the Vatican's ambassador to the Slovak Republic. He pleaded with the Nuncio to pressure the president to stop the trains. Father Tiso was still the local priest of his village, and thus continued to come under the jurisdiction of the Vatican.

The Nuncio replied that he did not take up secular matters on a Sunday. The rabbi, dumbfounded, burst into tears, for his wife and seven children were on that train. "Your Excellency! The lives of thousands of little innocent children are at stake, and you call that a secular matter?"

Eyes spitting hate, the Nuncio said, "There is no such thing as an innocent Jewish child. You'll all pay with your blood for the killing of our Saviour. Now get out, or I'll call the Gestapo!"

Rabbi Weissmandl also tells of the 82-year-old Archbishop Kmetko, to whom President Tiso acted as personal secretary for many years. An old rabbi, who was the same age and had known the archbishop for many years, was asked to go plead with him to stop the trains. To spare him, the rabbi was not told the real purpose of Auschwitz, but only that it was a labor camp.

The old rabbi said to the archbishop, "I understand that there is a war going on and the government needs labor — but what kind of labor can be had from women, children and babies?" The archbishop replied, "This is not merely a deportation. Where you are going you will not die from hard labor, hunger or epidemic. All of you — men, women, and children — will be murdered. It is a punishment that is due to you for the death of our Saviour! There is only one piece of advice for you: conversion to our faith. Only then will I try to stop the deportation!"

R' Michoel Ber Weissmandl

The true face of the clergy emerged on many different occasions. Here are just a few examples.

Dr. Lucas, a physician at Auschwitz, testified in court in his own defense, saying that he went on vacation to his native Austria, where he confided to the Archbishop of Asnabruck that he was injecting carbolic acid into the veins of Jewish children. The cleric's reply? "You are merely obeying orders."

The commandant of the Buchenwald concentration camp testified in court how he "confessed" to the clergy — including, specifically, the Archbishop of Insburg — to the effect that he'd killed Jews, including Jewish children. The archbishop replied, "You are only doing your duty."

Of the hundreds of chaplains in the German Army, both Catholic and Protestant, not one publicly protested or tried to stop the killings.

During the Eichmann trial in Jerusalem, the Israeli government assigned the Reverend William Hall, a Canadian missionary who'd been living in Jerusalem for 30 years, as personal chaplain to Eichmann. Reverend Hall failed to persuade Eichmann to return to his Church. Even in the face of impending execution, Eichmann remained to the last an unrepentant Nazi. Under questioning, Rev. Hall stated that, had Eichmann accepted his "Saviour," he would have immediately entered the gates of paradise without passing through purgatory at all.

Even though he had a hand in the murder of six million Jews? Hall was asked.

Had Eichmann embraced the Church before his execution, Hall replied, he would have been absolved of guilt and had a place in paradise.

And what of the souls of his six million Jewish victims?

They, Hall asserted, would certainly not have entered paradise; on the contrary, they were consigned to hell because they had not accepted the Church's "salvation."

Some, it seems, have placed a policeman at heaven's gates.

One Man's Search

I remember my search for Jews at the end of the war. The Soviet press had hardly ever made mention of concentration camps or the systematic destruction of the Jewish people. The first I heard of it was in Stalingrad, immediately after the Red Army had routed the Germans. I knew that there had been a thriving Jewish community there, for the *Rav* of my home town of Lomza had once served as *Rav* in Tzaritzin (Stalingrad's original name). As soon as I had the chance I went off in search of Jews — but couldn't find a single one. The local Russians told me how the Germans had rounded up all the Jews and shot them — men, women, and children. I didn't believe it!

As a soldier in the Red Army, I was totally cut off from civilian life and had no chance to further my search until I came to Berditchev, the town of R' Levi Yitzchak, the *Tzaddik* of

Berditchev. The gentiles had called the town *"Yevraiskaya Stolitze"* (the Jewish Capital) because 90 percent of its population was made up of Jews. As I traveled to the front, the trooptrain I was on made a stop in Berditchev. Our commanding officer told us we'd be staying there for three hours or longer. Off I went in search of Jews . . . *But I didn't find even one!* In the former "Jewish capital" I saw only Russians and Ukrainians.

In my officer's uniform

I remembered reading somewhere that R' Levi Yitzchak's *shtibl* was located on a hilltop. Looking around me, I saw that I was standing in front of a hill. I began to climb. At the top, I found only destruction — stones and bricks strewn around, the remains of a large, square building. Exhausted, I sat down on one of the stones.

It is not uncommon to see a soldier weeping. In the aftershock of battle, as he thinks of his lost and wounded comrades, the tears flow easily. And so, when those civilians passed by and saw a soldier in battle fatigues crying like a baby, they stopped to shake their heads, wipe away their own tears, and offer me food and schnapps. Little did they know that I was not coming from battle, but going into one.

It was time to *daven Minchah,* but there was a revolt churning inside me. How could I *daven?* The rumors about the total destruction of the Jews were true!

At that moment, I recalled an episode from my youth. My father had davened in the *Beis HaMidrash HaGadol,* with the *rav* sitting on the right side of the *Aron HaKodesh* and my father on the left. Next to the *rav* sat R' Alter Katzaneck, a gray old man who spent his entire day learning Torah. He lived on the monthly checks he received from his children in America. Hard of hearing, he would place himself on the bench directly in front of the *bimah* for the reading of the Torah, so as not to miss a word.

Once, as my friends and I ran around as small boys will do, he grabbed me. Screaming *"Shaygetz!"* ("Heathen!") R' Alter slapped me in the face.

After *davening,* my father walked over to the old man and said, "Reb Alter, you are right about the children making noise. But you have no right to give my Chaimke a *patch.* He is my child, and if a punishment is in order, I'll do it!"

Somehow, I couldn't shake off that episode. My heart was bleeding at the terrible reality around me. Inside I was all in a turmoil, yet the only words I could utter to Heaven were, *"Tatte in Himmel* (Father in Heaven)! Is this how You take care of Your children?"

I had a hard time overcoming my bitterness. When at last I *davened minchah,* it was more crying that praying, more complaining than pleading. I felt the presence of R' Levi Yitzchak; I was certain he had already mobilized the entire *Pamalya Shel Malah* (Heavenly Hosts), asking, "Where are the Jews of Berditchev?" Heartbroken, alone in the world, surrounded by enemies, I still had a Father to Whom I could cry, complain, and make demands!

On my arrival in America, the first thing I did was visit my father's friends and surviving alumni from Slobodka and Mir. My father had told me when I left home, "Wherever you go, seek out the *rav* or *rosh yeshivah.* He will surely be from either Slobodka or Mir, a friend of mine, and all doors will be opened for you."

My first stop was the East Side, to the home of our *Rav,* R' Moshe Shatzkes. He was visibly moved to see that one of Reb Alter Shapiro's sons had survived. As we sat down, I asked, "Does the *Rav* remember Reb Alter Katzaneck?"

"Of course. He was my *shochen* (neighbor) in *beis midrash.*"

I related the episode of Reb Alter and the *patch.* I did not have to spell out the parallel with recent events. The *rav* began to cry, but neither of us uttered a word. *Vayidom Aharon!*

The next visit was to my father's *chavrusah* (learning partner), R' Yechiel Mordechai Gordon, the Lomzer *Rosh Yeshivah.* I was amazed at his cheerful demeanor and ready smile, despite the still-fresh wound of the war just behind him. He embraced and kissed me, and in the course of the conversation invited me to join his *kollel*. Later, seated at his table, the revolt inside me burst out: "Does the *Rosh Yeshivah* remember Reb Alter Katzaneck?" I repeated the story; and again, I didn't have to finish it. He began weeping aloud, and so did I. I had re-opened the wounds, yet not a word was said. *Vayidom Aharon!*

R' Reuven Grozovsky

Next, I went to see my *Rosh Yeshivah* in Kamenitz and my father's *chavrusah* from Slobodka, R' Reuven Grozovsky. By then the Katzaneck episode had become my weapon, symbol of my inner revolt. When I told him of the episode, he raised his eyes to Heaven and said, "*Ah shtarkeh ta'aneh* — a strong argument! Truly, a powerful argument." And he burst into tears. Not another word was spoken. *Vayidom Aharon!*

R' Gordon suggested one day that I go visit Reb Yaakov Kamenetzky, whom I had never heard of. The *Rosh Yeshivah* explained that Reb Yaakov was my father's friend from their Slobodka days.

Reb Yaakov welcomed me warmly, but when he heard that I was Reb Alter Tiktiner's son, the welcome turned into a long embrace and a number of kisses. He said, "I'm glad you came tonight, for I have a guest from Seattle: Reb Alter Poplack, your father's best friend from their *yeshivah* days." Greenhorn that I was, I assumed that Seattle, Washington was a neighborhood of New York — like the Bronx — and easily accessible. To this day I can't forgive myself for not taking advantage of the occasion to ask Rabbi Poplack more about my father.

The two reminisced about my father, and spoke of the *sefer* he wrote on *Nazir*, as well as his *Piskei Tosafos* on *Nazir*. Then, as had

R' Avraham Kalmanowitz after the War. I am seated beside him. Standing behind us, L-R: R' Chaim Ginzburg and the Rav's three sons, R' Yisroel Yitzchok, R' Shraga Moshe, and R' Bezalel.

become my habit, I brought up my Katzaneck complaint, and the two burst into tears — tears of silence. *Vayidom Aharon!*

The following visit was to R' Avraham Kalmanowitz, the Rav of my second home town of Tiktin. The *"malach hago'el"* (redeeming angel) of the Mirrer Yeshivah, Rav Kalmanowitz had carried that *yeshivah* on his shoulders since 1914. He was also the founder of the Mirrer Yeshivah in Brooklyn.

R' Kalmanowitz was then sitting *shivah* for his father, who had passed away in Jerusalem. The crowd left at last, and there were just the two of us. He sat on a low stool, and I beside him. With his arm around me, we talked about Tiktin. I told him that I remembered how he had arranged for his parents, sister, brother-in-law, and their two children to leave the USSR during the Stalin regime — a veritable miracle. We spoke of the *yeshivah ketanah* (*yeshivah* high school) he founded, and which I had attended both before and after my *bar mitzvah*.

Against my will, the Katzaneck story shot out of me. *"Rebbi,"* I asked, "How could the Father in Heaven tolerate such a terrible *Churban?"*

He pressed me to his chest, kissed me, and a flood of tears flowed down his long white beard. We cried together for some minutes, until someone came in with the good news that the *rebbetzin* had given birth to a baby girl; mother and daughter were both doing fine. *Mazel tov!* . . . *Vayidom Aharon!*

I began to research the great men of our time. Had the *Gaon* R' Moshe Feinstein ever dealt, orally or in writing, with the Holocaust? The answer — "*Vayidom Aharon.*"

I asked the students of the Kletzker *Rosh Yeshivah*, R' Aharon Kotler, if he'd ever touched on the topic at *Shalosh Seudos* (the third Shabbos meal) or on other occasions, off the record. The answer, again, was "no." The three volumes of *Mishnas Reb Aharon* contain a total of 756 pages and 238 *ma'amorim* (articles). I checked every page, but not one talked about the *Churban*.

Vayidom Aharon!

Wedding in a D.P. Camp

It was in Nuremberg and Furth — which are actually twin cities — that I met a young girl with blue eyes and blonde hair and a face that lit up the darkness of those grim days. In the midst of the terrible postwar pain, so full of heartbreak, loneliness, and despair, she awakened in me feelings of fresh hope and optimism.

Her name was Haddasah, and like all survivors she had her story.

One night, the SS raided the Jewish homes of her native Sosnowiec in southwest Poland, and arrested all the Jewish girls. She was only 16 when she was torn away from her parents, four younger brothers and baby sister. She was sent to the city of Oberalshtadt in the Sudeten section of Czechoslovakia. The concentration camp housed some 2,000 girls; she was one of the youngest, the "baby" of the camp. She was put to work in a factory known as Etrich, which wove the flax into thread to make uniforms for the German army.

After three and a half years, Hadassah was liberated. She planned to return home — only to find that there was no longer any home to return to. Her entire family had perished at Auschwitz. She was the only one left alive. Apart from this, a trip to her native town posed a danger from the many Poles who did not hesitate to murder Jews returning from the camps, thus fulfilling their Christian duty and national obligation to "liberate Poland from the Jews."

In normal times, Jewish courtships had always begun with a *shadchan*. However, in those postwar days there were no families, no communities, and no economic base. The *shtetl* as we had known it was gone. Everything it had once encompassed had been utterly destroyed, including the matchmaking profession. Nevertheless, weddings took place almost daily in the Displaced Persons (D.P.) Camps, which were established and supported by the United Nations Relief and Rehabilitation Administration (UNRRA).

Young people, longing for family, for roots — aching not so much for a husband or wife as for a father and mother — were getting married. There was no family to check out on the "other side." There was no "other side." There was no family left alive to invite to the wedding. In fact, there was hardly even a wedding — just a rabbi and a brief ceremony!

So where does a penniless boy take out a penniless girl in postwar Nuremberg? To the Palace of Justice, of course. There the international court was in session, trying prominent Nazis. The entire building had been cordoned off by the American M.P.'s, with entrance by special pass only. I'd become close friends with Dr. Isaac Stone from Chevy Chase, Maryland, a linguist with the State Department — also known as the "Angel of Nuremberg" for his activities on behalf of the Jewish Displaced Persons. He supplied me with passes.

There we used to sit, Hadassah and I, glued to our seats and our earphones. (Each seat had a box with four buttons. One could listen to the court proceedings in any one of four languages: English, French, Russian, or German.) Directly across from us sat the accused, guarded by American M.P.'s: Marshal Goering, Jodl, von Ribbentrop, Streicher, and all the other Nazi murderers who had planned the destruction of our people — and almost succeeded, thanks to the cooperation of the Christian nations of Europe. There we sat, a boy and girl who dreamed of rebuilding from the ruins. That was our date!

In my officer's uniform

One day, an American captain came up behind me and whispered something in my ear. He must have been under the impression that every human being on this planet speaks English; I just looked at him, puzzled, not understanding a word. Apparently he thought I didn't hear him. He raised his voice. In the courtroom where you could hear a pin drop the captain's voice rang out, causing all heads to turn. Embarrassed, he crooked an index finger at me and motioned for me to follow.

I didn't know what he wanted. Perhaps he had noticed me pushing the Russian button on the translation box, or maybe the whole thing was just a mistake. However, when an American officer tells you to come, you come. I whispered to Hadassah, "There must be some mistake. Am I under arrest?"

She just shook her head, frightened. She didn't know any more English than I did.

"If I'm not back within the hour," I said, "go see Dr. Stone. He'll know what to do."

The captain took me to a room. There was Isaac Stone, along with three other men in civilian clothes. I was so relieved to see him that I blurted, "Am I under arrest?" It turned out that Dr. Stone had told someone I'd deserted from Russia and Poland, and the American officials wanted to ask me some questions.

In those days I knew nothing of the CIA or any other organ of military intelligence, but since all of their questions concentrated on Russia, I suspected that the trio of strangers were a unit of some sort of intelligence agency. Stone acted as my translator from Yiddish to English. I noticed that the men discussed each of my answers with a man they called Dr. Maza. Toward the very end of the interrogation, Dr. Maza — whom I presumed to be their chief — asked me in perfect Russian, with a Muscovite accent, if there was any possibility of a revolution against Stalin. I immediately decided that he was a native Russian, since no American could ever learn to speak the language with such perfection.

I replied in the same tongue, asking him in turn how many people, considering the huge size of the land and its enormous population, he thought it would take to stage a revolution. "Fifty thousand, perhaps? Ten thousand? One thousand? Five hundred? Fifty people? But, in Russia, there is a joke making the rounds: A man, unable to sleep at night because of his fear of a nocturnal knock on the door, gets out of bed, looks in the mirror, and says, 'One of us in an informer!' So how can there ever be a revolution against Stalin?"

The men thanked me, and Stone walked me to the door. Before I left, I turned to him and said, "Dr. Stone, I seldom forget a name. All this time, I've been racking my brain, trying to remember where I heard the name Maza before. Now it comes back to me. It was when I read about the Mendel Beilis trial. The czarist government accused Beilis of killing a Christian child and using the blood to make *matzah*. This infamous and heinous blood libel was aimed not only at Beilis himself, but at the Jewish people as a whole — and particularly at the Talmud! The star witness for the defense of the Talmud and of the Jewish people was Rabbi Yaakov Maza of Moscow. That man there speaks perfect Russian, and is called Maza. Is he by any chance related to that famous rabbi?"

Stone gave me a slap on the back. "Chaim, you have the memory of an elephant." This was the first time I'd ever heard that expression; I never knew that an elephant has such a prodigious memory! "Indeed," Stone went on, "he is related. He is the son of Rabbi Maza."

Curiosity — ever my weakness — took over. "I would like to talk to him."

Stone replied sadly, "There is nothing to talk to him about. He is totally Americanized. Totally assimilated."

On the way back to the D.P. camp, Hadassah was low spirited. The proceedings we'd been witnessing had brought to the surface all her fear, loneliness, and sorrow. I began to sing an old Russian song from the days of serfdom, when the master-owner would choose mates for his serfs:

> *Why did my mother give birth to me?*
> *Why did she raise me?*
> *If the one I loved*
> *He didn't give me?*
> *Separation! Oh, separation!*
> *In a foreign country*
> *No one will separate us*
> *Not war — not even death!*

Hadassah hardly understood Russian. When I explained the words of the song, she exclaimed, "Don't ever sing it again! I had one separation in my life. I couldn't face another one!"

I switched to another Russian song:

> *We met not for the first time*
> *Many springs smiled upon us.*
> *In sadness we both kept silent,*
> *Happiness we shared, half and half.*
> *Let the days pass, speeding year after year*
> *And if a sorrowful moment comes*
> *I shall embrace you, looking into your eyes,*
> *I shall ask, "Do you remember our first spring?*
> *That first evening at the river's cliff?*
> *Our song in the far distant sea?"*
> *I shall embrace you, looking into your eyes*
> *I shall ask, "Do you remember our first spring?"*

Hadassah liked that one better. Her face shone in the last rays of the setting sun. She ended that day happy, which made me happy also.

On another occasion, I dug up an old Yiddish song, which she liked best of all:

Because whatever has been, has been
And is not here anymore.
The hours, the years, are passing by
The happy years of youth, how fast they fly!
And you can't capture them again
Because whatever has been, has been
And is not here anymore.
You dress and primp and beautify
But you give no one but yourself the lie!
Because whatever has been, has been
And is not here anymore!

Hadassah did not dress up, nor did she wear make-up. She didn't have it, and she didn't need it! Her beauty shone through the rags. One day, Dr. Stone asked me, "Well, when are you two getting married?"

"As soon as she has a decent dress and I a decent suit," I replied. (Actually, she was "richer" than I, for I had only one suit, while she had a dress for Shabbos and a WAC uniform for every day.[1])

Stone was surprised and annoyed. "With all the packages of clothes you delivered to the various D.P. camps, you couldn't pick out a suit for yourself and a dress for her?" he roared in exasperation.

He was referring to my "job." People from all over America would send packages of clothes to Dr. Stone for delivery to the D.P. camps. Being an army man in military uniform, he ran into trouble with his general. How, his commanding officer demanded,

---

1. WAC stood for the Women's Auxiliary Corps of the U.S. Army. When the American military government announced that no civilian could wear a military uniform, I had the job of finding a dye factory to change the color of Hadassah's uniform to navy blue. The uniform is still hanging in our closet to this very day!

could one G.I. exploit the military post by receiving so many packages? After the general was done with him, he assigned Stone a garage for storage, and a jeep with a military driver. Since the driver was often drunk or not to be found, I was the substitute who delivered the packages.

A civilian driving an army jeep excited the suspicion of every M.P. To avoid trouble, Stone offered me his military uniform, but my lack of English made us scratch that idea. Instead, he gave me a certain document with my name on it and a secret code which helped me pass any roadblock without uttering a word!

Responding to Stone's accusation, I said, "In Russia, stealing is a way of life, a way to exist, yet I didn't steal. Do you expect me to start now?"

Soon afterward, Stone brought me a gray suit with the label of a dry cleaner in Brooklyn still attached to it, and a blue dress for Hadassah — "To match her eyes," he said. We set the date of the wedding so as not to interfere with his duties at the trial.

It's an old custom for orphans to visit the graves of their dead parents and invite them to the wedding. Hadassah and I did not know the location of our dear ones' graves. To travel to Auschwitz was out of the question, so we settled for a "Prayer for the Dead" under the *chuppah*. In the absence of a printed *"kesubah"* (marriage contract), I wrote one myself. Though my handwriting is fairly good, the old rabbi had a hard time reading the document, as it was dark and he needed glasses, which he didn't have. His slow reading was to my benefit. It gave me time to "invite" my family and Hadassah's to our *simchah*.

I could feel their presence. Father smiled, looking just the way I'd seen him in a dream in the Kyzil-Kum desert in Kazakhstan, when I was chased by a wounded beast. Mother was so peaceful, her lovely face glowing with love and goodness. Her strawberry-blonde hair had turned silvery-white, and I could see tears rolling down her face.

My little brothers — oh, how I would have loved to embrace them! They were all happy, wishing me, "*Mazel tov.*" I didn't pay attention to the crowd around us, or to the rabbi. I was immersed in my fantasy, busy with my "guests." And then there was her family, whom I had never met. In my mind I introduced the two sides.

I addressed my father: "Look at her. She is neither Russian nor Tatar, but a pure Jewish soul. All of you are resting in the highest and holiest place, sheltered beneath the wings of the Creator. I wasn't worthy of being with you. You sent me away. Now you've come to my wedding, to wish me and her '*Mazel tov*'!"

Cries of "*Mazel tov!*" rang in the air. I came back to reality — to my bride, to my friends, to wishes, kisses, and hugs. If I'd told anyone who had been with us at the ceremony, and with whom I had talked, they would surely have thought I was crazy. But I've repeated the same prayer and the same invitation at the weddings of each of my children. The feeling of my family's presence is always the same, and the conversation is the same. They come, indeed, to bless us with "*Mazel tov!*"

My beautiful bride wiped the tears from my face. Little did she know that I had just "met" her family and mine. She presumed that they were tears of happiness — and she was right.

Glossary

ani — poor person

apikorsus — heresy

arba kossos — four cups of wine one is obligated to drink at the Pesach seder

ba'al agalah, balagalah — wagon driver

ba'alei batim, balebatim — householders; congregants

ba'al mussar — a master of ethical thought and practice

ba'al tzedakah — philanthropist

badchen — entertainer who sings original couplets about the bride and groom

Bais HaMikdash — the Holy Temple

Bais Midrash — House of Study

bitachon — trust, esp. trust in G-d

blatt — a folio page of the Talmud

Bobbe — grandmother

chachamim — Sages

chassan — groom

chavrusah — learning partner

Chazal — our Sages

chesed — kindness

chesed shel emes — (lit. true kindness) burying the dead

Chevrah Kadishah — Burial Society

cholent — a stew traditionally eaten at the Sabbath morning meal

Chumash (pl. *Chumashim*) — book containing one or all of the five books of the Torah

chuppah — (lit. canopy) the wedding canopy; the marriage ceremony

darshan — public speaker

daven, davening — to pray

din Torah (pl. *dinei Torah*) — litigation

drashah (pl. *drashos*) — Torah lecture; speech

einikl (pl. *einiklach*) — grandchild

emunah — faith; belief in Hashem

Eretz Yisrael — the Land of Israel

erev Shabbos — Friday

evyon (pl. *evyonim*) — a pauper

ganav (pl. *ganavim*) — thief

gedolim — Torah personalities; Torah leaders

gemilas chasadim — lovingkindness

gezeiras tach vetat — massacres of 1648-9

goy (pl. *goyim*) — non-Jew

hachnasas kallah — financial assistance for indigent brides

hachnasas orchim — providing hospitality to guests

halachah — Jewish law and practice

hashkafah — ideology

Haskalah — the "Enlightenment" movement

haskamah — rabbinic approval

hechsher — seal of approval

iluy — genius

kallah — a bride

kapote — frock coat

kasha — buckwheat; question

kavanah — concentration

kavod — honor

kedushah — holiness

kehillah (pl. *kehillos*) — community

kesubah — marriage contract

kiddush Hashem — sanctification of God's Name

klal Yisrael — the nation of Israel

Kohen (pl. *Kohanim*) — priest in the Temple, a descendant of Aharon

kol haTorah — the sound of Torah learning

lechayim — "To Life!"; a toast

Litvak — of Lithuanian descent, non-chassid

Ma'ariv — evening prayers

machzor — holiday prayer book

Malach Hamaves — the Angel of Death

maos chittim — lit. money for wheat; fund for Pesach needs

mashgiach — headmaste; supervisor of kashrus

Mashiach — the Messiah

maskil (pl. *maskilim*) — proponents of the Enlightenment

mechaber sefarim — author of scholarly works

melamed — teacher, esp. of young children

meshuganer (pl. *meshugoyim*) — crazy person

meshulach (pl. *meshulachim*) — fundraiser

meshumad — convert to a different faith

mesiras nefesh — sacrifice

middos — character traits

mikveh — ritual bath

Minchah — the afternoon prayer

minyan (pl. *minyanim*) — quorum of adult males, required for communal prayer

mishebeirach — prayer on a person's behalf

mishmar — all-night study session

misnaged (pl. *misnagdim*) — opponent of the chassidic movement

mitzvah (pl. *mitzvos*) — Torah command, good deed

mizrach vant — eastern wall of the synagogue

moser — informer against his fellow Jews

mussar — ethics

nachas — pleasure

Nassi — president, leader of the community

neshamah — soul

niftar — died

ochrana — the tzar's secret police

Olam Haba — World to Come

Panie — Sir

parnassah — sustenance

patch — slap

pikei'ach — wise man

poretz (pl. *poritzim*) — [Yiddish] big landowner,

posek — halachic authority

psak — rabbinic judgment

rabbanim — rabbis

rabbanus — rabbinate

Rabbeinu — our teacher

Rashi — primary commentary on Scripture and Talmud

Rav-mita'am (*Rav mita'am hamemshalah*) — government-appointed rabbi

Rebbe — chassidic leader

rebbi (pl. *rebbeim*) — teacher

Ribbono Shel Olam — Master of the Universe

Rosh Yeshivah (pl. *roshei yeshivah*) — yeshivah dean

seder (pl. *sedarim*) — ritual festive meal on Pesach; study session; an order of the Mishnah

sefer (pl. *sefarim*) — books, esp. on Torah subjects

semichah — rabbinical ordination

sha'alah — halachic question

Shabbos HaGadol — the Shabbos just before Pesach

Shabbos Shuvah — the Shabbos between Rosh Hashanah and Yom Kippur

Shacharis — morning prayer

shadchanus — matchmaker's fee

Shalom aleichem — welcoming greeting

shammas — sexton

Shas — the Talmud

sheitl — wig

Shema Yisrael — a Jew's statement of his belief in God, recited during prayers, before retiring, and in times of danger

shiur (pl. *shiurim*) — Torah class

shnorrers — beggars

shtadlan — communal activist who mediated with government officials

shtetl (pl. *shtetels*) — small Eastern European village or town

shtibl (lit. a small house) — room or other modest location in which to pray

shtreimel — fur hat worn by chassidim

shtut — city or town; seat in a synagogue

siddur (pl. *siddurim*) — prayerbook

simchah — celebration, festive event

talmid (pl. *talmidim*) — student

talmid chacham (pl. *talmidei chachamim*) — Torah scholar

Tanach — Scriptures

tefillah — prayer

Tehillim — Psalms

terutz — answer; excuse

teshuvah — repentance

torbe — a sack; esp. a pauper's collection-sack

tregger (pl. *treggers*) — stevedore

treif — unkosher

trop — melody, cantillation

tzaddik (pl. *tzaddikim*) [f. *tzaddeikes*] — righteous one

tzedakah — charity

vasser tregers — water carriers

yachsan (pl. *yachsanim*) — man of impeccable lineage

yeshivos ketanos — Torah institutions for teen-aged boys

yetzer hara — evil inclination

yichus — genealogy

yiras Shamayim — fear of Heaven

Yom Tov (pl. *Yamim Tovim*) — holidays

zechus (pl. *zechuyos*) — merit

zemiros — Shabbos songs

Zohar — foremost Jewish mystical text

This volume is part of
THE ARTSCROLL SERIES®
an ongoing project of
translations, commentaries and expositions
on Scripture, Mishnah, Talmud, Halachah,
liturgy, history and the classic Rabbinic writings;
and biographies, and thought.

For a brochure of current publications
visit your local Hebrew bookseller
or contact the publisher:

Mesorah Publications, ltd

4401 Second Avenue
Brooklyn, New York 11232
(718) 921-9000